THE RHYTHMS OF BLACK FOLK

RACE, RELIGION, AND PAN-AFRICANISM

THE
RHYTHMS OF
BLACK FOLK

RACE, RELIGION, AND PAN-AFRICANISM

JON MICHAEL SPENCER

Africa World Press, Inc.

P.O. Box 1892
Trenton, New Jersey 08607

Africa World Press, Inc.

P.O. Box 1892
Trenton, NJ 08607

Copyright © 1995 Jon Michael Spencer

First Printing 1995

Book Design: Jonathan Gullery
Cover Design: Carles J. Juzang

Library of Congress Cataloging-in-Publication Data

Spencer, Jon Michael.
    The rhythms of Black folk : race, religion, and pan-Africanism /
by Jon Michael Spencer.
      p.   cm.
    Includes bibliographical references (p.) and index.
    ISBN 0-86543-423-9 (cloth). - - ISBN 0-86543-424-7
(paper)
      1. Afro-Americans- - Race identity. 2. Afro-Americans - -Music.
3. Afro-Americans- -Religion. 4. Pan-Africanism. I. Title.
E185.625.S7   1995
305.896 ' 073- -dc20
                                    94-40069
                                      CIP

To all who are the descendants of
Master Juba

Contents

PREFACE

I argue in this book that African rhythm, particularly African rhythm creolized in the New World, gives rise to the distinctive qualities of black cultures. These rhythms especially undergird and distinguish black music, dance, and religion, each of which is a means by which Afro-peoples absorb these rhythms and concretize them in other aesthetic ways. Since black music has been the primary carrier of our rhythms (both our religion and dance are dependent on black music), I contend that it is from our music that we glean what I call "rhythmic confidence," a phenomenon that I describe in my introduction as essentially equivalent to what we call "soul."

In reading African and African-American cultural history through this lens, through this rhythmic hermeneutic, I see our cultural reality as comprised of a dialectic between rhythmicity and arhythmicity. By this I mean that the rhythms of black folk have had, insofar as they are the source of our rhythmic confidence, a proclivity to push up against the "powers and principalities"—slavery, colonialism, and continued forms of systemic repression—that have attempted to squelch our humanity. But in this master-slave dialectic our rhythms have been persistent and have continued to give rise to important aspects of Afro-cultures. Sometimes these rhythms are explicit and insurgent, such as in rap music; others of these rhythms are subtly masked behind an outer Europeanism, such as when the spirituals are arranged in

European musical forms. Using terms borrowed from literary critic Houston Baker, I will describe these two strategies by which we have maintained our rhythmic traditions as the "deformation of mastery" and the "mastery of form."

My intent for reading the cultural history of Afro-peoples through this rhythmic hermeneutic is to clarify the cultural relationship people of African descent have to one another. In this era in which the concept of race or racial identity is being rejected by postmodern theorists, I want to show that the continuity of African rhythm is one way of demonstrating a linkage between Afro-peoples. In arguing this point I also seek to show that a transatlantic Pan-Africanism, one that includes African peoples of the continent and the diaspora, is a legitimate, rational idea. My premise is that to abandon the idea that we Afro-peoples are significantly related to one another is to forego the potential we have to overcome together our current existence as the wretched of the earth.

In writing on these topics of race, religion, and Pan-Africanism, I constantly thought back on the experiences I had during my two wonderful trips to Africa. The first trip lasted thirty days, from mid-May to mid-June in 1992, during which I traveled around Zimbabwe, South Africa, the Republic of Ciskei, and Kenya. I taught, lectured, preached, researched, book-shopped, conversed, and watched (I did a lot of watching). The second trip in mid-November of 1992 was to Malawi, where I attended a ten-day conference on "The Worshipping Church in Africa." The conference was held in Blantyre and was attended by Africans from the west, east, and south of the continent. Prior to and following the conference I was again able to spend a few days in Nairobi, Kenya. I have given these dates because throughout the book I insert passages from the diaries I kept during my travels, passages that reflect the thoughts of Africa that came to mind as I was writing on race, religion, and Pan-Africanism. These passages from my diaries interrupt the text (like thoughts interrupt discussion), but they are also very much a part of the ebb and flow of my writing. From the perspective of my rhythmic hermeneutic, these recollections create a call-and-response pattern, which is a pivotal characteristic of African verbal and musical traditions.

I have fashioned this kind of patterning because I enjoy being in sync with our Afro-rhythmic tradition. I enjoy this so much so that I have long made an attempt to allow our rhythms to find some resonance in my intellectual life. One means of attempting to accomplish this has been to write according to the "soul of method," as Molefi Asante names it in his book *Kemet, Afrocentricity and Knowledge* (1990). Asante says that when our rhythms are allowed to break the structured, lineal monotony of standard western research methods by investing research with "soul" then the rhythmized researcher is enabled to tease out insights that would have otherwise gone unnoticed (unfelt). I think the Africanist art historian Robert Farris Thompson would say of the "soul of method" and my quest for it: "This to me is an example of how love, and also religious passion as an aspect of love, far from destroying objectivity, can push us to an objectivity beyond all academic understanding."

Thompson also understands what I mean when I say that Afro-rhythms give rise to Afro-cultures. In an interview authored by Donald Cosentino (the source of his above comment) Thompson said that it was the Afro-rhythms of the hollers, blues, jazz, and especially mambo that prepared him for his profession as an Africanist art historian: "If you look at my scholarship, it amounts, in many respects, to nothing more or less than glossing mambo through the history of art." Thompson continues, "Through mambo, African-Atlantic traits became my analytic system, a way of viewing the whole world. And it occurred to me: if *I* was moved, imagine how it hit Amiri Baraka. In fact, I think one could prove that mambo is a secret engine behind a lot of famous people." Indeed, if Afro-rhythms became the pervasive hermeneutic for the analytic system of this white art historian then how much more could it possibly be proved that Afro-rhythms are the "secret engine" behind all our creators of Afro-cultures.

I believe our Afro-rhythms comprise the secret engine behind my own researching and writing, but I am also indebted to a community of soulful people who have pointed out those places in my manuscript where my rhythms were off-beat, not quite what I would have wanted them to be. I am grateful to my wife, Michele Bowen-Spencer, a burgeoning historian and cultural critic, who read and commented on this work while it was in its later stages of completion. Likewise, I am indebted to Kenneth Janken, a historian teaching in the Curriculum for African and Afro-American Studies at the University of North Carolina at

Chapel Hill, and Willie Jennings, a theologian and ethicist at Duke University Divinity School. Both of them read and commented on the final draft of the manuscript. After lecturing for Professor Jennings' class on "Contemporary Black Culture and Consciousness: Theological Investigations" in the spring of 1993, I realized that he would be an excellent reader. His interest in having his students ponder the status of black identity in the West is similar to what I try to accomplish in this book. My own class during the spring 1993 semester, "African and Afro-American Linkages," also provided me with a collegial forum in which to work out some of my ideas. For typing the manuscript beginning at its very earliest stages when my thoughts were but a few syncopated beats, I express my gratitude to my secretary, Gloria Huang, at the University of North Carolina at Chapel Hill.

I owe thanks to one other person whose words rekindled my inspiration at the very time I was doing my final rhythmic glosses on *The Rhythms of Black Folk*—Sandra Bagenda, of Uganda, who I met at the Blantyre conference in Malawi. She later wrote me from Kenya—after I lectured for Professor Jennings' course but before I completed the semester's course on "African and Afro-American Linkages"—saying:

> Jon, here is a situation: a woman wakes up in the morning and gets a baby—it is not very easy, some of us have to go through hell, pain and more than I can explain—but then one morning you wake up only to find that the precious child has been taken away from you.
>
> Not only that, the child goes forever: no contact whatsoever, no trace left behind apart from the imaginary pain which you can't even recapture properly.
>
> Every stranger you come across after so many years resembles your child. You search in possible places, until you give up in vain, but the pain remains forever, never to be erased from your mind.
>
> That is how I look at all the Afro-Americans (African Americans). To me someone deliberately denied them a chance of seeing their mother again (Africa).
>
> However much I try to come to terms with the situation, it seems every day I come out with a different theory.
>
> We all say home is sweet home, but how can we confirm that the millions of Afro-Americans are comfortable with America as "their sweet home"? What happened to the African Woman who breastfed her sons and daughters only to be snatched

away from her and taken for good? Is she in position to get them back?

This book seeks to become a partial answer to these questions.

INTRODUCTION

What I am proposing in this book is similar to a theology of culture, which holds that religion is not simply a compartmentalized part of culture but is all-pervasive in culture because it actually gives rise to culture. I argue that African rhythm, even in the diaspora where it is creolized, gives rise to recurrent dominant themes and traits in the cultures of people of African origin. In this respect, I think Leonard Barrett is basically correct in saying in his book *Soul-Force: African Heritage in Afro-American Religion* (1974): "The drum is Africa and the drumbeats of Africa were the prime method of Africanizing the New World." Barrett also suggests, as I argue in this book, that these drumbeats were carried on the wings of religion: "African religion danced its way into the New World culture and became the basis for the rhythmic pattern of our present culture." But how did the "drumbeats of Africa" survive the diaspora when the drum, in most parts of North America, was banned?

I argue in this book that the drumbeats of Africa endured the slave factories and the middle passage and were sold right along with the captive Africans on the auction blocks of the New World. African rhythm languished in the galleries of white Protestant and Catholic churches until it could "steal away" and release itself without reproach among those who possessed it. Thus, the diaspora generally de-drummed the enslaved Africans but it did not de-rhythmize them. With the drum deferred, the drumbeats of

Africa could still be manifested percussively by hand-clapping, foot-stomping, body-slapping, and dancing.

When African rhythm was manifested in that most crucial African retention—dancing—it produced, among other African-influenced choreographies, the ring shout. I contend, along with Sterling Stuckey in *Slave Culture: Nationalist Theory and the Foundations of Black America* (1987), that this counterclockwise choreography found throughout Africa and its diaspora became one of the initial sources of black community and black national-ism in the New World. But I am surpassing Stuckey's thesis by arguing that the African rhythm that gave movement, momen-tum, and meaning to the ring shout is a principal means by which we, then as now, sense a certain continuity in our Afro-cultures and in our conglomerate racial identity. I am claiming that *African rhythm* is the answer to the question W. E. B. Du Bois posits in *Dusk of Dawn: An Essay Towards an Autobiography of a Race Concept* (1940). Du Bois says that as he faces Africa he wonders, "what is it between us that constitutes a tie which I can feel better than I can explain?" I am arguing that it is the rhythm of Africa that he could better feel than explain.

***

I have been speaking of African *rhythm* in the singular as a way of representing the commonalities found in the rhythmic world of most continental Africans—multimetricity, cross-rhythms, and asymmetrical patterning, all articulated percus-sively, customarily concretized in dance, and involving some form of call and response. Conversely, when speaking in the context of New World Afro-cultures, I refer to the *rhythms* of black folk. By pluralizing the word I am representing the fact that African rhythm was dispersed in the diaspora where its patterns found new and multifarious means of manifestation in Afro-cultures. By pluralizing the word I am also attempting to clarify my posi-tion as regards racial essentialism. My intent is not to suggest that rhythm is the vital substance in an African or black ontology. It is simply to show that the rhythms of black folk—African rhythm in diaspora and creolized—reveal a cultural tie that binds conti-nental and New World Africans. In addition to the ancestral and historical ties that obviously bind us, this cultural tie (rhythm) suggests a kinship that can further serve to legitimate a transatlantic Pan-Africanism.

Certainly there are some readers who will hear my talk about the "soul of method" (in the preface) and about the "rhythmic pattern of our present culture" (in this introduction) as comprising a conjuring up of bygone doctrines of racial essentialism. But I insist that I have no intention of reintroducing the idea of the "Negro soul" or the "African personality," which were propagated by the negritude movement spearheaded by the Senegalese poet and politician Leopold Senghor. Negritude, as I understand it, was the quality or essence of blackness revealed in the psychology or personality of the person of African descent. It was that alleged deeper connection that allowed Senghor to feel a cultural kinship with the literati of the Harlem Renaissance and New Negro movements in the United States: Du Bois, Zora Neale Hurston, Mercer Cook, Langston Hughes, Countee Cullen, Claude McKay, and many others. All of these artists and scholars more or less adhered to Senghor's essentialist idea that the dynamic force of rhythm was so entrenched in the black psyche that it always found expression in everything blacks do. But clearly I am not saying what Senghor is saying about rhythm in his essay titled "Ce que l'homme noir apporte" ("What the Black Man Brings"). Quoted by Frantz Fanon in *Black Skin, White Masks* (1952), Senghor says:

> It is the thing that is most perceptible and least material. It is the archetype of the vital element. It is the first condition and the hallmark of Art, as breath is to life: breath, which accelerates or slows, which becomes even or agitated according to the tension in the individual, the degree and nature of his emotion. This is rhythm in its primordial purity, this is rhythm in the masterpieces of Negro art, especially sculpture. It is composed of a theme—sculptural form—which is set in opposition to a sister theme, as inhalation is to exhalation, and that is repeated. It is not the kind of symmetry that gives rise to monotony; rhythm is alive, it is free.... This is how rhythm affects what is least intellectual in us, tyrannically, to make us penetrate to the spirituality of the object; and that character of abandon which is ours is itself rhythmic.

These ideas about rhythm being a spiritual entity undergirding the black personality are not the ideas I am trying to convey in this book. While I appreciate the importance of the modernist movement of negritude, which evolved at a particular historical moment in order to exorcise white supremacist ideology and invert negative understandings of Africa, I do not hold rhythm to be the purest expression of life-force or essence. In fact, I understand the arguments that have been posited (especially by postmodernists) regarding our bad habit of echoing the racialist understanding of blackness created by 19th and early 20th century European and Euro-American anthropologists, missionaries, and colonialists. Therefore, if negritude was a transition and not a final ending, as Jean-Paul Sartre prophesied in "Black Orpheus"—that is, if negritude was the "antithesis" to the "thesis" of white supremacist ideology—then perhaps the "synthesis" in this dialectic is what I will be presenting in the ensuing five chapters and conclusion.

This much should be established then: My "synthesis" in the historical dialectic between negritude and white supremacist ideology distinguishes my contention from John Work's claim in *Folk Song of the American Negro* (1969) that in the character of the black person there is a quality that rhythm alone expresses. I am arguing that in the cultures of Afro-peoples there are characteristics that Afro-rhythms alone give rise to. In fact, I believe Afro-peoples have generally recognized and appreciated these characteristics to the degree that we have nurtured them and permitted them to constitute an Afro-aesthetic. For instance, when African Americans of all walks of life observe black youths dancing to today's hip hop and see their dance movements concretizing the rhythms of the music, most of us doing the observing (if we are not also doing the dancing) cannot help but feel some kind of cultural kinship with these Afro-rhythms. It is a kinship similar to that connection with Africa that Du Bois said he could better feel than explain. When we observe black youths dancing, we cannot help but to feel (whether we can explain the feeling or not) that these are the same rhythms that our parents appreciated in rhythm and blues and gospel and that their parents appreciated in the spirituals and the blues. There is this undeniable continuum that has its roots in African rhythm; there is this undeniable genealogy of African rhythm in the New World.

***

My Pan-Africanist claim regarding rhythm being the link that binds Afro-peoples should by now be recognized as being a derivative of Du Bois's Pan-Africanism. This means that my views are likely to draw the criticism that I am (like Du Bois is believed to have been) overly romantic about Africa. It will be said by some of these critics, as I show in this book, that the cultural cleavage between Africa and Afro-America is so vast that the ties that bind us are perhaps merely historical.

Much of this kind of critical discourse is coming from intellectuals involved in what I would like to call (to emphasize both the growth of consensus and its often pernicious nature) a postmodern conspiracy to explode racial identity. This conspiracy is the postmodern equivalent to the "melting pot" theory, which postulated that all Americans should melt into a single cultural identity. What makes the postmodern version just as disturbing as its "melting pot" precursor is that it too seeks to leave us with no alternative but to fulfill Frantz Fanon's prophecy in *Black Skin, White Masks*. "However painful it may be for me to accept this conclusion, I am obliged to state it," prophesies Fanon. "For the black man there is only one destiny. And it is white." Religion professor Alton Pollard concurs with my assessment that the postmodernists seem eager to rush us toward that destiny. He says in his essay titled "The Last Great Battle of the West: W. E. B. Du Bois and the Struggle for African America's Soul," published in Gerald Early's edited volume titled *Lure and Loathing: Essays on Race, Identity, and the Ambivalence of Assimilation* (1993):

> The belief in "color-blindness" is largely a post-Du Bois condition among African Americans, a quality or approach to establishing a sense of self or identity that implies certain rites (and rights) of social entry without regard to race. For many if not all adherents to this position, rainbow declarations of a "color-full" society (the postmodern recognition of otherness, social heterogeneity, cultural difference, distinctive gender views, and so on) are highly suspect, an odious and irrational deception.... The new breed of "color-blind" African American sings a refrain that is distressingly as simple as it is symptomatic: "Rather than cast our lot with the race, we race to leave the caste."

I have in mind, as I think Pollard does, such adherants to this position as Shelby Steele, Stephen Carter, Glenn Loury, and Stanley Crouch. There are others too, but it is these few whom Cornel West also finds it necessary to reproach in his book of essays titled *Race Matters* (1993).

Nelson George, black cultural critic for the *Village Voice*, also has some reservations about the writings of these few individuals, but he himself makes some comments in the course of his critique that we should momentarily contend with. In his book titled *Buppies, B-Boys, Baps and Bohos: Notes on Post-Soul Black Culture* (1992), George says:

> To label them buppie books is too pejorative and too narrow, though they are products of an era that made black urban professionals possible. I doubt they will have much philosophical impact outside their intended market. But as the generational and political distinctions within the African American community sharpen, Steele, Carter, and the rest loom as lovely targets for separatists. If you're into conspiracy theories—and they're proliferating in black America today—their assimilationist slant and overt or implicit antinationalism are certain to incite the fiery.

Steele, Carter, Loury, and Crouch do loom large as targets, but there is nothing "lovely" about having to contest their discourse. To presume that the only reason West, Pollard, and I target these writers is because we harbor separatist proclivities is to underestimate the power of discourse itself. It is to underestimate the power of whatever consensus these few are able to generate and the possible social and political policies that their writings are used to support.

While it is the discourse participated in by the likes of the above four writers that I reproach in this book, I spend more time contending with the arguments that philosopher Kwame Anthony Appiah presents in his book, *In My Father's House: Africa in the Philosophy of Culture* (1992). In this regard, I partly concur with Nelson George's comment that he doubts that the books of the aforementioned writers will have much philosophical impact beyond the intended market. Indeed, it is Appiah's book that will carry far more weight since it is a scholarly rather than "pop" cultural work. It was Appiah, and not the others, that Arthur Schlesinger, Jr. quoted at length in a lecture on March 29, 1993, at the University of North Carolina at Chapel Hill. He quoted Appiah, emphasizing his discipline of philosophy and his professorship at Harvard, in order to argue that black Americans are a part of American culture and not African culture. So, Appiah's philosophical arguments provide us with far more intelligent substance with which we must contend, including his arguments against the viability of a transatlantic Pan-Africanism. In arguing thus, he severely attacks Du Bois and Du Bois's contention that there exists some linkage between himself and his ancestral homeland that he can "feel." I believe, on the other hand, that it is upon Du Bois's ideas that we can continue to build a legacy of racial unity that has helped African peoples overcome the worst of human circumstances, including the holocaust of slavery. This will require some revising of Du Bois's ideas about race, religion, and Pan-Africanism, which I attempt to do.

But Appiah contends that the time has passed for black racialism—black identity based on the concept of race—to be an intelligent reaction to white racism. He simply does not believe that people of African ancestry can or even should create alliances based on the concept of the black person. Though he sees an African identity evolving on the continent as a product of Africa's shared ecological, economic, and political realities, he insists that this emerging African identity belongs solely to continental Africans: not at all to New World Africans, whom he believes erroneously view Africa as our natural home. My argument to the contrary is that New World Africans can in fact consider Africa our natural home, not only because of our ancestral rootedness there but because of our deep cultural connection with the rhythm of Africa. I argue, therefore, that a Pan-Africanism that embraces both the continent and the diaspora is philosophically intelligent. Pragmatically speaking, I think it is important to show Pan-Africanism to be philosophically intelligent insofar as Pan-Africanism is, as it was during the first half of this century, politically expedient: Afro-peoples worldwide are still viewed and treated as the wretched of the earth. In terms of our aesthetic interests, given that our survival during slavery and colonialism has always been helped by our creativity, a Pan-Africanist perspective legitimates our return to Africa as the primary source for ever-needed cultural reassertion.

My propositions will no doubt still sound unintelligent to the debunkers of race that I have been discussing. I think the principal reason they will find it necessary, almost out of sheer reflex, to reject my proposition that African rhythm—the rhythms of black folk—binds Afro-peoples on a cultural plain, is because they all tend to suffer from what Shelby Steele calls "racial fatigue" in his book *The Content of Our Character: A New Vision of Race* (1990). This fatigue, which Steele says especially plagues the black middle class, results from their having always to be burdened with "things racial" when race is no longer the obstacle it once was prior to the 1960s. At the root of the postmodernists' fatigue over "things racial" lies the burden of their feeling that their individual identities must succumb to our group or racial identity. Steele, for instance, would prefer that blacks interact only when there are reasons beyond the mere fact of racial similarity.

We can also find the theme of "racial fatigue" running through the writings of Carter, Loury, Crouch, and Appiah. For instance, Carter reveals in his book, *Reflections of an Affirmative Action Baby* (1991), that he is fatigued by the notion that blacks in positions of prominence are expected always to be representatives of their race:

> Black people who have attained a measure of success in the white world are assumed—and, indeed, expected—always and everywhere to represent the race, not in the traditional and still-important senses of serving as role models for those who will come later or opening doors by proving their worth, but in a strange new sense of bringing excluded voices into the corridors of power, thereby articulating the interests of a constituency.

But what is so new or strange about blacks who have gleaned a measure of prominence in the corridors of power giving voice to those who suffer the most from socially induced misery? Cornel West says in *Race Matters* that his basic aim in life is "to speak the truth to power with love so that the quality of everyday life for ordinary people is enhanced and white supremacy is stripped of its authority and legitimacy." In anticipation of the postmodernist reflex to this position, West adds that a love ethic has nothing to do with "sentimental feelings of tribal connections" but rather is "a last attempt at generating a sense of agency among a downtrodden people."

But those of us who wish to generate a sense of agency among our downtrodden people, by nurturing not only racial cohesiveness but a self-reconciliatory sense of racial pride, are accused by Steele of suffering from what he calls "integration shock" and "inferiority anxiety." Integration shock is the shock of our suddenly being individually accountable when integrated into mainstream society. This shock allegedly leads to an anxiety that makes us maintain the discourse of race and racial pride as a means of camouflaging rhetorically our individual incapacities. Crouch provides the most pernicious claim in this respect in his essay in Early's *Lure and Loathing* titled "Who Are We? Where Did We Come From? Where Are We Going?" Crouch suggests that those of us shocked by integration might actually long for the days when we were really oppressed so that we do not have to contend with our anxiety of feeling inferior to whites:

> Given the poorly thought-out and contradictory positions of *The Souls of Black Folk,* why are those ideas that Du Bois presents in such unconvincing fashion still so popular...? Is it because those ideas remove Negroes from the weights of modern life as they fall upon everyone? Is it because those turn-of-the-century ideas allow for the avoidance of individual responsibility and make it possible to see Negroes in something akin to a pure state, or at least a state in which all is very simply white and black, Western and Third World, oppressor and oppressed? Today...there might even be nostalgia for those times, or at least for the simpler ideas those times allowed.

Steele identifies as an instance of "inferiority anxiety" the way some of us claim and covet "soul." First of all, he wrongly describes soul by using metaphysical rather than cultural terms, claiming that soul is derived from a "mysterious spiritual connection" to human feelings and rhythms. By avoiding a cultural definition and positing a metaphysical one, Steele is able to say that these feelings and rhythms are a part of but not exclusive to black life. With these premises prepared he then goes on to say that sometimes our "denied racial vulnerability" can cause us to overrate soul to the degree that we sometimes claim superiority in this area. He concludes that this claim of (metaphysical) superiority is nothing but the refashioning of the "inferiority anxiety" into a "grandiose racial specialness" that supports our denial of the anxiety. But the idea of "inferiority anxiety" is insufficient to explain our talk of racial pride or to explain our alleged overrating of soul, because soul is really derived from an area of black life that Steele has bypassed via his metaphysical talk of "mysterious spiritual connections." Soul is the consequence of our Afro-rhythms.

As I will explain further in the book, the rhythms of black folk leave an imprint on us, which is manifested as soul or what I prefer to call "rhythmic confidence." I believe that we return regularly, on a normative basis, to sources that provide us with the rhythms we need and enjoy: the black church, blues joint, jazz club, home sound system, the car or walkman radio. We return normatively to these sources of Afro-rhythms much like we return to places of institutional religion for our fill of devotion and doctrine. From devotion and doctrine we, for the moment in this normative cycle, satisfy our religious yearning (our need for spiritual catharsis and answers to the Vital Questions). From rhythm, in a similiar normative cycle, we who adhere to the tradition of soul glean our sense of rhythmic confidence. The religious person is the one who returns to such sacred gathering places as the black church to ponder the Vital Questions, while the spiritual person is the one who returns to the sacred sources of Afro-rhythms.

***

The situation in which we find ourselves with regard to the postmodernists who conspire to explode our racial identity can be understood as part of our ongoing dialectic between the external suppression and internal reassertion of our rhythmic confidence. Had those Europeans who held our African forebears in captivity in the New World succeeded in the conspiracy to suppress our humanity, had they contrived some method of de-rhythmizing Africans, then in America we would have had no rhythmic confidence: no freedom marches, no black-consciousness movement, and no rap gnosticism (rap music positing existentially salvational knowledge). Had the slave-owners enacted laws strictly forbidding their slaves to drum, dance, sing, preach, pray, clap, stomp, sway, and even to cradle their infants in their bosoms to the rhythms of their heartbeats, and had they gone so far as to attribute those prohibitive laws to the divine Master, then after a generation or two the slave-owners would have succeeded in de-rhythmizing their captives: no black religion or Pan-Africanism, no places of nurture for our rhythmic confidence. Indeed, confiscating the drum was certainly a culture shock to Africans forced into diaspora, but to have seized African rhythm would have been the ultimate act of de-Africanization and dehumanization.

Without our rhythms the New World descendants of the enslaved Africans certainly would have been a people without cultural retentions or cultural identity. As rhythmless creatures, the theological notion that we had no soul may have convinced even us. I think this is what Barrett is saying in *Soul-Force:*

> The restless rhythm of the African soul will be the theme of this book. That rhythm was obvious to the white man from the day

the Africans came ashore in the Caribbean until the day Emancipation was declared. It surfaced in the drums of the Maroons in the Cockpit Mountains of Jamaica; in the conch shells of the Haitians calling the barefooted soldiers to unite against the elite French regiments "steeled" by the drums of Vodun. It became a movement bound for the African homeland under Marcus Garvey's messianic leadership and later taken up by the Rastafarians. It escalated to a worldwide sound in the sixties in a holocaust of movements, the tremors of which still linger with us.

That is the theme of this book as well. I will touch on our rhythmic confidence as it was manifested throughout our history in America: in our musical continuum that ranges from the spirituals to rap, in our social movements that range from the social gospel movement to the black-consciousness movement, in our insurrection of subjugated sexualities that range from blues lyrics to rap dramaturgy. In sum, I discuss the relevance that African rhythm and the rhythms of black folk have on three potentially unifying elements among Afro-peoples, which Du Bois emphasized in his writings: race, religion, and Pan-Africanism.

1

WHAT IS AFRICA
TO ME?

In terms of what Africa means to me and to millions of African Americans today, the racialist legacy of Joseph Arthur de Gobineau's *Essay on the Inequality of the Human Races* (1853) has followed us. I am not speaking of the book's postmodern equivalent that models a new liberal racism, Andrew Hacker's *Two Nations: Black and White, Separate, Hostile, Unequal* (1992); for we know that Gobineau's legacy has followed us in European genealogy: poet Carl Sandburg, journalist Olin Downes, philanthropist George Foster Peabody, political scientist Andrew Hacker. But I am referring to its having followed us via a genealogy of African and New World African scholars who adapted Gobineau's idea of black essentialism (the notion that there is a black essence that biologically or ontologically distinguishes us from other human beings). This legacy in the thought of Edward Wilmot Blyden, Alexander Crummell, W. E. B. Du Bois, Kwame Nkrumah, Leopold Senghor, Langston Hughes, and others is the basic premise behind Anthony Appiah's complaints in *In My Father's House*, which I will discuss critically in the next chapter. Briefly, the problem Appiah identifies is that the Europeanist thought to which these black scholars adhered left people of African descent with a self-denigrating notion: that we have an inalienable African identity derived from an inherently distinct history, tradition, personality, and purpose, which difference is imprinted upon our culture in traits of emotionality rather than intellectuality, sensuality rather than rationality, and inferiority rather than "superiority." While the intent of claiming that blacks were "distinct but equal" (Blyden) was to vindicate and liberate the Negro, these negritudinaires, so Appiah's argument goes, built their new myths about blackness on the foundation of Gobineau and thereby merely relativized the presumed inferiority of blacks.

Whether this is true or not, the "black personality" ideology of Senghor did play a part in reinforcing the distinctions whites made between the westernized black person and the "real" black person; and it was the "real" black person around whom they built their theories of blackness. These theories could become quite imposing, as Langston Hughes discloses in his autobiography, *The Big Sea* (1940), where he discusses his white benefactor:

> Concerning Negroes, she felt that they were America's great link with the primitive, and that they had something very precious to give to the Western World. She felt that there was mystery and mysticism and spontaneous harmony in their souls, but that many of them had let the white world pollute and contaminate that mystery and harmony, and make of it something cheap and ugly, commercial and, as she said, "white." She felt that we had a deep well of the spirit within us and that we should keep it pure and deep.

Pages later, Hughes continues regarding his benefactor. It should be noted, by the way, that his confession that he is "not Africa" but only "loved the surface of Africa" seems to imply that his essentialism was only a portrayal, an aesthetic, perhaps counterfeit. He writes:

> She wanted me to be primitive and know and feel the intuitions of the primitive. But, unfortunately, I did not feel the rhythms of the primitive surging through me, and so I could not live and write as though I did. I was only an American Negro—who had loved the surface of Africa and the rhythms of Africa—but I was not Africa. I was Chicago and Kansas City and Broadway and Harlem. And I was not what she wanted me to be. So, in the end it all came back very near to the old impasse of white and Negro again, white and Negro—as do most relationships in America.

Poet Carl Sandburg, wanting to maintain that old impasse of white and Negro, similarly distinguished between a genuine spirituality emanating in Paul Robeson's singing of the spirituals and what he considered to be Roland Hayes's more refined interpretations:

> Hayes imitates white culture and uses methods from the white man's conservatories of music, so that when he sings a Negro spiritual the audience remarks, "What technic; what a remarkable musical education he must have had!" When Paul Robeson sings spirituals, the remark is: "That is the real thing—he has kept the best of himself and not allowed the schools to take it away from him!"

Transgressing the Essentialist Color Line

> The South laments today the slow, steady disappearance of a certain type of Negro,—the faithful, courteous slave of other days, with his incorruptible honesty and dignified humility.

> —W. E. B. Du Bois, "Of the Wings of Atalanta"

We see the distinction between the westernized and "real" black person being made the first time musicians R. Nathaniel Dett and Dorothy Maynor together performed in New York at Carnegie Hall in April of 1928, Dett as the director of the Hampton Institute choir and Maynor as a chorister. Edward Cushing, writing for *The Brooklyn Eagle*, said Maynor's soprano solo in "As By the Streams of Babylon" was so striking that the piece had to be repeated; but music critic Olin Downes, writing for *The New York Times* on April 18, insisted that the "real" Negro had been eclipsed by white musical influences. Downes said that interpretation "more racial in quality" would have been welcome, after which he launched into his own racialist theorizing about the Negro. His comment sounds reminiscent of what I pointed out in the introduction as Senghor's claim that the "character of abandon" in black people is rhythmic and John Work's identical statement that there is a quality in the character of the Negro that rhythm alone expresses. To this effect, Downes says: "The negro's musical impulses are not those of the white. He is less restrained, and often more individual as well as spontaneous in his expression." Downes then proceeds to theorize authoritatively about the "real" spirituals: "Some negro spirituals

3

are wildly dramatic. Often they have rhythms and phrase lengths which cut entirely free from white tradition. Many of them are rollicking rather than pathetic or tragic in expression." Since the spirituals that the Hampton choir rendered were not of Downes's "real" kind, he then says of the performance: "Need last night's program have contained nothing but solemnly religious music? Could not certain of the harmonizations have been less formal, more exotic? For us there was too much evidence of the musical influence of the whites and not enough of the originality of the race which has given America the spirituals and the dance rhythms that have gone over the whole world." Downes finally concludes, but with hesitance (hesitance even after he has reestablished racial difference): "With these reservations, it must be said that the choir made an excellent showing."

Downes's complaint about the choir's rendition of the spirituals being too formal and Sandburg's complaint about Hayes's rendition of them being too imitative of white culture are akin to one journalist's response to the Hampton choir's performance in London's Queen's Hall on May 3, 1930. Writing for the *Manchester Guardian*, the journalist said:

> The negro spiritual and kindred music retains its human appeal, but one has long discovered that it does not amount to very much as art; in fact, the appeal diminishes in proportion to the amount of art that is expended upon it. Most of the arrangements heard were rather tawdry, nor could one, with all one's admiration for Dr. Dett's work as an obviously exceptional choral conductor, be much impressed by his own compositions. They make themselves extremely agreeable to the ambitious choralist, but have only an insignificant musical message for the listener, whatever the words may do to uplift him.

***

As a student of music at Hampton Institute during the mid-1970s—a little more than three decades after Dett's death in 1943 and about two decades from the years my parents attended Hampton—my Hampton colleagues and I were not left with this racialist legacy. The musical tradition that such musicians as Dett and Maynor helped nurture at black colleges and universities, beginning in the first half of the century, made a distinctive contribution to our education by challenging the commonly held views about the Negro personality. Although Dett described the spirituals as music that enunciates a universal feeling among Negroes, this universal feeling was not an essentialist racial trait but an essentialist religious one—hope. Thus, when Dett explained in his essay "Understanding the Negro Spiritual" that the spirituals embody a quality somewhat hidden from the naked ear, he was speaking theologically, not biologically:

> It seems universally true that the life of a thing is found at, or near its core. It is not an accident of nature that the heart is in the center of the body. But how many of us are there who think about the heart of a thing when contemplating its interesting externals? It is even so with the Negro spiritual. Novelty of text, rhythm, harmony, and tune all tend to make one forget that these are merely externals; the features of, but not consequently, the soul of the song.

The "soul" of the spirituals thus had nothing to do with the "Negro soul." The rhythm of the spirituals, as important as Dett tells us that rhythm is, does not help us penetrate to the spirituality of the object (the Negro soul). Dett was simply explaining that enslavement produced the common feeling of oppression, which produced in the spirituals common expressions of hope. So, because these thoughts about the spirituals and his musical representations of blackness stood in opposition to the racialist opinions commonly held by whites, Dett helped those of us who learned about him in college reject the residue of Gobineau's essentialism that had been passed on by the likes of Carl Sandburg and Olin Downes.

Dett and Maynor had the same impact on whites in America and Europe. As these two musicians were transgressing the essentialist color line at home and abroad (that is, crossing over the racialist beliefs of the day), whites were being forced inescapably to reevaluate their old racialist notions. In this regard, Dett's and Maynor's sophisticated renditions of the spirituals were an instance of what Houston Baker, in his book *Modernism and the Harlem Renaissance* (1987), terms the "mastery of form." In my own interpretation of Baker, the "mastery of form" occurs in one instance when an inner Africanism is masked behind an outer Europeanism. Musically speaking, Dett and Maynor mastered the form in such a way that the inner religious and rhythmic substance of the spirituals was maintained but encased within

European musical forms.

Careerwise, Dett and Maynor were paradigms of this mastery. To begin with, both of them mastered the extrinsic qualities of the trained European musician—academic credentials. Dett, born in Drummondsville, Ontario, in 1882, received his bachelor of music degree in composition in 1908 from the Conservatory of Music at Oberlin College. This training was followed by intermittent study at the American Conservatory of Music, Columbia University, University of Pennsylvania, Harvard University, and the Fountainbleau School in Paris. He culminated this graduate education with a master's degree earned from the distinguished Eastman School of Music in 1931. Following his degree from Oberlin, he continued in the Western tradition of music scholarship by holding a number of faculty appointments and by researching and writing on the spirituals. All of his academic appointments were at historically black colleges, where he served as director of music: Lane College in Tennessee (1908-1911), Lincoln Institute in Missouri (1911-1913), Hampton Institute in Virginia (1913-1932), and Bennett College in North Carolina (1937-1942). At each of these schools he formed and directed choirs that toured and sang many of his published arrangements of spirituals.

At Hampton, Dett developed the music department to where it began offering a bachelor of science degree in February 1928. Maynor entered the department as a student the following September, and two years later, in the summer of 1930, toured Europe with Dett's choir. The choir gave concerts in Rotterdam, Amsterdam, The Hague, Antwerp, Paris, Vienna, Hamburg, Berlin, Dresden, and Brussels, and in each of these cities sang some spirituals arranged by Dett. The better known of these arrangements were "Listen to the Lambs," "Don't Be Weary Traveller," "Let Us Cheer the Weary Traveller," "O Hear the Lambs," and "Don't You Weep No More, Mary." Maynor was the soloist for Dett's arrangement of "As By the Streams of Babylon."

The tour was sponsored by philanthropist George Foster Peabody, a longtime member of Hampton's Board of Trustees, who had access to financial resources through the Palmer Fund. At the expense of this fund, Peabody sent Hampton professor George Ketcham abroad for the purpose of investigating the possibility of the choir touring Europe, and Ketcham returned with the endorsement of some of the most influential people of England and Belgium. According to his statements to the press, Peabody's intent for the tour was to demonstrate to Europeans, particularly those with colonial "possessions" in Africa, that the Negro's natural musical skills could be developed with the kind of opportunity whites in America were affording them. Peabody's association with and intention for the tour are reflected in a resolution passed by Hampton's Administrative Board on October 23, 1929, which was sent to the Board of Trustees for their approval of the tour. The document begins:

> The Administrative Board of Hampton Institute is fully conscious of the steady and untiring interest of members of the Board of Trustees in considering and promoting all projects which are for the advancement of colored races.
>
> Heretofore the interests of Hampton have been chiefly devoted to the Negro and Indian people of this country. Now an opportunity is presented to promote the interests of the Negros of Africa through influential white people of Europe who are interested in Colonial and Native affairs.
>
> Mr. George Foster Peabody has for a period of some years shown a particular interest in the development of music at Hampton Institute. He has encouraged the Music School. He has furthered the work of the Choir. It has been largely due to his interest that the Choir has been presented before large and important audiences.

Dett did not outwardly contest Peabody's intentions but quietly developed his own ideas about the purpose and value of the tour. Dett's plans were more akin to what Albert Morini, the Paris-based manager of the 1930 tour, had in mind for a subsequent tour. Morini wrote the new president of Hampton, Arthur Howe, on September 5, 1935:

> Needless to say that the present time is the psychological moment for a tour of cultured negroes in Europe, the "moment" being, of course, the high interest concerning the cultured potentialities of the coloured race, which has been inspired by the Italo-Ethiopian conflict and Italy's claim that the negroes require colonisation as the pre-requisite to civilization.
>
> I have no doubt that the new choir conductor will be able to select a group of about 25 singers and train them so as to get them ready for a European tour in February or March. In view of the present situation in Europe, in regard to the negro race, you certainly can justify the expenses involved in such a European tour.

The very next day (September 6), Morini wrote to Howe again. He had just received a correspondence from the Societa Italiana per la Propaganda Musicale in Rome, the official agency of the Italian government, which inquired about the Hampton choir giving a concert in the Augusteum in 1936. He wrote to Howe:

> I wish to call your attention to the fact that this European tour would certainly be of the very greatest importance for the future development of the Hampton Institute inasmuch as this invitation is founded on a political basis. You should above all consider the importance of the fact that the first Negro Choir who is invited to visit Italy, under the present circumstances, is the Hampton Choir, and I feel sure that you will appreciate the importance thereof. I would be happy to see you take my advice given in the friendliest spirit and do your very best to overcome all obstacles that may be in the way of this European tour. Its importance is certainly great enough to justify it and your trustees cannot fail to realize this.

We need only examine Dett's program notes and other writings, where he discusses the musical nature and social value of the spirituals, to see that his concerns for the 1930 tour were far afield of Peabody's and significantly closer to Morini's. Dett especially expresses concern about the appropriate development of the spiritual—namely, the "mastery of form." Aware that the most appropriate rendition of any music results from a performer's understanding of the composer's intentions, and cognizant that the intentions of the creators of the spirituals were special because they were a people rather than individual composers, Dett suggested that the key to their modern interpretation lay in the sincerity of the rendition. Most important to his counter-racialist project was that Dett viewed his own sophisticated arrangements of the spirituals as a model of sincerity. He felt this as well about his two orchestral works written in classical oratorio form, *Chariot Jubilee* (thematically based on the spiritual "Swing Low, Sweet Chariot") and *The Ordering of Moses* (based on the spiritual "Go Down, Moses").

To be sure, Dett's oratorios, motets, and anthems were not instances of "sincere" black music simply because he was black. Dett disagreed with the position (today it would be a postmodern position) that black music is any music composed by a black person since there are no, and cannot be any, central themes of blackness. In holding this line, Dett both rejected the notion that "black" cultures have no central traits while also defying the essentialist notion that there is a particularly black way of being. If like can produce only like then the product of the black composer "naturally" is always black music, but Dett drew a distinction between black composers who imitated European music through and through and those (such as himself) who mastered an outer Europeanism while encasing therein musical Africanism.

Dett's concern for the compositional preservation of the distinctive musical features of black folk song points to another means by which he gave his own students (and those in the generations that followed) some clue as to what Africa should mean to us. Throughout his writings he held that all of America's black folk song is musically of African origin, rather than being of Anglo-Saxon origin as such white contemporaries as George Pullen Jackson argued. In addition to the call-and-response pattern typical of the spirituals, Dett identified the frequent use of the pentatonic scale and, above all, the rhythm as the prominent elements that reveal the spirituals' African roots. His is no negritudinal claim that rhythm is "the archetype of the vital element" or anything of such essentialist magnitude. He simply says of rhythm, in his essay "Negro Music," that African rhythm is "reincarnated and re-christened" with each new generation as syncopation, ragtime, jazz, and swing, and that the possibilities for the development of rhythm in black music seem endless. It is the rhythm, too, that especially distinguishes, in this regard, his published piano suites—*Magnolia* (1912), *In the Bottoms* (1913), and *Enchantment* (1922).

As with his oratories, motets, and anthems, Dett's piano suites are characteristically European only with respect to their outer form. In defense of this strategy, Dett says in an essay titled "The Development of Negro Religious Music":

> It occurred to the writer that if a form of song were evolved which contained all the acceptable characteristics of Negro folk music and yet would compare favorably in poetic sentiment and musical expression with the best class of church music, it would be a means of solving this peculiar problem, for, being created out of native material, it would save to the Negro and his music all the peculiar and precious idioms, and as work of art would summon to its interpretation the best of his intellectual and emotional efforts. These principles being fundamental, the appeal would be as great to white people as to the colored

people, while at the same time such composition would constitute the development of a natural resource.

It is important to note that while Dett believed that sophisticated arrangements of the spirituals would render them more befitting of the tastes of modern people, he made it clear that such arrangements did not "improve" the originals. This was a way of challenging the racialist presumptions that the European component (the allegedly rational, logical, and superior form) somehow improved the "Negro" element (the allegedly irrational, illogical, and inferior substance).

That the Africanism of the spirituals was maintained even when encased in an outer Europeanism is duly evident in the acclaim Dett's choral performances received from audiences in America and Europe. One such favorable review—of the choir's 1929 performance in Boston's Symphony Hall—appeared in the March 11 issue of *The Boston Evening Transcript:*

> These listeners were not disappointed.... They enjoyed...the racial ardor that is often the most moving element in a concert by negro singers. Yet they might have observed an artistic and technical approach similar to that of other choirs—say the St. Olaf Lutheran Choir, for example.... The elements that differentiated this occasion from others of similar intent were the racial overtones and undertones observable in vocal timbres, rhythmic pulses and spiritual concentrations.

The ability to master the form while savoring the substance of the spirituals was, as the foregoing review implies, helped by the choir's demonstration that it could also master the European classics. Journalist Allen Doggett discloses this in his review of the choir's performance in the chamber music auditorium of the Library of Congress in 1927:

> When a Negro choir sings a French folk song so that the applause is spontaneous, dispelling the prevalent impression that the spirit of such a piece cannot be given full value by an American choir; when a cultured audience coming primarily to hear Negro singers in a program of Negro folk music is carried beyond the race aspects of its performance into the realm of a universal art knowing no color line, a lasting impression in musical annals has been made.

Obviously Dett's strategy was working and he had good reason to ignore whites such as Carl Sandburg and Langston Hughes's benefactor. Such whites, in their theorizing about the difference between the westernized and "real" black person, questioned the authenticity of Dett's arrangements. As he prepared for his European tour, Dett thus had good reason to ignore George P. Phenix, the principal of Hampton Institute. On April 21, 1930, Phenix sent a letter to Dett as he was boarding the *S. S. De Grasse* for the choir's European tour. In its entirety the letter reads:

Dr. R. Nathaniel Dett
Passenger S. S. De Grasse
New York City

Dear Dr. Dett:
I have been thinking a good deal since you were in my office the other day about the suggestion I made in regard to the singing of spirituals and the more I think of it the more I am convinced that my suggestion has merit. I am confirmed in this feeling by some things that have happened since.
The other day after you were in my office one of our best colored people happened to be here and spoke about the Sunday evening concert in the most appreciative terms, but these words of appreciation were followed by a remark to the effect that there were no spirituals on the program, that they were so finished that their essential character had been lost. He expressed a wish that something might be done to retain the original quality of these songs. I have also heard recently that in Charleston, South Carolina, a group of white people have organized to sing Negro spirituals and to preserve them in their original form as folk songs.
A folk song to be real must be sung as it is sung by the "folk." These folk songs can of course be harmonized differently and modified and the material they contain be utilized in the most sophisticated sort of compositions, but when this is done they have ceased to be folk songs. As sung by the choir a week ago, our spirituals were in a sense de-spiritualized and it seems too bad that people on the other side should be given an erroneous idea of what these spirituals really are. As I intimated the other day, I believe if the choir could sing the spirituals without a conductor and in the same manner that they would sing them if they had come together by chance in South Carolina or some other place, that the contrast between them and the other songs on the program would be striking and would add to the dra-

11

matic value of the entire performance. I hope very much you will give this suggestion full consideration and at least experiment with it somewhat in your early concerts.

The letter ends, "Very sincerely yours, [*signed* George P. Phenix] Principal." Had Dett shown the "people on the other side" the spirituals as sung spontaneously by the folk, he would not have been able to challenge the essentialist idea that there is a "real" Negro.

Viewing the Hampton choir from the perspective of its "mastery of form" suggests that the choir's tours at home and abroad accomplished something other than to show whites (as Peabody wished) how to be more dignified colonizers, more righteous masters. Their tours facilitated encounters between whites and blacks, with the consequence of having challenged the prevailing racialist thought.

***

There were, in historical retrospect, only a few setbacks that resulted in Peabody's intention for the European tour overshadowing Dett's in this master-slave dialectic. The most prominent setback was when the choir gave honor to David Livingstone at his tomb in London's Westminster Abbey. According to a journalist whose words followed the headline "Cabin and Cloister," there were 3,000 Britons present to hear this people of the "cabin" sing in the Abbey nave ("cloister") where lay the remains of Livingstone: "For their part, the Hampton Institute students desired to lay a wreath of laurel on the tomb of David Livingstone...and with their songs to convey some of the gratitude which their race feels to the many Englishmen who have sought to guide them in their journey out of darkest Africa." The blunder on the part of the choir lay in the fact that "darkest Africa," a racialist notion that Dett's "mastery of form" had been strategically countering, was a Victorian invention popularized by the very man this people of the "cabin" were honoring. Livingstone's *Missionary Travels* (1857), as well as Henry Stanley's *How I Found Livingstone* (1872) and *In Darkest Africa* (1890), were culprits in this cursing of African peoples.

To mark the tragic irony of a black choir honoring Livingstone, we need only understand that the American equivalent of his writing is the "Local Color" fiction of the 1880s and

1890s. This American literary minstrelsy, which captured the domestic regionalism of the "local" South in a "colorful" way, perniciously caricatured and stereotyped black people. The portrayal of blacks as loyal, comical, pathetic, and affectionate—by the likes of Mark Twain, William Faulkner, Grace King, and Kate Chopin—was kindred to Livingstone's and Stanley's depictions of Africans (like Andrew Hacker's depiction of African Americans) as weak and pitiable and therefore needful of European colonization. In terms of the Hampton choir "desiring" to lay a wreath of laurel on Livingstone's tomb, the extent of the blunder was (as anyone could have anticipated) captured in the white press. A caption heading an article in (of all titles) *The Colonist* of Victoria, British Columbia, read: "Descendants of Slaves Honored Africa's Friend."

But even in this embarrassing moment when Peabody's aims for the European tour gained ground in the dialectic with Dett's, it is by the grace of two journalists with a hermeneutic inspired by the spirituals that Dett's side in this dialectic buoyed up from momentary submergence. In an article titled "Deserving," an editorialist for the *Musical Courier* quoted an editorial in *The New York Herald Tribune*, which read:

> One hesitates to assess the significance of the incident for fear of failing to do it justice. Westminster Abbey is the Valhalla of a race which enslaved the ancestors of these boys and girls so reverently listened to. In capturing it, as they did, they were in a sense paying off an old and bloody score, but in a coin such as revenge rarely employs.
> Compare the quality of these Negro spirituals with that of the hymns current in the Anglo-Saxon world on either side of the Atlantic! Is a comparison possible? Then consider their source in the sufferings and humiliations of a slave existence! What these colored choristers were offering before the altar of the white master, in his sanctuary of sanctuaries, were flowers plucked from the Gethsemane he imposed, flowers so exquisite that he must bow his head in their presence and acknowledge his inability to gather their equal.
> "Vengeance is mine, saith the Lord." Well, here it was in its divine form.

The editorialist for the *Musical Courier* then enters, also inspired by the spirituals in his hermeneutic:

The Herald here gives the Anglo-Saxon world a slap that it most justly deserves. We Anglo-Saxons on both sides of the Atlantic ought to be thoroughly ashamed of ourselves for the sort of music we have introduced into our churches and the sort of music we ourselves are composing for use either inside or outside of the churches. If ever a race ought to wake up and see itself as it is, that race is the Anglo-Saxon—musically speaking.

But not just "musically speaking." The "mastery of form," we must conclude, is a magnificent maneuver if "slaves" are able to garner the currency to compete, against the odds, with the "masters" who have imposed their Gethsemane; if "slaves" are ever to get "masters" to wake up and see themselves as they are. Given Dett's adeptness in this master-slave dialectic—making whites bow their heads in the presence of the spirituals and acknowledge the spirituals' "superiority"—it is not difficult to imagine that the overseas reviews of the choir portrayed blacks in a way that significantly differed from the invented Negro of the European imaginary. This is true even though some of the reviews were not all that favorable.

My selection of excerpts from reviews in newspapers of Holland, Belgium, Germany, France, Switzerland, and Austria certainly does not cover every perspective held by those who heard the Hampton choir sing. However, that there is a constituency that held these views, no matter how small that constituency, reveals the emergence of a different, more humanistic perspective on the Negro. The concert review in Holland's newspaper, *The Hague Het Vaderland*, said:

> I marvel first at the schooling, the exceptionally fine discipline, the ever-joyous tone sonorities and colors of such natural voices, and at the remarkable memory of the fine choir when not a page of music was used during the evening. It is beyond understanding how the effects were achieved, bringing forth the spiritual and the inner qualities. This is an exceptionally fine chorus.

Just as the above reviewer noted the choir's schooling and discipline, so did the reviewer for Belgium's *Brussels La Meuse* comment on the choir's perfect technique:

> From the standpoint of vocal technic the choir is perfect. It could easily teach many things to our own choruses. The queen was present at the concert and Dr. Dett was presented with a palm

leaf by the Musique des Guides.

The reviewer for the *Berlin Tageblatt* similarly noted the choir's "artistic training" and "perfect tone balance":

> The program was a great success; after the first number idle curiosity was turned into genuine enthusiasm and appreciation. The artistic training of these singers is outstandingly remarkable. There is perfect tone balance.

The recognition given to the choir's artistic training, discipline, and technique was important to Dett's scheme, but the "mastery of form" would not have been reached if Dett had not given expression to the inner Africanism—particularly the rhythm. Indeed, Dett was able to convey both intelligence and emotion, both rationality and sensuality, and thereby undermine the racialist distinction between inferiority and superiority. In this respect, the reviewer for France's *Lausanne La Fueille d'Avis*, like the reviewer for the Holland paper, recognized both the musical "mastery" and the music's "deeply moving" component:

> The mixed choir from Hampton Institute was a wonderful revelation. Conducted with real artistry by Dr. Dett, a composer of high attainments, the choir offered a beautiful program with an art particularly expressive and human. There was absolute mastery of the most difficult passages, incomparable blending, beauty of subtle shading, marvelous discipline, all united into the finest cohesion. We can compare the Hampton choir with the best Russian choruses and it has something even more deeply moving in expression.

We find a similar sentiment expressed by a former Virginian named Lewis D. Crenshaw, who was then residing in France and attended the concert in Paris's Theatre des Champs Elysees. Writing to the president of Hampton Institute on May 15, Crenshaw said:

> As a former Virginian now residing in France, I cannot refrain from sending you a word of appreciation of the splendid concert given last night in Paris by the "Hampton Choir," which I had the pleasure to attend.
> I heartily congratulate Hampton Institute on having trained such a group of singers, who are certainly worthy ambassadors of your school.
> I and my family were entirely surrounded by French people

and I can assure you that every number on the program gave them intense pleasure. I have heard "spiritual" songs for many years in various Southern States, but rarely have they made the impression that they did on me last night.

We were particularly pleased with the two numbers composed by Nathaniel Dett "Listen to the Lambs," and "Let us Cheer the Weary Traveller."

I suggest that the above French journalist's statement that the choir was a "wonderful revelation" and Crenshaw's statement that the choristers were "worthy ambassadors" of Hampton be understood as referring to Dett's masterful re-imaging of the Negro.

I also suggest, as I stated previously, that the choir's rendering of selected European classics played a role just as important as the arranged spirituals in Dett's capacity to traverse the essentialist color line. This is evident in the review that appeared in Switzerland's *Geneva La Tribune*. The writer initially seemed trapped in his racialist imaginary and drawn to the mythic Negro type, but the choir's perfect rendering of classical works precluded his being able to give a stereotypically essentialist portrayal of the choristers:

> The 40 Negro Singers directed by Dr. Dett scored a truly triumphant success at the Grand theater. The chief impression carried away is that of deep conviction and faith. Many of the Negro songs are simple stories from the Bible, however, the choir also sang the Russian "Kyrie Eleison" by Lvovsky to perfection. The ensemble is outstanding; the harmony, the attack, the articulation are absolutely faultless.

The following extract from Austria's *Vienne Der Tag* summarizes all that the foregoing reviews seem to have been indicating, and specifically what Dett was implying in stating that black music provides an important point of contact between the races:

> And now that the Negro singers from the renowned Hampton Institute proceed in triumph through European concert halls they are not looked upon as foreigners but as interpreters of human experience common to mankind.

Dett considered this triumph to comprise what he called "the emancipation of Negro music" in an essay of that title. This emancipation entailed the unchaining of black music from a half century of misunderstanding and low ideals set upon it by minstrelsy. The emancipation Dett actually engendered was, as I have been arguing, even more far-reaching than he and his contemporaries knew, even more significant than subsequent generations of Hampton students actually understood when we heard Dett's arrangements in music classes and at choir concerts. To be looked upon as no longer foreigners is to have transcendently transgressed the barrier of otherness that was rather immense and ominous during Dett's day.

***

These thoughts did not consciously cross our minds when we studied Dett or heard his music during the mid-1970s, but if these thoughts had even vaguely crossed the minds of those students who traveled with him abroad then certainly they had an impact on the way Dorothy Maynor interpreted her career as a concert soprano. In terms of the precedent Dett set for challenging the European racialist imaginary, Maynor's career may have been even more important than the touring of the Hampton choir. This is due to the fact that she was a black woman. In a way that the white racialist imaginary made concrete in their media descriptions of her, Maynor carried the mark of the Hottentot or Bushman African woman, whom 19th-century Europeans had made into the ultimate symbol of the supposed aberrant black female (and male) sexuality and distinct black biology.

Part of the Maynor portfolio that enabled her to undermine European's racialist essentializing of her (and the "Negro" in general) was her classic musical training. Born in Norfolk, Virginia, in 1909, Maynor began attending grade school at Hampton Institute when she was 14 years old. She completed high school there in 1929 and entered the Hampton music department that year as a student of Dett's. After graduating in 1933 with a bachelor of science degree, she pursued further musical training and received in 1935 another bachelor of science (in conducting) from the Westminster Choir School in Princeton. For a period of 25 years thereafter she performed in North America, South America, the Caribbean, Europe, and Australia. Her repertoire for these performances included German songs by such composers as Bach, Beethoven, Schuman, Schubert, and Brahms; French songs by such as Debussy, Milhaud, Poulenc, and Ravel; and opera arias by such as Handel, Mozart, and Verdi. Additionally, she customarily performed a group of spirituals, which were arranged by such black composers as Harry T. Burleigh, Clarence Cameron White, Edward Boatner, and Dett (almost always one or more by him in honor of his having first mentored her).

That Maynor masterfully re-imaged the "Negro" for white as well as black listeners, while yet maintaining the spirituals' African musical qualities, is exemplified in audience and critical response to her performances. Some white critics rebelled against her unwillingness to reflect her mark of inferiority with "authentic" renditions of the spirituals. On the other hand, black audiences and concert reviewers seemed to recognize in Maynor's performances of the spirituals the authentic qualities that distinguished this music. Blacks probably recognized in Maynor someone who knew the spirituals just as intimately as they did. If black concertgoers had read any of the press about her they probably knew she was raised the daughter of an African Methodist Episcopal minister and sang spirituals Sunday mornings in her father's church and Sunday afternoons when neighbors gathered at their parsonage.

It is true that during the first half of the century, prior to the mid-1970s when I was in college, prior to the black cultural awakening that began in the late 1960s, the members of mainline black Protestant churches tended to view the "slave songs" as too shamefully crude for formal worship and too recollective of the dehumanizing experience of captivity. But this does not change the fact that during the late 1930s and the 1940s black journalists reviewing Maynor's concerts did not seem hemmed in by the expectation of "natural" differences between the races. For instance, a concert review of November 25, 1939 that appeared in Norfolk's black newspaper, *The Journal and Guide,* just raved about Maynor's singing of the spirituals: "Her spirituals took the house also and, after a tumultuous applause, she sang 'Everytime I Feel the Spirit' and 'Were You There,' unaccompanied." On January 25, 1947, the same paper reported on another recital she gave in her hometown. The enthused writer insisted that the racial descriptive be omitted when referring to Maynor's accomplishments: "Dorothy Maynor is an artist. Leave out the adjective—just artist (period)." The writer went on to offer accolades for her renditions of German, Spanish, French, and English classics, as well as for her renditions of the spirituals. Of the latter the writer said,

"Few, if any single singer we've heard, can surpass her in interpreting this contribution of the race to the nation's culture."

Conversely, white critics and benefactors of the Negro could not seem to prevent the subjectivity of their racialist imaginaries from passing itself off as objective and rational criticism. But Maynor, with no blunders akin to that of the Hampton choir honoring Livingstone, continued to unbalance and unhinge their expectations. She accomplished this not only in her perfectly classical performances but in her perfectly rational interviews. When a reporter for *The New York Times* interviewed her following her professional "discovery" by Serge Koussevitzsky, conductor of the Boston Symphony Orchestra, the journalist seemed hopeful to chronicle an instance of Negro excitability bordering on youthful arrogance. He recorded the dialogue in the August 13, 1939, issue. "I suppose your ambition is to make an even greater success with your New York recital this Fall," the journalist prodded. "My work has nothing to do with that kind of success," Maynor calmly responded. "I hope to represent this art of song as well as I can. That's about all I can say. To accomplish that, to be a worthy representative of the best music—one feels so very small when one thinks of it." While there is in Maynor's response some of the expected humility of the Negro, her language nonetheless served to challenge the prevailing stereotypes.

Olin Downes, the longtime music critic for *The New York Times*, was one who repudiated renditions of the spirituals that did not reflect the "Negro personality" with its "natural" emotivity and sensuality (and inferiority). When Downes reviewed Maynor's professional debut at New York's Town Hall in the November 21, 1939, issue, he could find no flaw in her renditions of the European classics: "She proved that she had virtually everything needed by a great artist—the superb voice, one of the finest that the public can hear today; exceptional musicianship and accuracy of intonation; emotional intensity, communicative power." But in her renditions of the spirituals he had much that was critical to say: "It was inevitable that Miss Maynor would be asked to sing a group of Negro spirituals. Two of these, including the second 'By and By,' she did beautifully. But her voice, singular as it may seem, is not the ideal voice for Negro spirituals. It has not in sufficient degree the negroid coloring." The next year Maynor gave another recital in New York's Town Hall and Downes again praised her European renditions but criticized her spirituals. He wrote in the October 27, 1940, issue of the *Times:*

> There came the inevitable group of Negro spirituals apparently
> expected by the public when a Negro of either sex sings. As a
> rule, Negro spirituals sung in recitals are sung with an artiness
> that is discouraging. They lose their folk quality; they become
> self-conscious, theatrical, whereas no more sincere and inspired
> music has ever been written. Miss Maynor is to us refined to the
> point of self-consciousness when she sings these songs. Nor did
> we enjoy Nathaniel Dett's finicking and artificial arrangements,
> made for Miss Maynor, of the two spirituals, one with an echo
> effect at the end which is anything but congruous with the true
> nature of the music. The singing, without accompaniment, of
> the spirituals, "Swing Low, Sweet Chariot" and "They Crucified
> My Lord" were tonally among the most beautiful accomplish-
> ments of the evening. But it was conventionalized singing, and
> the melodic quirks bestowed upon the melody of "Swing Low,
> Sweet Chariot" did not make that haunting melody more irre-
> sistible than it is.

Despite Maynor's general success in challenging the white-con-
structed mythologies of blackness, despite her lack of blunders of
the magnitude of the Hampton choir's honoring of Livingstone,
the white racialist imaginary was not easily redeemed. The day
after Maynor's New York debut, a reporter named Michael Mok
interviewed her for the November 22 issue of *The New York Post.*
He wrote stereotypically of her "childlike humility" and said she
had "the glow and shy gayety of a jungle bird." Mok, we see,
imposes a difference, and the image he chooses—Negroes as
equivalent to children—permits him and his white readership to
feel secure again. It permits them to feel secure because the stereotypical image restores the moral imbalance in favor of what the
archracist Gobineau called the "adult" white race. Mok continued
in the mode reminiscent not only of Harlem Renaissance literature—exotic images of the sun, jungle, wild animals, and
rhythm—but also reminiscent of the colonial literature of
Livingstone and Stanley and the Local Color fiction of Twain and
Faulkner: "There's sun in her skin of gold-powdered tan, in her
melting deep-brown eyes, in her slightly husky sing-song speaking voice, in her smile that reminds you of a child bewildered by
too many toys and sweets on Christmas morning."

Similarly, the November issue of *Life* magazine featured a
photograph of Paul Robeson sitting with Maynor at the reception

following her Town Hall debut, under which the caption read: "Paul Robeson, baritone, heard Dorothy Maynor. So did Roland Hayes, tenor. Marian Anderson sent a wire. These Negro singers would make an unsurpassed quartet." Again, the writer imposes a difference, and the image chosen—the four-person faceless monolith possibly reminiscent to whites of minstrel performances—again permitted whites to feel secure in the idea of "natural" racial differences.

To proceed further, this *Life* magazine article is suspect for far more villainous reasons. It says of Maynor at one point, "She is 4 ft. 10 in. tall, weighs 145 lb. In operatic arias, she stands in conventional fashion, hands folded in front. But when she comes to spirituals, she leans elbow on piano, jounces her chunky body up and down as she sings" (this is accompanied by a photograph that places too much emphasis on her bustline "jouncing"). Immediately following this description is another photograph that shows Maynor from the posterior. She is bent over, taking a bow, and her buttocks are protruding. The readership has now seen this black woman jouncing her breasts up and down and bowing with her buttocks protruding. These images, whether or not intentionally stereotypical and crude, could not help but conjure up the 19th-century European icon par excellence of the Negro: the buttocks (and large breasts) of the famous female Hottentot of 19th-century Paris, Sarah Bartmann. By publishing these photographs of Maynor jouncing and bending and by describing her height and build as they had, the *Life* article was conveying to the sexualized imaginary of racialist whites Maynor's likeness to the "Hottentot Venus." The connection of images is inescapable, since representations of the physiognomy of the Hottentot woman enters the 20th century in such art as Pablo Picasso's *Olympia* (1901), and since Bartmann's buttocks and genitalia remain to this day on display in the Musee de l'homme in Paris.

Given this history and the continued racialist claims about black sexuality (which I return to in Chapter 5), we should not overlook this probable symbolism when such publications as *Newsweek* and *The New York Post* begin articles on Maynor by describing her as "a short and plump Negro woman." Neither should we overlook the supporting evidence: the similar need *The Boston Herald* had to consult an anthropologist for racial theorizing following Maynor's successful New York debut. The article read, "Prof. Earnest A. Hooton, the Harvard anthropologist, believes we should recognize—rather than overlook—distinguishing racial traits, and when they are beneficial, as in the case of the Negro's affinity for music, encourage them." This, by the way, was the very same message George Foster Peabody wanted to convey to Europeans, especially those with colonial "possessions" in Africa, in sponsoring the 1930 European tour of the Hampton choir.

Such perceptions as Hooton's and Peabody's notwithstanding, I contend that Maynor's successful "mastery of form" was all the more an event of far-reaching racial significance given the fact that she was "a short and plump Negro woman." Racial mythologies do not easily disappear, but I believe that the attenuation of the customary view of the "Negro personality," and specifically Maynor's contribution to that attenuation, is, for instance, what paved the way for her to be asked to sing the national anthem at the inauguration of President Dwight D. Eisenhower on January 20, 1953. Maynor, the first black person ever to have done this, represented a profound symbolism, and there should be no doubt that this symbolism and generally her "mastery of form" were instrumental in helping set the context in which the civil rights movement could ignite.

So, what is Africa to me? Africa has never been the will behind a mythical black ontology and rhythm has never been the means of penetrating to the spirituality of that black ontology; for I was raised with the legacy of R. Nathaniel Dett's and Dorothy Maynor's "mastery of form." I have understood Africa as, as Dett taught, the loins from which the spirituals sprang, the rhythm of the spirituals having been "reincarnated and re-christened" even in the arrangements of the spirituals that Dett's choir and Maynor sang. The "Negro soul" aside, I contend that what Africa is to millions of African Americans can serve as rational legitimation for a cultural Pan-Africanism that would keep Africans of the continent and the diaspora in some form of dialogue and within the reach of cultural, social, and political solidarity.

The Alleged Agony of Africa

And, finally, need I add that I who speak here am bone of the bone and flesh of the flesh of them that live within the Veil?
—Du Bois, "The Forethought"

In the summer of 1992 I spoke at a church in South Africa's southwest township, Soweto.

May 24: The bishop introduced me.... When he said I was teaching in the African and Afro-American Studies Curriculum, with emphasis on "African," the congregation responded favorably. I looked up and smiled.

Afterwards I joined the church membership as a gesture of solidarity with the black struggle, the elders of the church filed by to greet me and one of the women whispered "Welcome home."

May 24: I joined the church, the congregation said "Amen." The bishop sent me on home, "no longer a slave," to proclaim the story of the African struggle.

Everywhere I went in South Africa, Zimbabwe, and Kenya I was given this kind of reception. It was the kind of reception that an African American named Al Price said he felt each time he returned to Africa. In an essay titled "At Home in Africa," Price says:

It has become commonplace to hear African Americans describe feelings akin to spiritual experiences when they land on African soil for the first time. I have visited Africa seven times over the last ten years and on my first visit, I had the feeling of coming home after having been away for centuries, a feeling that far outlasted the warm welcome I received at the airport in Nairobi, capital of Kenya. It struck me again and again on subsequent visits.

Each time, I have discovered more examples of beauty and people who are as friendly and helpful as always.

I naturally felt especially "familiar" among Africans who spoke English and had interests and education similar to my own, just as I feel most "familiar" with such African Americans. Similarly, I felt a greater cultural gap and least "familiar" when I stayed the night at a rural village in Zimbabwe, just as I feel least culturally comfortable among African Americans who maintain a rural way of life. On another level, I felt greater political kinship with Africans (as with African Americans) who are involved in the kind of insurgent intellectual struggles against imperialist ideologies that I am involved in and who consider their religion (whatever it may be) to be relevant to that struggle. I certainly felt more culturally at home in South Africa, Ciskei, Zimbabwe, and Kenya—and, upon another trip, in Malawi—than I felt when I visited Belgium, England, and Germany. In fact, it is when I am in Europe that I find myself especially longing for Africa. While Dett's and Maynor's transgressing of the essentialist color-line in Europe certainly helped make Belgium, England, and Germany a more suitable place for me to visit, I am also indebted to them for re-imaging the Negro (and therefore the African) so that young African Americans of my generation could find Africa to be an attractive rather than repulsive place.

But the tradition of portraying Africa as repulsive, in a sense that has nothing to do with essentialism, is returning with the postmodern conspiracy to explode racial identity. It is now vogue to claim that African Americans are overly romantic about Africa and to support that claim by showing Africa as it allegedly really is—mired in misery. The September 7, 1992, issue of *Time* magazine, under the headline "The Agony of Africa," has as its cover photograph a naked, wailing African child standing against the lifeless background of drought-worn soil.

> *June 13: Pete Onteng took me to Mathare Valley (in Nairobi), where we walked through the inner neighborhood, where children walked barefoot through sewage.... I bought a pair of sandals made of car tires for 25 shillings. Many in this area are to be seen wearing them. We walked the narrow corridors, stepping over the raw sewage, dodging barefooted children, some playing or searching in the garbage.... When I returned to the room I wrote a few cards, one to Milagros Pena began, "Home hurts sometimes: Africa's aching. I hurt too."*

After reading the first of the *Time* cover stories, "Africa: The Scramble for Existence," by Lance Morrow, the interpretation likely to be brought to comprehending the cover photograph is that the child is suffering from Africa's "contending dooms": AIDS, overpopulation, tribal conflict, drought, starvation, economic mismanagement, and political corruption. Because of these "contending dooms" in this land revealing "some foretaste of apocalypse," Morrow deems Africa "the third world of the third world," "a vast continent in free fall." An equally pessimistic piece is "A Continent's Slow Suicide," a compendium of news excerpts in the May 1993 issue of *Reader's Digest*.

In another of the feature articles in *Time*, "In African-American Eyes," Jack White claims that every African American who travels to Africa seeks, as he himself had sought, an answer to the classic question "What is Africa to me?" He concludes that Africa for African Americans is not so much a "lost continent" (stolen away from the memory by slavery) as it is an "imagined one." Unable to claim any particular region, tribe, or language as our own, African Americans, says White, sometimes transgress the boundaries of rationality by adopting the entire continent as "home."

> *November 9: In going through the baggage check the Malawian guard asked me where I was from. I said the United States. He said he thought I was Kenyan.... Also, when I said my nationality, he said that I was from Africa long ago. I said, "yes!"*

The claim that we are overly romantic when we adopt the whole of Africa as "home" supports the contention that even the racial epithet "*African* American" is a romantic idea. In *The Content of Our Character* (1990), Shelby Steele says:

> Now we are to be African-Americans instead of, or in conjunction with, being black Americans. This self-conscious reaching for pride through nomenclature suggests nothing so much as a despair that follows real advancement. In its invocation of the glories of a remote African past and its wistful suggestion of homeland, this name denies the doubt black Americans have about their situation in America.... In the name "African-American" there is too much false neutralization of doubt, too much looking away from the caldron of our own experience. It is a euphemistic name that hides us even from ourselves.

Later Steele adds, "It is easier to be 'African-American' than to organize oneself on one's own terms and around one's own aspirations.... No black identity, however beautifully conjured, will spare blacks this challenge."

Stephen Carter, like Steele, prefers the term "black." "*African-American,*" Carter says, "I place in the same category as Leopold Senghor's and Aimé Césaire's *negritude* and Kwame Nkrumah's *African personality*—a tantalizing clue to one's reaction to an identity rather than an identity itself." Carter is reiterating Jean-Paul Sartre's critique of negritude in his essay "Black Orpheus," where Sartre says negritude is not the end all but rather only the "antithesis" in the dialectic with the "thesis" of white supremacy. So, for Carter to allude that some of us call ourselves African Americans and have an interest in Pan-Africanism only so we can feel good about ourselves is to interpret similarly the interests expressed in this book as nothing more than the "antithesis" in a dialectical moment with the white supremacy "thesis." Whereas, I see

African-American reaffirmation in the context of a Pan-Africanism as an end point itself. I think it is up to the likes of Carter—the journalists and all the rest—to explain why this should not be an end in itself.

One young black history professor, in telling newspaper reporter Mark Schultz about the expectations he had upon visiting West Africa, played right into the hands of those who chant our incompetence and our self-induced apocalypse. The professor said he was extremely eager to arrive in a land where he might run into long-lost relatives but that he found he felt little sense of kinship with Africans. To support his contention, he also commented that the idea of kinship bonds among Africans themselves is disproved by the fact that Africans sold their continental kin into the European slave trade. Stanley Crouch said the very same thing in his article in Gerald Early's *Lure and Loathing* that I mentioned in the introduction:

> Central to Pan-Africanism is a politics of race that assumes some sort of inevitable fairness in a group possessed of a commonality of complaint founded in struggling against the mutual ruthlessness of colonialism in Africa and the racial injustice of the Western Hemisphere. It purports a victimized but essentially royal "we." The brutal totalitarian history of postcolonial Africa should make clear just how naive that idea was, not to mention the way the corrupt and irresponsible Marion Barry so cynically called for racial unity and claimed racism in an attempt to manipulate the black majority of Washington, D.C.

Just as Dett and Maynor re-imaged the Negro and were thereby instrumental in helping set the context in which black people during the civil rights movement could begin to be seen by whites as human beings, so does it rest upon our shoulders to challenge the postmodern conspiracy to explode the racial identity that Dett and Maynor so painstakingly helped to reinvent. Contrary to those who point to African atrocities to awaken us from our alleged unrealism, African atrocities do not preclude the possibility of our kinship with Africans. Neither does African involvement in the slave trade, no matter how painful the fact, preclude this possibility.

Other co-conspirators have tried to cut into the alleged romanticism of African Americans by pointing out that some African societies engaged in the cruel practice of female circumcision. Stanley Crouch does this in an essay titled "Into Africa" in his

26

Notes of a Hanging Judge (1990). But in the West, retorts Egyptian womanist Nawal El Saadawi, is still to be found the existence of a misogynist "psychological clitoridectomy"—that is, painful, patriarchal female circumcision carried out systematically by means that range from the suppression of women's capacities to spousal abuse and rape.

Notwithstanding this logic, when the black professor's expectations were not satisfied he drew a conclusion fully antithetical to his initial enthusiasm, and did so rather than attempting to find some reasonable middle ground. Regarding African and African-American kinship, he said: "The cultural cleavage is vast. The ties that bind us are perhaps merely historical." The scholarly and mass media communities entrenched in the ideology of white supremacy feast on such statements, just as they did the blunder of the Hampton choir "desiring" to lay a wreath of laurel on Livingstone's tomb. The negative aspect of the history professor's statement is its implication that we have no significant cultural root beyond what we imitated of white American culture during the centuries of our captivity. In stating that the ties that bind African Americans with Africa are "perhaps merely historical," is it not being suggested that we abandon our African past and become "unraced"—a term Toni Morrison uses to describe white Americans? Is it not being suggested that we return to the years prior to anthropologist Melville Herskovits contesting the myth that black Americans have no past in his 1941 book, *The Myth of the Negro Past?* I think we would not be doing justice to those before us, such as Dett and Maynor, both of whom carried out the delicate balancing act of defying the essentialist notion that there is a particular black way of being while also rejecting the (postmodern) notion that "black" cultures have no central traits.

There is little doubt that Africa—as many African Americans know it (indeed as the world knows it)—is partly an "invention." As I said in the beginning of this chapter, the racialist legacy of Gobineau has followed us via a genealogy of African and New World African scholars who adapted Gobineau's idea of black essentialism: Blyden, Crummell, Du Bois, Nkrumah, Senghor, Hughes, and so forth. To be more accurate in terms of our current situation, it is certainly true that there is some misconception regarding Africa that has resulted from our "miseducation."

Because of the way Africa has been portrayed in history texts and popular culture, even people of European origin sometimes imagine Africa to be a paradise of big-game hunting or a last vast wilderness of primordial rhythm through which young adventurers can hitchhike. Some still perceive Africa to be the "dark continent" in which they, as missionaries, can work out their salvation by washing black souls "white as snow." With *Time* magazine's article of January 26, 1987, "Everyone's Genealogical Mother," in which it was reported that biologists, working with mitochondrial DNA, speculate that Eve lived in sub-Saharan Africa, some whites who visit the continent seem themselves romantic about setting foot on the land of lands wherein the primeval Eden was to have been. This is true on a cultural level as well. In an article titled "Out of Africa! Should We Be Done with Africanism?" in V. Y. Mudimbe's edited *The Surreptitious Speech* (1992), French scholar Denis-Constant Martin says:

> For many among the Western public, Africa is again in fashion, as it was during the heyday of colonial exoticism about sixty years ago. Through music classified as African, but reworked in European or American studios, the West offers material (as yet not much used) for the dreams of uncertain youths who, furthermore, find an opportunity to pour out their generosity in spectacular events of rock music meant to highlight the African "misery," even though they know nothing more about these misfortunes.

So, when the claim is made that African Americans' perceptions of Africa tend to be mere romanticism, a double standard and often a stereotype have been imposed. To this effect, Martin says in his article "Out of Africa!":

> With what right can the French, the Europeans, or the Americans denounce the "endemic effects" of an Africa that "is off to a bad start," "sick," "strangled," "tormented by the demons of tribalism," "ravaged by the misdeeds of corruption" and "lost its compass?" I mean, with what right can they generally denounce, globally condemn Africa, and not, of course, legitimately rise up without complacency in the name of the universal rights of man against a specific event, against a particular practice in Africa, as one would do for anything similar happening elsewhere? But it is not frequently so: on the contrary, from the heights of a clear conscience, they judge Africa on the basis of what has occurred during the span of one generation, thereby "forgetting" the past, even recent, of their own societies, offsetting what may be happening still in their own

countries. France giving amnesty to the "Carrefour du developpement" embezzlements, America of the Reagan scandals, and Great Britain eroded by the Irish canker: how dare they denounce African corruption, negligence, and tribalism!

So, a double standard and often a stereotype have been applied to critiques of African Americans' supposed romanticism about Africa. It is a double standard because African Americans alone are made to appear uncritical in our understanding of political, economic, and social realities; to appear dysfunctional in our tendency to exaggerate the African heritage. However, if we put the notion that African Americans are overly romantic about Africa into a critical context by critiquing the stereotype and the double standard, we will find that African Americans are no more romantic when they adopt the entire African continent as "home" than are white Americans when they so adopt Europe, not to mention white Americans' romantic notion that Europe is a continent or a "community" (the "European Community"). Parts of Europe might accomplish a political federation and a unified economy but not a "community," given the same reality that precludes "community" in the entirety of Africa: the myriad cultures, languages, religions, political factions, ethnic rivalries, and civil wars.

White Americans also have romantic history-book images of Europe that range from its geographical size to its historical significance in the development of Western culture. In terms of Europe's size, most Americans are familiar with the world's continental dimensions depicted in modern derivatives of the Mercator map, developed in 1569 by the German cartographer Gerhard Kremer. Because the equator is placed below the middle of the map, the northern hemisphere, where whites have quantitatively outnumbered people of color, receives unequal prominence. This results in Europe appearing to be nearly the same size as Africa, when Africa (11.6 million square miles) is about 8 million square miles larger than Europe (3.8 million square miles).

In terms of Europe's "size" in the development of Western culture, Europe has not only produced no so-called "Western religion" (despite its avid guardianship of Christian "orthodoxy"), it has an infamous history of unreligious and antihumanistic behavior: slavery, colonialism, holocaust, world war, and fatal xenophobia. To consider the esteem some African Americans have for Africa to be overly romantic because of the problems plaguing the African continent is equivalent to considering the esteem whites have for Europe to be overly romantic given Europe's deeply entrenched history of pseudo-humanism.

The element of hypocrisy, implicit in any such application of a double standard, is also demonstrated when those who herald the claim of African-American romanticism turn out to be the same who oppose multiculturalism; when multiculturalism is the educational process that could begin to correct misconceptions about Africa by giving it critical attention. We find this to be the case with *Time* magazine when we read "The Agony of Africa" in the light of the July 8, 1991, issue of the magazine headlined "Who Are We?" In that issue of *Time* are two feature articles that favor the "conservative" perspective in the debate over multicultural-ism. The first, "Whose America?" by Paul Gray, has a prominent caption above a painting of the "founding fathers" (all white males) signing the Declaration of Independence. The caption reads, "A growing emphasis on the nation's 'multicultural' her-itage exalts racial and ethnic pride at the expense of social cohe-sion." Ensuing is an "opinions" section in which multiculturalism is both supported and contested mostly by academics. One of the nonacademics is Henry Grunwald, former editor-in-chief of *Time*. Grunwald says, "Certainly we must become more aware of other cultures and their contributions. But the top priority should be to equip children for life in the modern world, to preserve and expand the unity America needs to function better, for the sake of all, and to avoid the destructive effects of intellectual tribalism." This attempt at objectivity (this conservative slant) characterizes the "good and bad" aspects of multiculturalism in the second and final feature article, Arthur Schlesinger, Jr.'s "The Cult of Ethnicity, Good and Bad." The historian states, "The eruption of ethnicity is, I believe, a rather superficial enthusiasm stirred by romantic ideologues on the one hand and by unscrupulous con men on the other." Ensuing this tilt toward the suppression of information about such "other" cultures as Africa's comes—in such forms as *Time* magazine's "The Agony of Africa"—the wag-ging finger heralding a dysfunctional "romanticism" on the part of the African-American masses and intelligentsia.

This maneuver is reminiscent of the journalism found in southern newspapers during Dett's early professional days when blacks, with a new sense of self-determination, commenced the great black migration to northern cities. One means the white press employed to prevent the continued diminishment of the

South's source of cheap labor was the political drawing, which typically contrasted the balmy and "friendly" old South with the cold and costly new North. But the founding editor of *The Chicago Defender*, Robert S. Abbott (a graduate of Hampton Institute like Maynor), collected these pieces and reprinted them in his paper for the purpose of dissecting and disgracing them. At present, the self-determinative migration among increasing numbers of African Americans involves a psychological exodus to Africa, not to mention the increasing numbers of us actually visiting or living there; and like the *Defender* editor, today's cultural critics must police the pages of the white press in order to counter the subtle message that there is no cultural connection between Africans and African Americans and that there is nothing in Africa worth the attention of African Americans. We must also give retort to those black Americans who are part of the postmodern conspiracy to explode black racial identity.

Parts of Africa may be suffering miserably by "contending dooms," but the human suffering should not diminish any sense of historical and cultural kinship. When I stayed the night at a village in rural Zimbabwe and heard eight teenage boys and girls sing in the village church in their Shona tongue, "God bless Zimbabwe, it is now being destroyed by AIDS and hunger," my sense of connection with these rural-dwellers did not widen, it deepened. Likewise, neither any expanse of physical distance or historical time nor any feeling of familial unacceptance preclude the reality of African-American historical and cultural kinship with Africans. Children who have been separated from their parents at birth and raised by foster parents cannot expect to feel at home when, as adults, they finally find their biological parents. Nevertheless, the romance of children and parents brought together in new relationships can be nurtured, so that as the historical and cultural linkages become recognizable to the diaspora children and their continental parents the transatlantic cleavage can be increasingly closed. Many African Americans, such as myself, are involved in this kind of romance with Africa—a romance that depends on the possibility of a Pan-African perspective—but we are not otherwise overly romantic about Africa.

There is in fact something truly romantic and indeed perfectly legitimate about reconciling a severed relationship with the homeland of one's ancestry, something rewarding about being amidst peoples who remember various cultural aspects of the African past without interrupted lineage, something revealing about recognizing the cultural roots of what in the diaspora often remains a remnant or residue of the original fruits. If in the reacquaintance of African Americans and Africa there is an aspect of emotionality, it does not necessarily have anything to do with the political, economic, ecological, or epidemiological turmoil on the continent; it has something to do with long-lost children (who did not leave their homelands as immigrants but as captives) returning as near as possible to the land and the loins from which their foreparents sprang.

If cultural critics were to substantiate fairly and fully, without stereotyping and hypocrisy, the claim of African-American romanticism toward Africa, they would first have to distinguish between romanticism and what is often either false expectation, miseducation, or romance. In contending with actual romanticism, they must delve beneath its surface and consider the religious sensibility that undergirds it: *hope*—hope that transcends rationality because it arises within the interstices of oppression and alienation. Given that it is a psychology of hope and an insurgent spirituality that undergirds this "romanticism," one can only criticize any uncritical view of Africa in the same way one would criticize people's uncritical view of their religion—in an enabling way, with love.

***

There is probably no better a potential challenge to the points I have made regarding how we view Africa than in Eddie Harris's book titled *Native Stranger: A Black American's Journey into the Heart of Africa* (1992). If we could pull a narrative from the young black history professor—who was eager to arrive in a land where he might run into long-lost relatives but found he felt little sense of kinship with Africans—it would probably be much like Harris's *Native Stranger*. In fact, Harris's views become a paradigm with which I can discourse, in that they probably represent a response that many African Americans would have if we had the chance to spend such a protracted period traveling throughout the continent.

The book has as its first sentence a statement that we would expect to hear from the postmodernists I have been discussing: "Because my skin is black you will say I traveled Africa to find the roots of my race. I did not—unless that race is the human race, for except in the color of my skin, I am not African. If I didn't know it then, I know it now. I am a product of the culture that raised me." By the end of his journey, which lasted nearly a year, Harris was exhausted from having been hassled at borders, arrested in Liberia, physically depleted by malaria, and angered by the powerlessness of African people under oppressive African regimes. He hated these aspects of Africa and felt that he could never live there, that he was fortunate to be able to live comfortably in the United States. He made this clear when he was aboard a boat in Zaire and he and an Englishman named Justin were taken to the captain for taking unauthorized pictures. The captain forbade them from taking any more pictures and gave Harris a preachment about the necessity of his moving to Zaire to help the country grow. Harris writes:

> "The most advanced black man in the world is the American black man," he said. "We need you. This is your home. This is where you belong."
> I was shaking my head. I could never live in Africa, I told him. I had been here too long already.
> "You prefer to live with the whites?" he said. He pointed his thumb at Justin. "His ancestors stole your ancestors from this place and took them to America as slaves. How can you live with them?"
> Thinking quickly back on all I had seen and all I had felt, I turned to Justin and thanked him. The spell was broken.

Harris said he had known all along that if he got too close to Africa it might lose its magic—that the pyramids of Egypt, for instance, would turn to nothing more than a pile of neatly arranged rocks.

Based on what Harris has said thus far, postmodernist thinkers who contend that the tie that binds Africans and African Americans is merely historical and that there is no such thing as the black race will feel their arguments affirmed. Upon a closer look, however, we see that Harris simultaneously resents and loves Africa (the same way he and many others of us feel about America). Though he is not African, he does believe there is a line that connects this place we have come from (which he calls the "motherland") and the place in which we now find ourselves; and he is curious as to what portion of being black was carried out of Africa. He says, "There is in all of us some profound craving to know where we come from. On the grandest scale, we seek to understand the origins of the universe, the evolution of mankind. At a simpler level, an adopted child wants to know the woman who gave him life and birth. We trace family trees. We visit the neighborhood where we lived as children. We look back as far as we can." Harris says he is not African but that somewhere deep inside of him Africa beats in his blood and shows itself in his hair, skin, and eyes. He concludes, "Africa's rhythms are somehow my rhythms." There was enough to remind him, he says, that what he carried within him had come in part from Africa. "I did not feel African, but was beginning to feel not wholly American anymore either."

The acknowledgment of this "double consciousness," which Du Bois spoke of back in 1903, is really what Harris is communicating when he speaks about the contradictions Africa makes one feel and when he says he sometimes feels he has more in common with the Dutch Afrikaner than the black South African: "After almost a year in Africa, I have no answers. Only this one question remains: *Who am I?* I have more in common, it sometimes seems, with the Dutch Afrikaner, the Boer." The fact that he could leave Africa with no answers but only this question leads him to conclude: "If you cannot know yourself, how can you expect to know a place like Africa? You can't. You cannot know this place in such a short time, such a short passing through—or should I say, these *places*. Africa is a myriad of people and ways. And Africa is more than that. Africa is change. Africa is contradictions. And Africa brings out the contradictions in the traveler." The young history professor who visited Africa could have said these words, and Du Bois would have understood.

When Harris entered Senegal from Mauritania, coming across the Senegal River, one among a group of men spoke to him while shaking his hand. It was the kind of welcome that I said earlier I was given everywhere I went in South Africa, Ciskei, Zimbabwe, Kenya, and Malawi. The Senegalese man said to Harris: "You are American? Welcome home. We are happy that you have come." As he pondered the welcome, Harris thought to himself that coming to Africa was not exactly like coming home, that Africa was in fact not his home, but simply that he had an awareness that it was the land of his ancestors.

Now a "native stranger" in the "body of Africa," which is the land of his ancestors, Harris was now looking for its heart and soul. Being more figurative than essentialist, he said: "I smelled the earth and listened to the wind and felt for the rhythm of Africa coming up through the ground like a heartbeat." That rhythm manifested itself from his subconscious in a dream and he awoke as he was dancing in his sleep. "Suddenly, deep in the night, I woke up dancing," he recalls. "I was sitting up straight and I was bouncing, sleep-dancing in my dreams, to music I could not hear, to rhythms I could only feel." That rhythm was not Senghor's "archetype of the vital element," for the night he awoke "sleep-dancing" he had been listening to a Senegalese woman singing and rocking while working on the streetside. Essentialist notions of rhythm aside, Harris's episode of sleep-dancing to rhythms he could only feel tells us something very concrete, as I will argue momentarily with reference to art history, archaeology, and the sociology of dance.

I think Harris's remark was unknowingly the answer to his earlier question, "Who am I?" Harris, I argue in this book, is someone in whom the rhythm of Africa evidently resonates because of the African-American culture in which he was raised. Perhaps he is correct that if we cannot know ourselves then we cannot expect to know Africa; but if he can know this about himself—that he is someone in whom the rhythm of Africa culturally resonates— then perhaps he can also know at least this much about Africa: The rhythm of Africa is at the heart of the rhythms of black folk.

The Archaeology of Rhythmic Confidence

> Herein lie buried many things which if read with patience may show the strange meaning of being black here at the dawning of the Twentieth Century.
> — Du Bois, "The Forethought"

I see African American culture not as a myth to make us feel good about who we are, but as a creolized continuum of myriad African cultures that merged during the era of slavery in the New World. My position is not an instance of a black person being overly romantic about his African cultural roots, but is a position supported by evidence that ranges from the archaeological remains of our earliest African ancestors of colonial America to the artistic corporeal and visual traditions of New World Africans.

Robert Ferris Thompson, in his book titled *Flash of the Spirit: African and Afro-American Art and Philosophy* (1983), identifies Yoruba, Kongo, Dahomean, Mande, and Ejagham influences of West and Central Africa on the art and other visual traditions of African peoples throughout the New World. The Kongo-Angola influence is especially identifiable in the decoration of graves in black traditional cemeteries, which Thompson has observed in such cities as New Orleans, St. Louis, and Jacksonville (Florida). Yoruba art can be found in such cities as New York and Miami, some of the cultural transfer coming not directly from Africa but from Cuba through Cuban migration to the United States. There is also the indirect continuation of African visual traditions via artists of the black New World deliberately turning back to these traditions for ideas and inspiration. Thompson says that as African-American artists awaken to the Yoruba traditions of Atlantic black art history they will be able to extend these in the New World, just as when African-American architects increase their knowledge of Mande-influenced round houses in Africa and the Americas they will be able to turn these historical presences into opportunities for homage and creative elaboration. This is the potentiality of cultural reassertion that I spoke of in the introduction.

Anthony Appiah would not contest the notion that there are these cultural transfers, for he holds that the African-American traditions that are African-derived come from specific African cultures. But he does claim that since the African-American traditions come from specific African traditions they therefore are not common black possessions. Thompson, on the other hand, helps us see that it is in fact appropriate for African Americans to speak of black Africa as a whole rather than of specific African traditions, since our heritage is comprised of the syncretization of myriad African ethnic traditions (not forgetting the Native American, Asian, and European influences). This is why Thompson calls Haitian vodun "Africa reblended": Vodun, along with its creole visual tradition of sacred art, is comprised of a mix of influences from the religions of Kongo, Dahomey, and Yorubaland. Similarly, some African-derived art, such as in Rio de Janeiro, is comprised of a fusion of Kongo, Angola, Yoruba, and Dahomean, as well as Roman Catholic and Native American references. Thus, "the agony of Africa" notwithstanding, the degree to which African Americans claim Africa as a whole can be comprehended as corresponding to the degree to which we value not only our ancestral history but also our collective cultural heritage. This could remain true among African Americans even if we, after protracted travel throughout Africa like Eddie Harris, felt in the end that we were "native strangers."

Given Thompson's remarks, it is also appropriate that when we speak of the roots of black rhythm we refer to Africa rather than to specific African traditions. This claim is at the foundation of my Pan-Africanism which allows me to speak of "the rhythms of black folk." Thompson parallels this Pan-Africanism of mine by performing his Afro-art history with a musical sensibility that is cognizant of African rhythmicity in the various visual traditions of the continent and its diaspora. He presents his rhythmic hermeneutic in his book's introduction:

> Since the Atlantic slave trade, ancient African organizing principles of song and dance have crossed the seas from the Old World to the New. There they took on new momentum, intermingling with each other and with New World or European styles of singing and dance. Among those principles are the *dominance of a percussive performance style* (attack and vital aliveness in sound and motion); *a propensity for multiple meter* (competing meters sounding all at once); *overlapping call and response* in singing (solo/chorus, voice/instrument—"interlock systems" of performance); *inner pulse control* (a "metronome sense," keeping a beat indelibly in mind as a rhythmic common denominator in a welter of different meters); *suspended accentuation patterning* (offbeat phrasing of melodic and choreographic accents); and, at a slightly different but equally recurrent level of exposition, *songs and dances of social allusion* (music which, however danceable and "swinging," remorselessly contrasts social imperfections against implied criteria for perfect living).
>
> *Flash of the Spirit* is about *visual* and *philosophic* streams of creativity and imagination, running parallel to the massive musical and choreographic modalities that connect black persons of the western hemisphere...to Mother Africa.

Thompson is making no claim of the nature that, for instance, rhythm makes us penetrate to the spirituality of the object of African creation. In his book titled *African Art in Motion: Icon and Act* (1974), he explains:

> I am not arguing, however, that musical quality is consciously suggested by textile-makers, for there is no evidence to that effect, nor am I suggesting that visual quality is transcendentally African.... Nevertheless, it seems to me that it would be irresponsible not to attempt to sharpen awareness of staggered and suspended pattern in some forms of African cloth by reference to off-beat phrasing of melodic accents in music, or in dance.

It is in the chapter titled "Rhythmized Textiles" in *Flash of the Spirit*, which covers the Mande and New World Mande-influenced cloths found in Georgia and Mississippi, that Thompson applies his rhythmic hermeneutic with explicit musical language. He speaks of the "rhythmized, pattern-breaking textile modes" and says the "spontaneity in design" (improvisation) constitutes a tendency towards "metric play and staggering of accented elements." These designs, which he says are virtually intended to be scanned metrically, are visually resonant with the "off-beat phrasing of melodic accents in African and Afro-American music," a musico-visual idiom he says is unique to the black world. Speaking summarily of the "visual sound" of the textiles found across the Mande Atlantic world, Thompson states: "Thus as multiple meter distinguishes the traditional music of black Africa, emphatic multistrip composition distinguishes the cloth of West Africa and culturally related Afro-American sites."

But what about African statuary that gives the impression of stillness, statuary that does not lend itself to being scanned metrically? In *African Art in Motion* Thompson explains: "The inferential leap from complexity in motion to complexity in sculptural rendering must be handled gingerly. Sculpture stops time. This makes impossible the objective determination of multiple meter in the plastic arts even if it were implied.... If multi-metric dancing is impossible to convey in figural art, nevertheless, in highly sophisticated African civilizations, many acts can be intuited within a single piece of sculpture."

In *African Art and Motion* (1974), a museum guide with a similar title to the aforementioned book, but prepared by a group of art scholars for an exhibition at the National Gallery of Art, Thompson and his coauthors identify the interaction between art (sculpture and dress) and movement (dance and mime). It is visible to the eye that the sensuousness and spontaneity of African dance tradition is reflected in African statuary that portrays bent knees, flexible or supple hips, disposed arms, and even dance postures—that is, "the phrasing of the body." Statuary comprised of depictions of supporting (on the head) portrays what I would like to call rhythmic functionality. However, apparent stillness also implies a kind of rhythmicity. Statuary comprised of depictions of balancing, for instance, reflect the ability of Africans to move confidently with an object balanced on the head. The writers say, "Thus, at a higher level, African balance symbolizes transcendental equilibrium, enabling a person to communicate both physical vitality and mental calm." The authors make a similar point regarding Ghana's Akan priests, who dance balancing on their heads a vessel filled with magical substances and water: "While the art of maintaining physical balance is obviously required, the presence of a higher form of balance, relating man's intellect, to the mind of God, also is suggested." In terms of this statuary being "danced art," then, the apparently immobile figures imply, in the "choreographed universe" of the African world, a macro rhythm of cosmological balance. Perhaps this is what Leopold Senghor meant (essentialism aside) when he claimed that there existed in the plastic arts analogies to musical syncopations and off-beat rhythms.

Apparent stillness or nonrhythmicity in certain African statuary can perhaps be understood as corresponding to the phenomenon of the "break," which is that moment of nonrhythmic pause that appears in African drumming traditions as well as in African-American jazz, gospel-chorus singing, and dancing. Just because rhythm or movement is suspended at the moment of the "break" does not signify arhythmicity, for there is rhythm on each side of the break, and the break actually enhances the rhythm when it recommences. I would also contend that the imprint of rhythmicity outlasts the break (if the imprint is not in fact quasi-permanent). As Thompson suggests in *African Art in Motion*, there is at the macro level a rhythmic balance between action and inaction: "Icons serve to communicate that men and women in Africa recognize that certain balances must be sustained. Assertion and collectivity, 'riding tall' and 'getting down,' being beautiful and being productive—these are some of the essential balances which are struck in life and art." So, statuary depicting sitting—which communicates composure, wisdom, authority, and permanence— have the equivalent in various New World Afro-cultures to what is called "cool" in Afro-America. Statuary comprised of figures that are apparently still thus imply not arhythmicity but rhythmic control and discipline. Like religion, which gives rise to culture but is not always visible, rhythm is not always visible as a visual representation of movement.

But rhythm does not only bind people of African ancestry— Du Bois, Dett, Maynor, Eddie Harris, myself. In this regard, I omitted an important segment of the above extended quote from Thompson's *Flash of the Spirit*. Thompson says his book discusses the visual and philosophical streams of creativity that parallel the musical and choreographic modalities that connect black people of the West to Africa—"as well as the millions of Europeans and Asian people attracted to and performing their styles." Black rhythm, whether manifested in our visual art, clothing, or music, is what seduces rather than segregates. I will discuss this fully in Chapter 5.

***

Just as Thompson applies this rhythmic hermeneutic to his reading of African and Afro-diasporan visual linkages, so can this hermeneutic be applied to African-American archaeology as I contest the postmodernist conspiratory claims that African-American culture is a myth and that the "African" in our racial designation is a cultural misnomer. Though we would presume that rhythm, like music, is forever irreclaimable after its manifestation in performance, I contend, with the help of the foregoing information from Thompson, that African rhythm left its own imprint in the earth in which archaeologists dig. I was led to this conclusion after coming to terms with a question anthropological archaeologist Leland Ferguson asked and answered in his book, *Uncommon Ground: Archaeology and Early African America, 1650-1800* (1992):

> However white Southerners and others responded to the Civil Rights Movement, one thing was true: it commanded respect. Black leaders were courageous, dignified, and articulate. But where did their strength come from? How was it created? Most whites could not say.... How could American Negroes—supposedly primitive at worst and poorly educated at best—gather the strength to fight the establishment and win? The answer, of course, was that beyond the eye and mind of the white majority, African American culture was vibrantly alive, and had been alive for more than three hundred years. Through that span, African Americans combined African legacy with American culture, and along the way they left stories in the ground.

Through his study of the earthen story of 17th- and 18th-century southern plantations, Ferguson confirms that the material culture of enslaved Africans laid the domestic foundation for an African American culture that gave its adherents what Ferguson calls "power." I think this "power" is what I have termed "rhythmic confidence." We can also see how closely Leonard Barrett's notion of "soul-force" corresponds with Ferguson's foregoing answer to the question of where our strength came from when we were so direly oppressed. Barrett says:

> We began our study by reviewing our African heritage under the heading, "Source of Soul." In this discussion we established the fact that the sons and daughters of Africa did not come to the New World from a cultural wilderness but from a land with well-established cultural institutions, and that it was the transplantation of these culture dynamics in the New World that enabled the Africans in diaspora to preserve their sense of humanity in the face of the devastating assault of chattel slavery.

Ferguson says the material culture that was African-derived—tools, pottery, basketry, dwellings, and so forth—constituted symbols of power that reinforced the enslaved's views of themselves as Africans who were culturally distinct from their captors: "While many slaves may not have overtly resisted their enslavement on a day-to-day basis, most did ignore European American culture in favor of their own, and in doing so they also ignored and resisted the European American ideology that rationalized their enslavement. Archaeological research helps us see the contrast between the world the slaves built and the one they rejected." So, the extent to which contemporary African Americans claim Africa as a whole is not only the extent to which we value our ancestral history and our cultural heritage, but also the extent to which we continue to reject, with rhythmic confidence, the culture of our oppressors.

I claim, then, that the social advances of the civil rights movement came through a confidence derived from our heritage of rhythm. Dett and Maynor were contributors to that tradition. I believe also that this confidence was especially nurtured in the context of religion. Ferguson's archaeology lends some validity to my thesis in scientific terms:

> While objects like engraved spoons and African-style shrines seldom were mentioned in written documents, artifacts excavated on plantation sites, coupled with our discoveries of Bakongo-style marks on bowls from lowcountry sites suggest that the preserved remains of many shrines and rituals must lie buried underground across the South. Archaeological evidence of African-style religious practice in America reinforces and

makes tangible our sense that slaves brought to the Americas not only a variety of practical skills, but also elements of their African spiritual beliefs.

In my project of arguing for the viability of a transatlantic Pan-Africanism, the archaeological evidence reinforces and makes tangible my sense that the enslaved brought to the Americas not only their spiritual beliefs but the rhythms that undergirded and circumscribed those beliefs, as well as the rhythmic confidence that allowed for the sustained articulation of those beliefs. The rhythms of religious ritual did not disappear but were carried with Africans in their gait and their language, and it appeared in their visual traditions.

I am probably proceeding beyond a scientific reading of the archeological record, but I am still not trespassing on the essentialist notions of negritude. The record shows, for instance, that the dwellings of the enslaved Africans in the tobacco country of Virginia were more European than African in size and design because the African minority worked and lived side-by-side with white indentured servants and Native American slaves; while in colonial Carolina the African majority lived in small African-styled dwellings with clay walls and gabled roofs. The point is, no matter whether Euro-American culture dominated the process of creolization in Virginia because of a certain history and demography or whether the opposite was true in colonial Carolina, the rhythms of black folk—African rhythm at its heart—remained, in my assessment, a dominant gene. Similarly, when the culture of early 20th-century northern elite blacks, who had been emulating white culture, met with the culture of the southern working class blacks who migrated north en masse beginning in 1915, the culture of the latter became the dominant strain.

Before this dominant strain made its trek northward, it had been made distinctive by a different rhythmic worldview. For instance, in early 19th-century Carolina when the dwellings of the enslaved moved from being African-styled to European-featured, most of the family activities continued to occur *around* the dwelling, in a traditional West African way, rather than *in* the dwelling. This traditional relationship between Africans and their dwellings accounts for a different rhythmic worldview—a different "choreographed universe," to use Thompson's words—than that of Euro-Americans who lived *in* their homes.

Far fewer African Americans live around, rather than in, their homes in the late 20th century; but this tradition that nurtured African rhythmicity continued long enough for that rhythmicity to proliferate into other manifestations, such as the blues. Whether the rhythmized, pattern-breaking textile modes of the Mande and New World Mande-influenced cloths can be found in locations other than in Georgia and Mississippi, the point is that this tradition, with the help of other African-derived visual traditions, continued long enough for that rhythmicity to influence what Katrina Hazzard-Gordon, in her work on African-American dance, calls "the jook continuum." Thus, Africa can be legitimately understood as our natural—cultural and historical—"home."

***

Hazzard-Gordon explains in *Jookin: The Rise of Social Dance Formations in African-American Culture* (1990) that social dancing has provided a stronger link between African Americans and our African past than any other aspect of our culture. The jook joint has its roots in this African past and is the prototype of Afro-America's secular dance arenas. This important facet of African-American core culture, which emerged in southern towns principally for the entertainment of a rural workforce, is the forerunner of the honky-tonk (the first urban form of the jook), the after-hours joint, the rent party, and the black-owned club. Hazzard-Gordon concludes that no institution has matched the importance of the jook continuum, in that it was in this institution that "core black culture"—its music, dance, food, language, fellowship, and mate selection—found sanctuary.

The juke continuum has its immediate beginnings in the clandestine and public slave dances. The majority of the dance steps among the enslaved were distinctly African in character, and similarities in West African dance vocabulary eased interethnic assimilation on the plantations. Hazzard-Gordon says that after slavery the jook became perhaps the most significant development in the history of African-American secular music and dance, in that it became the central place of refuge during the post-Reconstruction years of intensified, terroristic white supremacy. Since the jook was the only dance arena that accommodated the emerging culture of southern black freedpersons, it served as common ground for the mixing of any remaining strains of African culture along with those additional elements that developed during slavery.

These remaining strands of African culture included "African movement motifs" in such dances as the Charleston, the shimmy, the snake hips, the funky butt, the black bottom, the twist, the itch, the buzzard lope, the fishtail, the camel walk, the slow drag, and the grind. The same motifs can be observed in African and African-American dance to this day. The African dance vocabulary first nurtured on the plantations was therefore constantly recyled. The contemporary soul train line, like the ring shout, had its beginnings among many West African ethnic groups; but while the ring maintains a sacred reference, the line was secularized early on. Hazzard-Gordon explains that the itch, which can be traced back to the Winti people in Suriname (whose dancers tug at their clothing as though scratching), was incorporated into the breakaway of the lindy hop by the late 1940s, only to return as an embellishment to rhythm-and-blues dances of the 1950s. The plantation dance called wringin' and twistin', she says, became the basis of the twist, and the leg gestures of the Charleston appeared in the mashed potatoes of the late 1950s and early 1960s. The hip gestures of the black bottom appeared as an embellishment in the lindy hop and jitterbug, later in the mooche, and even later in the four corners of the late 1960s and early 1970s. The camel walk, concludes Hazzard-Gordon, is a step similar to the Adowa, a Ghanaian funeral dance of the Ashanti people.

The African movement motifs were probably reinforced when newly imported Africans exerted a cultural influence that resulted in the re-Africanization of creolized plantation dance forms. These dance styles, which were therefore more broadly African than specifically derived from particular ethnic groups, were proliferated after slavery by traveling black performers in the southern tent and medicine shows. During the great migration southern blacks brought these African-based dances north. As the jook and honky-tonk evolved into the after-hours joint, rent party, and black-owned club of the urban North, the dances began losing their rural characteristics, says Hazzard-Gordon, and the remnant of group dancing diminished in favor of individualized and increasingly sexualized partner dancing. This practice continued in Afro-America's commercial urban continuum, which is comprised of block parties, membership clubs, night clubs, and dance halls. However, Hazzard-Gordon shows us that the African movement motifs continue in African-American dance up to the present.

My contention is that our acknowledgment of the rhythmic connection can make legitimate our repeated return to Africa for purposes of cultural reassertion and simply for the cultural renewal of our dance forms and other aspects of African-American culture. This is particularly the case when we see that African rhythm has returned full circle to Africa in such genres as rap, which is very popular in urban cities across the continent, as are African-American heroes such as Malcolm X and Muhammed Ali, about whom rappers rhythmize. I will return to rap in Chapters 4 and 5.

2

RACIALISM AND PAN-AFRICANISM

There is a religious tradition among blacks in America in which Africa has been the banner we have needed. This tradition includes the "African" churches of antebellum beginnings, such as the African Methodist Episcopal (AME) Church and the African Methodist Episcopal Zion Church, which have evolved to the present day to be pseudo-Pan-Africanist denominations with undeveloped (indeed faltering) relations with the people and cultures of their African namesake. Henry McNeil Turner, the 19th-century bishop of the AME church, was, on the other hand, an avid colonizationist and a forerunner of Marcus Garvey. During the 20th century this tradition of Africa being the needed banner extended to include Garvey's United Negro Improvement Association (UNIA), George Alexander McGuire's African Orthodox Church, and the Black Jews. Garvey was the most important of these, in that Africa meant not only a unifying banner but the place of destination for the millions of black Americans willing to follow him there. Garvey was also a forerunner to the Harlem Renaissance literati, who were the first African-American aesthetes to recognize cultural and racial bonds with Africa. Like these literati who succeeded him, we cannot underestimate Garvey's influence on what Africa means to us any more than we can ignore the influence of Blyden, Crummell, Senghor, Du Bois, Hughes, Dett, or Maynor.

When Africa Has Been the Banner We Need

> This is the history of a human heart,—the tale of a black boy who many years ago began to struggle with life that he might know the world and know himself.
> — Du Bois, "Of Alexander Crummell"

With the Great Migration under way, bringing large numbers of southern blacks into Harlem, and with many of the black churches championing a new social, political, and intellectual awareness, the atmosphere had been prepared for the arrival of Marcus Garvey, who became one of the greatest leaders of the black world. Garvey, a Jamaican, arrived in Harlem in 1916, then a follower of the self-help pragmatism of Booker T. Washington. The following year he founded the UNIA, which sought to instill in black people a strong sense of racial self-identity and self-determination in part by postulating a doctrine of racial Pan-Africanism. The organization's principal point of connection with the masses of black Americans was its close affiliation with Christianity. In defense of his strategy to have the UNIA remain nondenominational, Garvey removed George Alexander McGuire from the office of Chaplain-General because McGuire wanted his African Orthodox Church to be the UNIA's official religious body. Garvey simply refused to put his followers in a position where they would have to choose between the UNIA and their established denominational affiliations.

Since his relationship with the UNIA had ended, McGuire put his educational training and his experience as a former Episcopal priest to full use for the African Orthodox Church, where he began to develop his own Pan-African interests. In 1924, three years after founding the church, McGuire was elevated to archbishop. Three years hence, while Garvey was being deported following imprisonment for alleged mail fraud, McGuire's Brooklyn-based church was continuing to expand. In 1931, McGuire opened the Holy Cross Pro-Cathedral in Harlem. It was there that he was funeralized three years later. Archbishop Robertson, McGuire's successor, gave the eulogy, calling McGuire a man of "extensive knowledge" who had a "generous heart." An editorial titled "Rev. McGuire, Prelate, Dies," appearing in *The New York Amsterdam News,* said of the well-known prelate:

> Archbishop McGuire was known as a learned metropolitan, but will be remembered as the pioneer who first declared for certain rights denied to Negroes by the Episcopal Church in America.
> He was proud of his race, and because he knew that the Pope would always be Italian, the Archbishop of Canterbury an Englishman, the head of the Russian Orthodox Church a Russian, and the metropolitan of the Greek Church a Greek, regardless of ramifications in other countries, Archbishop McGuire decided to establish the African Orthodox Church as an autonomous institution with a Negro at its head.

McGuire left as his administrative legacy twenty churches in North America, ten in Africa, a jurisdiction in Cuba, a mission in Venezuela, approximately fifty ordained clergy, and several bishops and archbishops. Despite his prolific administration and Pan-African interests, however, McGuire's long-term influence was not to reach that of Garvey. Even after approximately two-and-a-half year's imprisonment, followed by deportation in 1927, Garvey was recognized as one of the world's greatest promoters of black nationalism and Pan-Africanism. The year of Garvey's deportation, Howard University educator Kelly Miller, a rather conservative commentator for the *Amsterdam News,* wrote for the April 27, 1927, issue of the paper: "Garvey, the black, was monarch of all that he surveyed. No Negro has ever reached such a pinnacle of renown with so great a following at his feet." The professor continued on May 4, 1927, "No Negro, not even Booker Washington, ever received such national notoriety.... The Garvey Movement became international in its involvements." The Garvey movement also proved to be resilient in its endurance. Following a convention in Kingston, Jamaica, in 1929, the UNIA was reorganized. In September of the next year Garvey's New York followers organized a parade through Harlem's streets celebrating the first anniversary of the reorganization.

Just as Garvey had worked with and influenced the black nationalist and Pan-Africanist doctrine of the founder of the African Orthodox Church, so had he previous contact with and influence on one of the early leaders of the Black Jews—Rabbi Arnold Josiah Ford. Ford, a West Indian who was formerly the

UNIA's choirmaster, was the pastor of a Jewish congregation called the Beth B'nai Avroham (Abraham) congregation. According to Harlem's leading figure among the Black Jews, Rabbi W. M. Matthew, who was interviewed at length by Edgar Rouzeau for an article titled "Black Israel," the organization known as the Commandment Keepers was the forerunner of this and Harlem's other black Jewish groups. The organization was founded in 1919 and incorporated the following year with Rabbi Matthew as the president. In 1923 Rabbi Mordecai Herman organized the Cushin congregation of Black Jews. When this group underwent a schism in 1925, Rabbi Herman's followers merged with Rabbi Ford's Beth B'nai Avroham, which had been organized a year earlier. Up until 1929, when Rabbi Herman was taken to court by Rabbi Ford for allegedly misappropriating funds, Beth B'nai Avroham had been gaining prominence. Though the charge against Rabbi Herman was dismissed, the incident divided the group. Eventually the congregation disbanded when Rabbi Ford allegedly departed for Ethiopia and Rabbi Herman died. The years that followed, according to Rabbi Matthew, saw the growth of the Commandment Keepers. By mid-1934 they had more than 500 members, and branches of the organization were opened in other parts of the eastern United States as well as in the West Indies.

Rabbi Matthew's Black Jews, Garvey's UNIA, and McGuire's African Orthodox Church each was far in advance of the mainstream "African" churches and all the other black churches in the search for a black theology and Pan-Africanist identity. Their legacy, particularly that of Garvey, has no doubt left a residue that has been inhaled by Pan-Africanist Christians throughout the world. In the United States this would include the denomination called the Shrine of the Black Madonna, founded in the early 1950s by Albert Cleage, and the African American Catholic Congregation, founded in 1989 by George Augustus Stallings, Jr. I believe that these denominations that nurture a connection with Africa, despite whatever particular problems critical scholars have identified with each of these denominations, can serve as models to be taken seriously in the search for a viable Pan-Africanism. But before I can make the claim, I would do well to fend off the arguments made to the contrary by Anthony Appiah.

Fending Off Theologies of the Powerful

> The more I met Alexander Crummell, the more I felt how much
> that world was losing which knew so little of him. In another
> age he might have sat among the elders of the land in purple-
> bordered toga...
> — Du Bois, "Of Alexander Crummell"

In Appiah's book, *In My Father's House: Africa in the Philosophy of
Culture,* we have what is perhaps the most recent and careful critique of the sometimes uncritical view of Africa by continental
and New World Africans. As I critique Appiah's work, I will also
have in mind the intent of Henry Louis Gates's edited volume,
"Race," Writing, and Difference (1986), which includes an earlier
version of one of the chapters in Appiah's book. The intent of
"Race," Writing is stated by Gates in his introduction. He says (as
Appiah states elsewhere) that when we speak of race we appear
to be uttering an objective term of classification, when really it is
a dangerous biological misnomer which, in inscribing allegedly
"natural" differences, has left in its wake the slaughter of millions
of human beings. In his conclusion to the volume he says, "our
task is to utilize language more precisely, to rid ourselves of the
dangers of careless usages of problematic terms which are drawn
upon to delimit and predetermine the lives and choices of human
beings who are not 'white.'" Still, it is Appiah's book, more than
any other, that makes the protracted philosophical arguments
regarding postmodernism and racial identity. Furthermore,
Appiah ties this whole postmodernist perspective to the question
of Pan-Africanism.

Appiah, who is a Ghanaian, warns against our perceiving
Africa's modern identity as a unity based on notions of culture or
race. He begins by arguing that black racialism—the concept of
race derived from 19th-century European thought—is no longer
an intelligent reaction to white racism. Though his statement suggests that there was a time when black racialism was possibly an
"intelligent reaction" to white racism, he assails Crummell and Du
Bois (and Garvey and McGuire by implication) for developing a
Pan-Africanism based on the racial concept of the black person.
He follows Du Bois's discarding of biological notions of race
through to his adoption of a concept of race as an elusive entity
that can be better felt than explained. To this effect, Du Bois says
of Africa in *Dusk of Dawn:* "On this vast continent were born and

lived a large portion of my direct ancestors going back a thousand years or more. The mark of their heritage is upon me in color and hair. These are obvious things, but of little meaning in themselves; only important as they stand for real and more subtle differences from other men. Whether they do or not, I do not know nor does science know today." To be more generous than Appiah, this racialist response to the experience of racism is what Jean-Paul Sartre called "antiracist racism" in *Black Orpheus* with reference to Senghor's negritude. Nonetheless, Appiah fears that the consequence of even "antiracist racism" will be nothing short of continued self-evaluation within the confines of our presumed racial inferiority.

I would contend that Du Bois's criterion for a Pan-Africanist nationalism that is simultaneously continental and diasporan—his idea of black people having a common "social heritage" of slavery, discrimination, and insult—is still possible as an "intelligent" reaction to racism. But Appiah finds something disconcerting in the view that what Africans share in common is the fact that European imperialism exploited them. Appiah seems especially resentful that Crummell's and Du Bois's racialist Pan-Africanism was exported to Africa where it was embraced and proliferated by African nationalists such as Ghana's Kwame Nkrumah. Appiah says, "Since they conceived of Africa in racial terms, their low opinion of Africa was not easily distinguishable from a low opinion of the Negro, and they left us, through the linking of race and Pan-Africanism, with a burdensome legacy." The nature of this legacy is explained by V. Y. Mudimbe in *The Invention of Africa* (1988): "In effect, in the early 1960s, the African scholar succeeded the anthropologist, the 'native' theologian replaced the missionary, and the politician took the place of the colonial commissioner. All of them find reasons for their vocations in the dialectic of the Same and the Other." Mudimbe continues, "These paradoxes reveal that we are dealing with ideology. Modern African thought seems somehow to be basically a product of the West. What is more, since most African leaders and thinkers have received a Western education, their thought is at the crossroads of Western epistemological filiation and African ethnocentrism. Moreover, many concepts and categories underpinning this ethnocentrism are inventions of the West." When Appiah discusses the commodification of neotraditional African art and literature by the West, he insists that we reject the commercial demand for an invented Africa of exotic mysteries and a sentimentalized past. Part of the difficulty with this burdensome legacy of race is that it was created to oppress blacks, which is why Appiah decries the fact that we have unwittingly bought into Europe's racial fictions. He most probably would decry the racialism of Garvey, McGuire, and Matthews, and appreciate the challenge that Dett and Maynor gave to the likes of Carl Sandburg and Olin Downes on this account. Though he concedes that the identity of every people is historically constructed and has its share of invented histories, biologies, and cultural affinities, he feels that the "falsehoods" about Africa being an organic community (doubtless including the "falsehoods" poeticized by the Harlem Renaissance literati) are too serious for intellectuals to ignore. Appiah fears the possibility of these folk theories of race, these mythologies of an Africa unified by a glorious past or a shared metaphysics, being presumed to be true. If people of African ancestry can come together around the concept of the black person and create productive alliances, we might presume that any theoretical objections should give way to the practical value of these alliances; but Appiah insists that there is every reason to doubt that such alliances can endure.

One reason the concept of the black person is inadequate to Appiah is because it creates interracial boundaries with other people of color; while intraracially it leaves us unprepared to handle conflicts resulting from our different economic realities. This is the reason Appiah finds the theories of the Afrocentric Egyptianists, such as Cheikh Anta Diop, to be disabling: They require us to see the past—the Egyptian pharaonic civilization—as the location of unity and wholeness to the degree that we are diverted from creatively confronting the problems of the present.

Not only is it objectionable to Appiah that all people of African ancestry unite around the concept of the black person, but also for Africans to do so. After Africans opposed European colonialism during what was a rare historical moment of African solidarity, they were left at the time of independence with European-created states that nationalized peoples of differing ethnic traditions and languages. This accounts for much of the difficulty Africans have had in attaining national unity and in fashioning a continental Pan-Africanism. In the postcolonial years there were not only the precolonial variances of ethnicity to contend with but also the variances formed by differing experiences under the colonial regimes. Appiah contends that the experiences of Africans under the British, French, Portuguese, and Belgians were so vastly different that basing a Pan-Africanism on rhetoric about European atrocities is insufficient to capture the imagination of Africans who did not have overwhelmingly negative experiences with the colonizer. He explains that many Africans living in villages amid their families remained relatively untouched by cruel forms of colonialism and therefore did not harbor the kind of resentment toward Europeans that South Africans and African Americans did.

Appiah uses the same reasoning to discount the viability of a transatlantic Pan-Africanism based on a presumed common racial experience among black people. He says that the rhetoric that resulted from the enslavement and segregation of black people in America does not necessarily have special meaning to Africans, who may not have experienced those same forms of insult and injustice. Despite the dissemination of colonial Christianity and education, the cultures of the vast majority of Africans, says Appiah, only felt shallow penetration by the colonizer. The colonials may have attempted to stigmatize African traditional religious beliefs but Africans conspired against them, concealing their disregard for much of European Christianity by camouflaging their religious traditions behind a thin veil of Christian belief. As I will discuss in the next chapter, however, that veil was not so thin after all, just as it was not so thin among enslaved Africans in the New World; for in both Africa and America there is but a minority of Christians who are trying to bring to Christianity more of the beliefs and rituals of traditional African societies.

Despite the possibility here for a common Pan-African project among such Afro-Christians trying to re-Africanize Christianity, Appiah thinks otherwise. In an effort to argue for a Pan-Africanism that does not function on a common heritage of European imperialism or white oppression (and consequently on the basis of race), Appiah raises some reasonable facts about the different colonial experiences of Africans and the distinction between those experiences and the American slave experience. Because Appiah's conclusion is that the Pan-Africanist projects of Africa and the New World must go their separate ways, we should, before accepting what is to me an extreme solution that plays into the postmodernists' interests, examine closely the presuppositions that allow him to argue as he does. Certainly if I wish to make my Pan-Africanist claim that rhythm—as something that endured the slave factories and the middle passage—culturally binds African peoples, continental and diasporan, I must examine closely Appiah's premises.

Appiah's first assumption is that the majority of Africans, who did not have extreme colonial experiences, do not feel a personal sense of insult resulting from a knowledge that if they were in, say, South Africa or America they too would be victims. Only the affected or the enlightened, Appiah presumes, would be sufficiently informed so as to feel this "mediated sense of insult"; and those Africans who do feel this are not, Appiah says, feeling anything more than could decent whites holding the thought that if they were black they too would be victims. Certainly, however, the number of whites who have had this thought are relatively few, and the number who have been led to struggle against racism because of this thought are even fewer.

> *May 22: After dinner we went to the Market Theatre in Johannesburg to see the musical Sarafina, by Mbongeni Ngema. It is fascinating that there is such a mixed crowd of blacks and whites....*
> *Throughout the second half of Act 1 I could not contain my tears. The hurt they have suffered and share with us, I feel. I wonder if the whites here feel it, and if so what they will do about it. I will do more, more than I have been doing. I will draw from their pain and history and struggle, connect it with our own in America, and tell my people to sing a new song of liberation—not a song of complaisance but of freedom.... If this is not the message of Jesus the prophet then I cannot be a Christian.*

In implying that it is an act of racialism for blacks to have empathy for only other blacks just because decent whites can also feel our insult, Appiah has set up the premises that permit him to discredit the thoughts of Du Bois about the oppression of the entire nonwhite world: If there exists this common experience of oppression by European imperialism then why does Du Bois write as if he has to choose association with Africans over other groups of color? This, Appiah says, is exactly the narrow choice that racialism imposes on us. On this matter I only go so far as to concur with Cornel West in *Race Matters*, because West recognizes the logic behind this mindset of Du Bois:

> Instead of a closing-ranks mentality, a prophetic framework encourages a coalition strategy that solicits genuine solidarity

with those deeply committed to antiracist struggle. This strategy is neither naive nor opportunistic; black suspicion of whites, Latinos, Jews, and Asians runs deep for historical reasons. Yet there are slight though significant antiracist traditions among whites, Asians, and especially Latinos, Jews, and indigenous people that must not be cast aside. Such coalitions are important precisely because they not only enhance the plight of black people but also because they enrich the quality of life in America.

What Appiah fails to consider, however, is that there is a caste within the nonwhite world—caste which, nurtured by global white supremacist ideology—places Africans and their continent at the bottom of the world order. In the September 7, 1992, issue of *Time* magazine (the aforementioned issue titled "The Agony of Africa"), Africa is referred to as "the third world of the third world" and "a vast continent in free fall." This rhetoric points to the reality that, to a degree significant enough, every other people of color are permitted in this global system of white supremacist ideology to distance themselves hierarchically from people of African descent. Again Hacker, despite his own liberalist racism, understands. He says that all nonwhites can detail the discrimination they have suffered from whites but that a distinction is permitted by whites who hand out the racial memberships. He continues, "members of all these 'intermediate' groups have been allowed to put a visible distance between themselves and black Americans. Put most simply, none of the presumptions of inferiority associated with Africa and slavery are imposed on these other ethnicities."

We should take these admissions wherever we can find them, even if they come from postmodern Gobineaus such as Hacker. But Appiah seems out of touch with racial reality in this country in which he has lived and taught for more than a decade. In terms of the racial politics in Africa, he seems equally unwilling to consider the arguments of the novelist Ngũgĩ wa Thiong'o. He rejects what he calls the literary "nativism" of the Kenyan novelist because he sees this "nativism" as a reflection in academic literary criticism of the romantic racialism of Crummell and Du Bois. This "nativism" holds that to write in European languages is to remain colonized, as Ngũgĩ puts it in *Decolonising the Mind* (1986):

But the biggest weapon wielded and actually daily unleashed by imperialism against that collective defiance is the cultural bomb.

The effect of a cultural bomb is to annihilate a people's belief in their names, in their languages, in their environment, in their heritage of struggle, in their unity, in their capacities and ultimately in themselves. It makes them see their past as one wasteland of non-achievement and makes them want to distance themselves from that wasteland. It makes them want to identify with that which is furthest removed from themselves; for instance, with other peoples' languages rather than their own.

Appiah criticizes Ngũgĩ for requiring that these languages be abandoned by intellectuals, based on Ngũgĩ's suspicion that a hostile spirit remains at work in them. Appiah is no doubt thinking of the passage in the latter book where Ngũgĩ speaks of the power of imperialism: "In my view language was the most important vehicle through which that power fascinated and held the soul prisoner. The bullet was the means of the physical subjugation. Language was the means of the spiritual subjugation." Appiah contends, conversely, that the European languages need not transmit the imperialist visions of their original speakers, that these languages instead have been turned against that imperialism like double agents.

An instance of European languages in the service of new masters—an instance of this linguistic "mastery of form"—occurs when African intellectuals write europhone literature that is specifically about themselves or their cultures. Appiah says that the languages of the colonizers can also be creolized and their imperialist visions playfully subverted in the lyrics of popular song (I specifically discuss this as the "mastery of form" in Chapter 4). It is obvious that Wole Soyinka writes in English, for example, but it is difficult to determine whose English it is, claims Appiah: "In Soyinka we hear a voice that has ransacked the treasuries of English literary and vernacular diction, with an eclecticism that dazzles without disconcerting, and has found a language that is indisputably his own."

I agree, as someone who believes in the viability, if not necessity, of the "mastery of form." I made my position on this clear in Chapter 1 with reference to Dett and Maynor. That is to say I agree that even if it were argued that Soyinka writes a Briton's English, he and other contemporary African writers would still have a project that is distinctly different from that of a British writer. In other words, there would still be inside the outer Europeanism an intrinsic Africanism. While the European writer engages in a search for the self via an inner voyage of discovery, explains Appiah, the African writer engages in a search for an African culture. While the European writer asks "Who am I?" and may feel that the problem of who "I" is can be a personal problem, the African writer asks "Who are we?" believing that "my" problem is "ours." For the African writer the project that is "ours" derives, Appiah says, from a set of problems common to African peoples: recent colonialism, the nationalizing of multifarious ethnic groups, and the persistence of foreign languages that belong to colonizers who defined Africans by race as inferior.

***

Overall, this common project for African intellectuals involves the transition from traditional to modern life and loyalties. This transition, forced by colonization and postcolonial interaction with the West, includes the growth in literacy and the modern economy and the change from communalistic (oral) to individualistic (literary) cultures. Involvement in the West's institution of publishing agitates this struggle, explains Appiah, since an author, despite rootedness in the "we" tradition of oral culture, is expected to become the authoritative "I." Thus, the transition from oral to literary culture requires the resolution of the tension between individualistic cognitive styles that tend to be more adversarial in nature and the communitarian worldview that tends to result in more accommodative behavior. Appiah says that this transition also requires a resolution in the tension between traditional belief and natural science, including the question of how much of the traditional world of the spirits must be given up or assimilated—for instance, transformed into ceremony devoid of literal belief in the invisible. In this project that draws them into a common, Pan-African sphere, says Appiah, African intellectuals must contend with either the difficulty or impossibility of believing both in modern development and in the preservation of the best of their cultural heritage.

In the realm of art or music, this meeting of the traditional and the modern can be seen in the "neotraditional," which Appiah says is produced specifically for the West. In the realm of literature this neotraditionalism involves a postcolonial African intelligentsia of Western education writing in European languages, employing Western literary techniques, depending on the promotion of the Western publisher, and, in so doing, offering the West a commodity comprised of its mythic portrayals of Africa. If there is a lesson in this cultural exchange between Africa and the West, says Appiah, it is that the two are already "contaminated by each other," that there is no longer a fully traditional African culture awaiting salvage by African artists—just as, he says, there is no American culture without African roots.

It is the reality of an Africa in transition from the traditional to the modern, an Africa irrevocably "contaminated" by the West, that Appiah says is the basis of commonalities for a rational Pan-Africanism; not an Africa whose societies are presumed to hold a common stock of cultural knowledge. With respect to a Pan-Africanist literary culture, then, writers should be referred to as African only to the degree that they grapple with these common problems in their writing. Appiah argues likewise concerning the unresolved question of what African philosophy is. First of all, he says there is no overall African philosophy in the continent's so-called folk philosophies, because different cultures have varying concepts regarding God, gods, evil, justice, knowledge, life, reason, truth, and so forth; secondly, this so-called folk philosophy is, to Appiah, little more than folklore. To presume that there is something otherwise organically African to be done in philosophy is, contends Appiah, to digress to the racialist notion that because there is a philosophy that whites have claimed as their intellectual property then there must be some aspect of the intellectual life that belongs to blacks.

Just as African writers are in search of a culture rather than of the self, so can a distinctly African philosophy be based on the postcolonial situation: specifically the syncretism of tradition and modernity and of traditional religious world outlooks and natural science. That Appiah thus redefines the limits of commonality for a Pan-African philosophy—a common sociohistorical situation comprised of the vast continent in transition—is part of the reason he disagrees with the Afrocentric Egyptianists that Egyptian philosophy should be the foundation of an African philosophy. He sees Egyptian philosophy as possibly nothing more than a folk philosophy and contends that there is no evidence that the Egyptians were dealing with the same problematic of transition that faces Africa today.

Thus, trying to return to a unified precolonial African identity, in an effort to discover a basis for an *African* writing and philosophy, is erroneous to Appiah, since precolonial diversities hardly allowed for a unified African culture. But he believes an African identity is in fact evolving—as a product of Africa's shared ecological, economic, and political realities—on which a rational Pan-Africanism can be based. However, this emerging African identity belongs only to continental Africans, not to New World Africans, whom Appiah believes erroneously view Africa as our natural, racial home. He argues that a Pan-Africanism devoid of the mystifications and mythologies he deplores, one based on the sociohistorical commonalities he lays out, must separate a Pan-Africanism of the African continent from any Pan-Africanisms of the continent's diaspora. For instance, African-American culture is not African in the sense of what Appiah argues is actually common to continental Africans: "Shared traditions do not help: the traditions of African Americans that are African-derived are derived from *specific* African cultures, and are thus not a common black possession; and the American-ness of African-Americans has to do with traditions developed in the New World in interaction with the cultures brought by other Americans from Europe and Asia."

November 13: Antonia Okono said something interesting as a response to my question of African unity. She said she feels a greater sense of unity with other Africans as a continental African than as a citizen in her own country of Kenya because of tribalism. Hardly a day goes by, she said, when one is not reminded of who he or she is.

What I am claiming is that the rhythmic tradition of African Americans is a common black possession, that the rhythms of black folk are fundamentally African in the broadest sense.

***

The consequence of Appiah's desire to separate African and African-American Pan-Africanism would be to remove from the African-American worldview the kind of stability that mythologies (that religion) provide. I am perhaps saying the opposite of what Appiah means when he comments, "'African solidarity' can surely be a vital and enabling rallying cry; but in this world of genders, ethnicities, and classes, of families, religions, and nations, it is as well to remember that there are times when Africa is not the banner we need." I am suggesting that, for reasons Appiah does not address, there are times when Africa, within the context of a racial mythology, *is* the banner we need, and that Garvey, McGuire, and others recognized that. Since we disagree, and especially since Appiah's argument is worrisome to me (someone concerned about the unification of peoples of African ancestry), I can at least lessen the grip of his logic by showing the presence of a double standard in his argument.

Appiah contends that African peoples can accept the imposition of the European languages, which are now a unifying factor in nations of multiple ethnic tongues, because we have indigenized these languages. We have indigenized them even to the degree that we are able to employ them to deconstruct the European imperialism these languages once carried. He contends that since it is too late for Africa to escape European "contamination," we might as well use to our advantage this situation that history has thrust upon us. I agree, but contend that the same logic holds regarding the notion of race. Here I am glossing what Frantz Fanon says in *Studies in a Dying Colonialism* (1959). Even though he (akin to me) was not a proponent of cultural negritude, Fanon states: "It is the white man who creates the Negro. But it is the Negro who creates negritude." Appiah admits there is no reason to believe that by denying the existence of race that racism will be obliterated, that Africans could escape the stigma of the centuries, because racism does not require the actuality of races. This becomes pointedly clear when we examine the words of a white teenaged "gaybasher" of Houston, who was interviewed on the January 9, 1992, edition of the CBS television show *Street Stories*, anchored by Ed Bradley. The youth said that the gays did not seem human, that they seemed like "their own race." I am not suggesting that we return to the essentialist doctrines of race—biological or ontological—but since we cannot escape contamination by Europe's concept of race and we have creatively indigenized the concept (not so much biologized race as theologized it), we should seek to use creatively this unifying factor to our advantage.

Our having creatively theologized race is what has resulted in accusations against Stephen Carter, Shelby Steele, Glenn Loury, and Stanley Crouch that they are "not black enough": They do not subscribe to that core motif of liberation theology that teaches us to lift up "the least of them"—those who are "black," as James Cone defines them symbolically. Cone says in his first book, *Black*

Theology and Black Power (1969), "In America, blacks are oppressed because of their blackness. It would seem, then, that emancipation could only be realized by Christ and his Church becoming black. Thinking of Christ as nonblack in the twentieth century is as theologically impossible as thinking of him as non-Jewish in the first century." Since the notion of racial inferiority was originally theorized theologically rather than scientifically, reinventing "black" in this way is a powerful reversal in the face of continued subjugation.

We have always known that few whites are "black," but for those who have the markings—the gross morphology—that generally signal an existential understanding of the underside of history, this neglect of such others is shocking. While on the one hand Loury is struggling to resolve the dissonance between his personal identity and the socially constructed definition of who he is supposed to be as a black American—namely, the dissonance of being seen by many other blacks as "not black enough"—he, on the other hand, calls himself a Christian (which certainly involves a socially constructed definition of who he is supposed to be as a follower of Christ). In an essay in Gerald Early's *Lure and Loathing,* titled "Free at Last? A Personal Perspective on Race and Identity in America," he defines himself as "a husband, a father, a son, a teacher, an intellectual, a Christian, a citizen." I am suggesting that "racial fatigue" is unchristian, and it is shocking to blacks to find other blacks who are unchristian in this way: believing, as Carter wishes to believe about himself, that they can be in solidarity with the "least of us" by simply being successful individuals (who *happen* to be black) or by being good role models in the ivory tower. Thus, for blacks to say that Carter, Steele, Loury, and Crouch are "not black enough" really has no more to do with essentialism than it has to do with actual skin color. It is a metaphor for saying they are not "my kind" of blacks, which means theologically that they are not "my kind" of Christians. It is not a flaw in their racial identity; it is a flaw in their Christian proclivity.

Since we have creatively theologized the concept of race, then, there is no need to discard this unifying factor. The same logic holds regarding Christianity, a religion that Appiah does not challenge but passively accepts. If we were to apply the postmodernist criticism of race to Christianity we would have to explode the whole notion of monotheism, so that the concept of a Christ—a single messiah that requires us to model our identities after him—would have to be abandoned. If Christianity in Afro-

America and Africa can be, as Appiah believes, creatively adapted when being a Christian involves a socially constructed definition and Christianity is a Western hand-me-down largely acquired during slavery and colonization, then so can the idea of race be creatively developed. Appiah has not dealt with this challenge to his argument because he has not adequately responded to Ngũgĩ's challenge to both colonial languages and Christianity, especially in *Detained: A Writer's Prison Diary* (1981), *Barrel of a Pen: Resistance to Repression in Neo-Colonial Kenya* (1983), and *Decolonising the Mind: The Politics of Language in African Literature* (1986). In *Barrel of a Pen* Ngũgĩ says:

> The colonial education system denies that the colonized have real human languages. These are described as vernaculars meaning the languages of slaves or merely barbaric tongues. So the children of the colonized are punished and ridiculed whenever they are caught speaking their mother's language, and rewarded when they speak the language of the master, French, English, Portuguese or Italian as the case may be. This had one aim: to make a child despise his language, hence the values carried by that language, and by implication despise himself and the people who spoke a language which now was the cause of his daily humiliation and corporal punishment. By the same token he will admire the language of the conqueror, and hence the values carried by that language and the people who evolved the language of his daily reward and praise.
>
> But these values are reinforced by Christianity, particularly the version brought by missionaries. To the European colonizer the African has no religion, he knows not God. He is superstitious, and worships idols and several Gods. There is only one God, though he has a Son, begotten by the Holy Spirit. This God is white: his angels are white; and when the saved finally go to heaven, they will wear white robes of purity. But the devil is black; his angels are black; sin itself is black; and when the sinful finally go to Hell, they'll be burnt to black charcoal. Is it surprising that the African converts sing in pleading terror: Wash me Redeemer and I shall be whiter than snow? Is it any wonder that African converts wear white robes of virgin purity during their white wedding? And is it any wonder that African women often buy red, blond or brunette wigs to hide their black hair? And is it any wonder that African women and men will apply *Ambi* and other skin-whitening creams to lighten their dark skins? Whiteness

becomes a Christian virtue as in Smith's Rhodesia and Botha's South Africa.

Because Appiah has not adequately answered Ngũgĩ, he is permitted to see as nothing more than a veiling of his earlier appeal to biological notions of race, Du Bois's claim that the gross morphology (color, bone, and hair) of Africans "stand for real and more subtle differences" in peoples of African ancestry. On the other hand, I see Du Bois's "subtle differences" as being comprehensible in cultural terms. I am claiming that in culturalizing rather than biologizing race, one factor in our creative conception of "race" can be our rhythm. I am not in this instance theologizing "race" because that would throw us back to Senghor's essentialist ideas about rhythm—rhythm as the "archetype of the vital element" and as that which distinguishes our allegedly natural "character of abandon." All that I had learned from Dett and Maynor would have been for naught.

***

Appiah's basic argument against my proposition, notwithstanding, is that the time has passed for black racialism to be an intelligent reaction to white racism.

> *November 21: At 4:00 Phyllis Byrd had dinner guests—Shanta (from the United States) and two Africans, one from Nigeria and the other from Rwanda. We had a good time. I felt as at home with them as I do when we have African-American guests to our own home....*
>
> *I asked about how at home the Nigerian and Rwandan feel here in Kenya, and both said that despite the cultural differences they still feel they are among other Africans. Particularly when it comes to the Europeans and Indians, they feel that Kenya is their country because it is part of Africa. They said, in the words of the Nigerian, that they do not feel like foreigners.*

But for whom really has the time passed? If we read Appiah carefully, the time has passed for intellectuals for whom inconsistency in belief—belief that does not stand up to logical argument—is a sign of irrationality. The time has passed for intellectuals who hold up rationality as, like Appiah seems to, the object of requisite faith:

Rationality is best conceived of as an ideal, both in the sense that it is something worth aiming for and in the sense that it is something we are incapable of realizing. It is an ideal that bears an important internal relation to that other great cognitive ideal, Truth. And, I suggest, we might say that rationality in belief consists in being disposed so to react to evidence and reflection that you change your beliefs in ways that make it more likely that they are true.

Appiah concludes that while we cannot change the world only by evidence and reasoning, we certainly cannot expect to change the world without these things. His esteem for the new god of the West leads to a third argument of his, in which there is room for opposing views.

While Appiah presents evidence that the old gods have not always served Africans well and that literal belief in spirits has often resulted in tragic consequences which rationality could have prevented, he withholds evidence regarding the myriad failures of the new gods rationality and truth. Appiah at least understands the complexity of the project he proposes, for he says that for new truths from the West to become the basis of national life and policy, they must be believed; and whether or not these truths will be believed will depend on how intellectuals are able to assimilate traditional beliefs and the modern ideas that "rush at us from worlds elsewhere." I contend that the idea of rationality and truth completely replacing the mythologies and mystifications of African or black identity is, in being one of those ideas that rushes at us from worlds elsewhere, utterly otherworldly. Appiah is considering neither the global evidence that human beings are still fundamentally religious human beings nor the cultural pattern that the oppressed require mythologies and mystifications (including our rhythms) to fend off the theologies of the powerful. In not considering this, it is understandable that Appiah would state in a negative rather than positive connotation that African Americans need Africa as a source of validation.

Appiah, in sum, rejects the prospect that racism could be countered by accepting the categories of race. So does Henry Louis Gates, whose argument we should hear first because it is much simpler and is actually the premise of Appiah's more complicated argument below. Gates simply says, "When we attempt to appropriate, by inversion, 'race' as a term for an essence—as did the negritude movement, for example...—we yield too much: the basis of a shared humanity." But we can agree that race is not an essence but rather a metaphor pointing to, I would say, cultural differences as well as to experiential differences, given that blacks and whites have been on the opposite ends in the master-slave dialectic. But my concession that I refer not to essence would not satisfy Gates or Appiah because the word "race" itself is fraught with implications too inseparable from hierarchical understandings of races.

But this argument alone has as its end the verification of Ngũgĩ's claim that we need to abandon the European languages because they are replete with problems surrounding gender, race, class, and empire. If we follow Gates' argument, is not the next step (if it is not in fact the same step) to claim that the term "African" is too dangerous a word because of its historic devaluation, the implication of a "dark" essentialism? Is not the next step (if it is not in fact the same step) to claim that the term "black" is too dangerous because of the predominance of Western religious symbolism where "white" is equivalent to good and "black" to evil? Is it not the next step to abandon the traditional disciplines coming out of Europe, which carry in their theory and methodology a tainted legacy of racialism, particularly the disciplines of anthropology, sociology, psychology, and history? The word "ethnic" is no better than the word "race" because everyone is ethnic except whites—the unethnic, the "unraced" (as Toni Morrison states). I think Houston Baker's response to Appiah's essay in *"Race," Writing, and Difference* is, in this regard, equally a response to Gates. Writing in the same volume, Baker says:

> In the presence of Appiah's essay, one wants to exclaim, "He is teaching us! He is teaching us!" But depression quickly sets in when one realizes that what Appiah—in harmony with his privileged evolutionary biologists—discounts as mere "gross" features of hair, bone, and skin are not, in fact, discountable. In a world dramatically conditioned both by the visible and by a perduring discursive formation of "old" (and doubtless mistaken) racial enunciative statements, such gross features always make a painfully significant difference—perhaps, *the only* significant difference where life and limb are concerned in a perilous world.
>
> In short, Appiah's eloquent shift to the common ground of subtle academic discourse is instructive but, ultimately, unhelpful in a world where New York cab drivers scarcely ever think of mitochondria before refusing to pick me up.

Appiah's argument, though based on Gates' above premise, proceeds into the sphere we might expect of a philosopher and contends with the ideals of Truth and Rationality. In Appiah's estimation, those who do not hold to his faith have fallen into temptation and intellectual apostasy: "One temptation..., for those who see the centrality of these fictions in our lives, is to leave reason behind: to celebrate and endorse those identities that seem at the moment to offer the best hope of advancing our other goals, and to keep silence about the lies and the myths. But...intellectuals do not easily neglect the truth." This claim that intellectuals do not easily neglect truth is another one of those ideas that rushes at us from alien worlds. History shows that intellectuals reveal only part of truth, often only enough truth to camouflage the mythologies of race, gender, class, and empire that stabilize their privilege. The reality regarding Appiah's assumption that truth predicated in the academy trickles down in the form of national policy to fashion increasing quality of life for the masses is that only *some* of the truth trickles down. Perhaps the most important truths are guarded by intellectuals who have ideological agendas and class interests to protect. Certainly Appiah is correct that our societies profit from the academic institutionalization of the imperative that truth not be neglected, but we cannot expect the unprivileged and oppressed to discard their mythologies and rhythmic mystifications and to tell their truths before the privileged and powerful do.

Here is where I also disagree with those postmodern coconspirators who seek to explode racial identity. In his aforementioned article in *Lure and Loathing,* Stanley Crouch informs us that he is at odds with "the patronizing idea that Negroes are somehow so incapable of existing as adults in the contemporary world that they should always be handled like extremely fragile children who must be fed the myths that 'make them feel good about themselves.'" It must be conceded, however, that the best defenses for the oppressed are theological ones (stated with rhythmic confidence), without which we would stand unguarded to fend off the wicked truths that rush at us from other worlds. In this regard, Sengelese historians Mamadou Diouf and Mohamad Mbodj understood Cheikh Anta Diop well, where Appiah fails to appreciate his significance. In their article "The Shadow of Cheikh Anta Diop," published in Mudimbe's *The Surreptitious Speech,* they say: "Diop's work postulates a theology and does so from the start."

We can understand Appiah's worry, then, that in denying the reality of races, particularly the race of the black person, there are black nationalists who will treat him as though he were proposing genocide, as though he were obliterating all people who claim to be black. Indeed, there may be reason to believe that without a viable replacement the denial of the concept of race would, in further dividing us along lines of class and gender, have the effect of a measure of genocide. The factor of genocide would enter when the black middle-class, with its eyes on the prize of the American Dream, would leave the black poor (already abandoned by white America and the likes of Shelby Steele) to fend for themselves against the mounting social, political, economic, and epidemiological odds that rush at them. Neither do I think we can abandon race without an adequate replacement, when some of our most important institutions—the NAACP and particularly the black church—are built upon it. The black church, with its cultural heritage of rhythms different from the white church, is deeply rooted in the rhetoric and existential reality of race. Without this tie that binds us, what would have become of the social gospel movement in the black church, which was so crucial to our sustenance through the great depression and which prepared us theologically for the civil rights movement?

Historical Amnesia Regarding Race and Progress

> "What then becomes of all your argument, if there are no races and we are all so horribly mixed as you maliciously charge?" Oh, my friend, can you not see that I am laughing at you.
> — Du Bois, *Dusk of Dawn*

We cannot erase the life-saving race work carried out by the Harlem ministers who preached and practiced the social gospel: Reverdy C. Ransom, Adam Clayton Powell, Sr., W. W. Brown, Hutchens C. Bishop, and others who were "my kind" of black people because they were "my kind" of Christians. Ransom, a minister in the AME Church, was one of Harlem's earliest practitioners of the social gospel. His first real pastorate in this tradition of progressive Protestantism, the Institutional Church and Social Settlement, was located in Chicago from 1900 to 1904. As an outgrowth of this prophetic ministry among his people he joined another man of rhythmic confidence and Pan-Africanist leanings in founding the Niagara Movement in 1905, the venerable Du

Bois. The Niagara Movement was the nucleus of that important race institution founded four years later, the NAACP.

In 1907, Ransom moved to Bethel AME Church in Harlem, where he remained the pastor for five years. During this time he began practicing his social ministry among the people of his race in the most impoverished parts of Harlem through the mission he founded, the Simon of Cyrene Mission. Regarding this challenging work, Ransom wrote in his autobiography, *The Pilgrimage of Harriet Ransom's Son:*

> It is hell, but we have plunged into it, and never have we known such joy in the service of our blessed Lord, as we find in offering the lifeline to the poor human derelicts who have suffered moral shipwreck and have been dragged by the treacherous undertow of degeneracy or vice, out where the rescuers from the life-giving stations (the churches) rarely, if ever, venture.

In carrying out this ministry in the black community, Ransom intentionally avoided representing Christianity as being evangelistic and moralistic:

> My wife and I lived in daily contact with the people there. We said nothing about religion whatever. We met all the people in the spirit of brotherly kindness. We visited the sick, the saloons, the houses of prostitution, the gambling joints and all other places we could find that had never known the friendly touch, or the personal interest from people connected with the churches.

The mission was kept open every night of the week and Ransom often held services on the streetside during the summer. Ransom could really preach! He continued this work until he was elected a bishop in 1924, a post that hardly any but a man with rhythmic confidence and preaching abilities could attain.

Adam Clayton Powell came to Harlem in 1908, the year after Ransom had come. He, too, could preach! Soon he, like Ransom, began to establish himself as a practitioner of the social gospel among the "least of us." A sermon he preached some years later to his Abyssinian congregation was excerpted in *The New York Amsterdam News,* on February 28, 1923, in an article titled "Abyssinian Church Holds Services in New Community Edifice." Powell's proclamation was:

> A New Testament Church is one in which the members recog-

nize themselves as the agents through which God supplies the needs of men and women in the community where it is located. The duty of the Abyssinian Church is to meet the needs of the people in Harlem whether they be social, economic, or spiritual. It is just as truly the duty of this church to help the people of this community to become economically efficient as it is to help them to become spiritually fervent. The same Bible which exhorts us to be fervent in spirit also urges us not to be slothful in business. It is just as much our duty to get men and women good positions as it is to get them to join the church.

Displaying the kind of rhythmic elocution that came to be expected of the black Baptist preacher, Powell continued with his theology of liberation that calls into question the Christian proclivity of those postmodernists who feel "racial anxiety":

A man hungry and cold will not have much patience with a lecture on spirituality. If I had no shoes on my feet I would not want any of you to tell me about the golden slippers of the new Jerusalem. If I did not have warm clothes, your sermon on long white robes and golden girdles of Heaven would fall upon deaf ears. If I did not have anything to eat and was starving, your essay about the bread of Heaven would aggravate my appetite.

Powell did not stop at preaching a good and rhythmic message but put his theology to practice with rhythmic confidence. His church maintained a home for the elderly and a social center called the Community House, which housed evening training schools for religion teachers and Red Cross nurses. During the summers the Community House hosted the largest Vacation Bible School for youths in the city. The evening school for religion teachers, called the Harlem Teachers Training School for Religious Workers, offered an impressive curriculum for the black community. During its winter term of 1929, for instance, it offered courses on the New Testament, Church School Administration, Development of the English Bible, the Bible Message of Today, the Teaching Work of the Church, and more. Powell received much acclaim from the black community for the work of the Community House, as a newspaper editorial, "Changes in the Church," reflected:

In the new Abyssinian Baptist Church and Community House, just completed at a cost of three hundred and twenty-five thousand dollars, provision has been made for a gymnasium,

70

shower baths, reading rooms, classes in domestic science, stenography, typewriting, civil government, beauty culture and for an unemployment bureau.
What does this mean? Simply that Rev. A Clayton [Powell], the pastor, and his followers realize that God has no objection to an intelligent Christian and that it is easier to serve Him when one is in good health and gainfully employed, than when one is sick and unemployed. The Community House will provide clean, wholesome amusement and diversion for thousands of young men and women in Harlem who otherwise might seek pleasure in places of questionable repute.

Powell was also one of six Harlem residents to win the 1930 Harmon Award, the incentive awards given by the foundation of William E. Harmon to blacks who distinguished themselves in the areas of business, education, and art. Powell won the bronze medal for religious service.

Another black preacher of the social gospel era was Rev. W. W. Brown, pastor of the Metropolitan Baptist Church. Brown was not as well-known as Powell, and it is difficult to say if he could preach like Powell, but he was known for his involvement in Harlem's economic concerns. Brown repeatedly made "Buy Property!" the theme of his sermons. The reason this message was so important, and the reason the involvement of the black church in this impetus was so crucial, was that too large a percentage of black income left Harlem each week in the hands of white property- and business-owners—people who, Appiah should understand, saw themselves, then as now, as bound together by their race.

The most distinguished of Harlem's churches involved in buying real estate was St. Philip's Protestant Episcopal Church under Rev. Hutchens C. Bishop, who served the church from 1886 to 1933. St. Philip's owned a substantial amount of property in Harlem, including $640,000 in apartment buildings extending a full block on 135th Street. The church's financial capacity was due to the fact that more blacks of educational attainment, and therefore financial means, worshipped at St. Philip's than at any other black church in the city. Because Bishop put his church's income to good economic use for the community, he, like Powell, received well-deserved adulation from his colleagues. Rev. Imes, the pastor of St. James Presbyterian Church, stated in a January 6, 1926, article in *The New York Amsterdam News*: "The best thing that can be said about a churchman is that he believes in the church as adaptable to every phase of human need and experience. This we believe Dr. Bishop has earnestly tried to put into living reality." What tie, then, other than the concept of race, could have bound black people together and otherwise given Ransom, Powell, Brown, and Bishop the impetus to serve their people through that race institution called the black church?

***

The social gospel, preached rhythmically in the black church and practiced confidently in the black community by such distinguished clergymen as the aforementioned, helped prepare Harlem's churches to contend with the Great Depression when it hit in 1929. All of that rhythm binding black church folks together—the preaching, the praying, the singing—was about to pay off in a substantial way. What happened, let me emphasize, needs to be weighed against Appiah's doubt that productive alliances created around the concept of the black person can endure. What happened also needs to be considered in terms of a contemporary model for Afro-Christian churches of the continent and the diaspora, where similar conditions prevail (I am speaking of a common Pan-Africanist agenda). What happened is that in September 1930, St. Mark's Methodist Episcopal Church, a black congregation, hosted a mass meeting in order to determine ways of alleviating the economic depression and of creating jobs. Within a couple of months a centralized movement had been organized, the Harlem Co-operating Committee on Relief and Employment, directed by Shelton Hale Bishop. Bishop, the assistant pastor of St. Philip's Church, was the son of the pastor, Hutchins C. Bishop. Under his youthful leadership the Committee solicited clothing, food supplies, and monetary contributions from Harlem's churches for immediate relief of families in the Harlem black community.

Bishop carried out the coordinating work of the committee expeditiously. Practically every social service agency in Harlem was involved alongside many of the churches, including such organizations as the Urban League, the Association for Improving the Condition of the Poor, the Charity Organization Society, and the Young Men's (YMCA) and Young Women's Christian Association (YWCA). A station was set up to distribute clothing, and a number of churches initiated feeding programs that were coordinated through the central committee. Among these churches were Mother Zion, Bethel, St. Mark's, St. James, and St. Philip's. St. Philip's was the first to start offering breakfast to needy school children who presented cards from their school principals. In the months ahead other black congregations joined in the feeding program.

Abyssinian Baptist Church, given its size and prominence in Harlem, ran its own relief bureau. It was headed by the pastor's son, Adam Clayton Powell, Jr., who coordinated the work with that of the larger committee under Bishop. Describing the results of his church's relief program, the senior Powell said this in the local paper under the headline "Abyssinian Pastor Says Ministers Should Give Jobless Aid":

> In response to the solicitation of this bureau many members of our church have opened their homes to the homeless.
>
> Through the generosity of the Seward Prosser Committee, this bureau has been able to place on an average of 100 half-time workers each week. Others are sent to clean houses, wash windows and do other work for our members who are in good circumstances, and these members pay 50 cents an hour for the services rendered.
>
> At a Sunday morning service two weeks ago the pastor pledged $1,000 of his salary to open a free food kitchen. Within a few minutes, without any urging, church members and church organizations raised in additional pledges and cash $1,500. The relief bureau now has $2,500 in hand or in sight and will open the kitchen Dec. 26, and will keep it open for the next three months or as long as the need exists.

Abyssinian's dramatic club, the Romeo Dramatic Players, also played its part by presenting two one-act plays on timely subjects, "The Employment Office" and "The Man on the Curb." The proceeds from the admissions receipts were donated to a food kitchen that provided free meals for the unemployed.

While many of Harlem's churches, following the lead of Abyssinian and St. Philip's, responded to the economic crisis through social outreach programs, some churches evidently chose not to become involved. The senior Powell, endorsing a statement by Nannie H. Burroughs, founding president of another race institution called the National Women's Training School (located in Washington), castigated those churches that showed indifference toward the crisis. Complaining about "racial fatigue" was simply unacceptable given the seriousness of these circumstances. Powell said in the same newspaper piece, "Every close observer will admit that the situation is the most tragic we have faced since the emancipation.... If the churches do not answer this challenge they ought to shut up and close up."

The junior Powell, who could preach like his father and followed in his father's footsteps, had long taken Nannie Burroughs's challenge to heart. Having been raised in a household in which the social gospel was the standard of ministry and in a church where the preaching maintained black folks' tradition of rhythm, he was already emerging as a man of rhythmic confidence and as the model for social concern and community activism. In a letter to the local press, a Harlem resident named E. Elliott Roberts said of him: "Hats off to the Rev. A. Clayton Powell, Jr. My heart skipped a beat when I saw him picketing Woolworth's 125th street store for refusing to employ Negro clerks in the Harlem establishment. He is the type of preacher Negroes need. He is fearless, courageous and sincere." The church still needs those kinds of preachers and the black community still needs those kinds of black people.

Strong with rhythmic confidence nurtured in the bosom of the black church, the junior Powell eventually carried his fearless style of social concern into the United States Congress, where he represented Harlem from 1945 to 1971. Here we could proceed into an analysis of the black politician—from Reconstruction, through the civil rights era, up to the present—noting the nurturance of the black church and other rhythmic forms of black core culture on their styles of self-confidence. But this recollection of the bygone era of the social gospel—when race, rhythm, and a latent Pan-Africanism were operative—should lead us to call into question Appiah's historical amnesia, his ahistorical postmodernism. It certainly should lead us to call into question Carter's, Steele's, Loury's, and Crouch's religion.

Historical amnesia and "racial fatigue" aside, by the mid-1930s the mainline churches were increasingly being discussed as regards the growing need for Christianity to be more applicable to the needs of the masses. George E. Tait, in a guest editorial in *The New York Amsterdam News*, wrote: "In these days of rising juvenile delinquency, of deplorable housing conditions, of economic catastrophe and political ignorance, the Negro church should abandon selfish interests and wield its influence wisely to guide the people to economic salvation and political freedom."

Tait concluded, "It is a narrow conception of Christianity that preaches a doctrine of heavenly glory in the midst of economic, political, moral and social enslavement on earth." Another editorialist argued in an article titled "The Church Today" that the black church was more important to the black community than the white church to the white community:

> The responsibility imposed upon the Negro church is greater than that of the white church because, in addition to salvation, the Negro needs many other things the white race already has with more limited means of getting them. It must not content itself with merely pointing the way to life hereafter lest many of its followers be overcome and fall by the wayside in the battle of life.

James Weldon Johnson, then executive secretary of that venerable race institution, the NAACP, made the same comment in a lecture at St. Philip's Church. His words were recorded in the local paper under the headline, "Young People's Fellowship of St. Philip's in Three-Day Session":

> The power of the church is the greatest and most influential among mankind in the world. But the Negro church is relatively more powerful, not because of Christianity, but because it occupies a more commanding position in the life of the Negro.
> In most communities Negroes look to the church for guidance on almost every subject, whereas the white race has a great many avenues, sources and approaches to life. Therefore, the church is still a more dynamic and compelling influence in the life of the Negro than in the life of whites. And this brings a greater responsibility upon the Negro minister than upon the white minister.

***

Given that I have been avidly pointing out instances where the concept of race has worked in our favor, I should explain that Appiah admits there are contexts in which stating that race is nonexistent is politically inopportune, contexts in which the truth can do more harm than good. Evidently, then, the matter is that Appiah and I disagree on what those contexts are. The era of slavery, Reconstruction, and post-Reconstruction were such contexts in which stating that race is nonexistent would have been politically inopportune. With reference to the social gospel movement,

I have been arguing that the first half of the twentieth century, when the black church recommitted itself to its racial ties, was such a context.

For instance, many of Harlem's white churches made it clear by their discriminatory practices that they did not want black members in their congregations. St. Matthew's Protestant Episcopal Church, in Brooklyn, actually posted a notice in its printed bulletin of Sunday, September 15, 1929. It was reported in *The New York Amsterdam News* a few days later under the caption "Rector Hides Behind 'Smoke Screen' in Raising 'Jim Crow.'" The church bulletin read: "The Episcopal Church provides churches for Negroes. Several of these churches are within easy reach of this locality. They are in need of the loyal support of all true Negro Churchmen, therefore the rector of this parish discourages the attendance or membership in this church of the members of that race." This blatant act of racial discrimination did not go without further critique by blacks in Harlem who felt a sense of racial solidarity with blacks in Brooklyn. A political drawing titled "Ku Klux Klan Robes Free," published a few weeks later in the same Harlem paper, reflected the black community's disgust. It depicted the bulletin outside St. Matthew's as displaying a well-known biblical text as presumably interpreted by the supremacist hermeneutic of the church's white members: "Come unto me all ye who are white and heavy laden." The caption above the drawing added to the parody by announcing that the church was distributing Ku Klux Klan robes free of charge. We can see, too, that the black press was (and remains) one of those race institutions that has been a crucial component in helping us fight off the theologies of the powerful that rush at us from their world.

The point I am making is that if Appiah can (as I can) conceive of "antiracist racism" being a possibly intelligent response in 1930, then why not now? What has really changed between then and now? Are we yet judged by the content of our character rather than by the color of our skin? Clearly, the racist American milieu as well as neocolonized, ethnic-torn Africa are today such contexts where it is politically inopportune to posit postmodernist notions that explode racial identity among blacks. While Appiah, like Gates and others, believes that race is both a useless and dangerous falsehood, I believe it could be dangerous not to continue to embrace and expand creatively the notion. After all, whites, as Appiah knows, are not going to discard the notion of race just because a few postmodernist theorists (particularly black ones) suggest that the concept is outmoded or irrational.

As I will point out in my conclusion, with reference to John Hope Franklin and Derrick Bell, racism (consequently the notion of "race") will be with us in the 21st century, and Bell presumes permanently. "As a popular colloquialism puts it," says Bell, "it is time to 'get real' about race and the persistence of racism in America." I agree with John Hope Franklin that "there is nothing inherently wrong with being aware of color" (or race) "as it is seen as making distinctions in a pleasant, superficial, and unimportant manner" (by which I presume he means a nonessentialist manner). "It is only when character is attached to color, when ability is measured by color, when privilege is tied to color, and a whole galaxy of factors that spell the difference between success and failure in our society are tied to color—it is only when such considerations are attached to color that it becomes a deadly dreadful, denigrating factor among us all."

***

I believe I find support for my argument in two of the essays in Bell Hook's book *Yearning: Race, Gender, and Cultural Politics* (1990), "Postmodern Blackness" and "The Chitlin Circuit: On Black Community." Hooks, like myself, understands the necessity of deconstructing the "master narrative" of racial essentialism in order to escape colonial imperialist paradigms that portray blackness one-dimensionally and thereby sustain white supremacist ideology. She says that the postmodern critique of essentialism is useful for African Americans wishing to reform narrow, outmoded notions of racial identity that have been imposed not only from the racial outside but from within our community, so that blackness can be understood to encompass multiple experiences and identities that permit diverse cultural productions. She says that the concept of "soul," for instance, can be, but need not be, a problematic notion:

> We cannot respond to the emergence of multiple black experiences by advocating a return to narrow cultural nationalism. Contemporary critiques of essentialism (the assumption that there is a black essence shaping all African-American experience, expressed traditionally by the concept of "soul") challenge the idea that there is only "one" legitimate black

experience. Facing the reality of multiple black experiences enables us to develop diverse agendas for unification, taking into account the specificity and diversity of who we are.

But Hooks also believes the concept of soul can be cherished, as long as it is not essentialized. Those in the black community who faithfully embody such aspects of our cultural legacy can even pass it on, she says. This can be one of those "habits of being" traditional to the folk experience of blacks that we can reenact, not as a gesture of passive nostalgia, she says, but as a historically viable survival strategy. Leonard Barrett conveys this message in his book *Soul-Force:*

> The term "soul" is a popular word in today's Black revolutionary language, but it has also been taken up by the wider American society. "Soul" is a germinal idea, born out of deep social conflict; yet all such ideas seem to spin off into ridiculousness, to take on broad and vague connotations and the term "soul" is no exception.... However, in the true world of Black experience the word conveys a potent and very special quality of feeling that is unknown to those who are not Black. However, in order not to appear left out, the wider society uses the word, but only for form's sake and certainly without tuning in on the "peculiar" feeling that properly defines it.
> "Soul-force"...describes that quality of life that has enabled Black people to survive the horrors of their "diaspora." The experience of slavery, and its later repercussions still remain to be dealt with; and "Soul" signifies the moral and emotional fiber of the Black man that enables him to see his dilemmas clearly and at the same time encourages and sustains him in his struggles. "Force" connotes strength, power, intense effort and a will to live. The combined words—"soul-force"—describe the racial inheritance of the New World African; it is that which characterizes his lifestyle, his world view and his endurance under conflict.

Accepting this purview, Hooks opposes postmodernist cultural critique that devalues the importance of the legacy of soul by dismissing its authenticity—for instance, by suggesting that the concept of soul is experientially inauthentic or utterly illusory. She concludes that black folks, already coping with feelings of alienation and fragmentation, cannot afford the luxury of such dismissal. This is what I have been saying about the concept of race: We simply cannot afford the luxury of such dismissal. Speaking of Appiah and other writers in Gates's *"Race," Writing, and Difference,*

Houston Baker, writing in the same volume, makes our point:

> The scenario they seem to endorse reads as follows: when science apologizes and says there is no such thing, all talk of "race" must cease. Hence "race," as a recently emergent, unifying, and forceful sign of difference *in the service* of the "Other," is held up to scientific ridicule as, ironically, "unscientific." A proudly emergent sense of ethnic diversity in the service of new world arrangements is disparaged by whitemale science as the most foolish sort of anachronism.
>
> For example, at a recent symposium at the University of Pennsylvania, two of that university's leading anthropologists insisted that talk of "racial" differences as a *positive* aspect of Afro-American life sounded like biology "some two hundred years ago." Complementing their smug condescension was, of course, a myopic and racist insensitivity that kept them from realizing that the discourse set in motion in the name of science "two hundred years ago" contained no Afro-American speaking subjects. Further, they left the symposium immediately after their presentations, patently (indeed, almost blissfully, it would seem) ignorant of the practical vulnerability of their claims....
>
> No, what the anthropologists heard was not two-hundred-year-old talk, but inversive discourse—talk designed to take a bad joke of "race" (produced, in large measure, by *their* discipline) and turn it into a unifying discourse. This discourse would produce a black *group* initiative contrary to the interests of the academically isolated whitemales who have always done whatever was necessary...to make science work.

This point is where Hooks and I differ with Appiah: in our insistence that anyone exploring the implications of postmodernism on racial identity respect the lessons of history and consider the impact that the identity explosion will have on the oppressed groups; and in our insistence that the "politics of difference" not be separated from the "politics of racism." In this respect, it is curious that, on the one hand, Appiah is so concerned with holding up an academic ideal—maintaining the philosopher's proper relationship to truth and rationality—while, on the other hand, nonchalantly accepting the fact that in denying the existence of race there is no reason to believe that racism will be obliterated. Hooks, conversely, believes that a postmodern critique of identity can result in a serious challenge to racism, and this makes all the more humanizing her petition for African Americans to begin to articulate new and varied forms of bonding that cut across boundaries of gender, class, and race.

Unlike Appiah, Hooks also understands the suspicion that some African Americans, such as myself and Houston Baker, have when these postmodern critiques are surfacing at a historical moment when many subjugated people seem to be gleaning a voice for the first time: multiculturalism, Afrocentrism, political correctness, womanism, rap, and black film. Hooks says:

> The unwillingness to critique essentialism on the part of many African-Americans is rooted in the fear that it will cause folks to lose sight of the specific history and experience of African-Americans and the unique sensibilities and culture that arise from that experience. An adequate response to this concern is to critique essentialism while emphasizing the significance of "the authority of experience." There is a radical difference between a repudiation of the idea that there is a black "essence" and recognition of the way black identity has been specifically constituted in the experience of exile and struggle.

***

As I explained in my introduction, I repudiate the idea that there is a black essence, particularly that there is an ontological quality in the black person's character or personality that rhythm best expresses. I do not subscribe to Senghor's notion about rhythm being the "archetype of the vital element" anymore than I subscribe to Schopenhauer's notion that music is the objectification of or the immediate language of the Will, the Will being the innermost nature of the world that gives rise to all reality. However, I do believe that African rhythm, as a cultural continuity appearing in the rhythms of black folk, has been, from the time we set foot on these shores as enslaved people, a source of apparent "racial" unity. I believe this rhythmic commonality, overwhelmingly evident to us in a vast part of our culture in the sacred and secular spheres of our lives, helped glue together a "racial" identity that gave impetus to fairly unified responses to white racism: the black social gospel movement of Ransom and Powell and the black nationalism and Pan-Africanism of Garvey and McGuire. Though we want to be careful to remove the archaic residue of essentialism, as I believe Dett and Maynor did, I hold that the common culture of rhythm shared by Africans of the continent and the diaspora can still serve as a core commonality on which to build certain Pan-Africanist alliances. The Afro-Christian church, which I will now discuss, would be one place to begin.

3

WORSHIP IN THE PAN-AFRICAN CHURCH

When I attend black churches of various socioeconomic levels, I often witness a kind of preaching ritual that Reverdy Ransom and Adam Clayton Powell evidently practiced, a kind of preaching ritual that certainly has its roots of musicality and rhythmicity in Africa. Looking back at accounts of antebellum slave preaching documented in the journals and diaries of southern planters and their wives, we can, as I document in my book *Sacred Symphony: The Chanted Sermon of the Black Preacher* (1987), find that a correlation has always existed between black preaching and the antebellum spiritual. In fact, it is most probable that a substantial number of spirituals actually evolved through the preaching event of black worship. Although it is likely that apart from worship slave preachers and other individuals worked at composing the songs that later came to be called spirituals, it is probable that the more frequent development of these folk songs came from extemporaneous preaching (and praying) that intensified little by little into intoned utterance.

This melodious declamation, delineated into quasi-metrical

phrases with formulaic cadence, was customarily enhanced by intervening tonal responses from the congregation. Responsorial iteration of catchy words, phrases, and sentences resulted in the burgeoning of song, to which new verses were contemporaneously adjoined. What facilitates this contemporaneous composing is that black sermons and prayers have been traditionally comprised of formulaic units that include repetition, extension, variation, sectional transition, tonal modulation, and thematic recapitulation. Spirituals created in such a manner, especially favorable creations, were likely remembered and perpetuated through oral transmission. There is no telling, then, how many of the spirituals sung in our churches today might have spontaneously evolved out of the event of preaching in the antebellum "invisible" and institutional black church. Perhaps there is no way of proving that the spirituals still sung today (or which ones) really did evolve out of the black preaching event, but what is certain is that traditional black preaching is itself musical and shares in common with the spirituals and African folk song certain melodic, rhythmic, and textural traits.

The use of melody in sermons and prayers is especially traditional among black preachers dating back to the antebellum era. That which is variously referred to in contemporary black preaching circles as whooping, intoning, chanting, and tuning is none other than the melody that was heard in black preaching. This melody is comprised of a series of cohesive pitches that have continuity, tonality, quasi-metrical phraseology, and formulary cadence. The principal melodic mode that from antebellum times continues to be employed by black preachers in their traditional "tuning" is the pentatonic, a scale common not only to uncountable black spirituals but also to African folk song.

Rhythm, which has always been a seminal element in African music and language, is the single ingredient that gives the melodiousness of black preaching its momentum. Scholars who have written on black preaching have generally concurred that rhythm is the fundamental musical component of this vocal genre. Black preachers such as Ransom and Powell who have been knowledgeable of the spiritual and aesthetic value of traditional rhythmic usage have generally sought to become skillful at fitting their sermonic phrases and sentences into quasi-metrical units. This is accomplished by squeezing together and stretching out words in the same way that is done by modern rap artists, who are the linguistic kin of the black preacher. Preachers often accompany this quasi-metered delivery of their text by striking the lectern or stomping the foot. Thus, the rhythmicity of traditional black preaching (like black rapping) includes kenetic, linguistic, and metric manifestations, all of which create a contrapuntal multi-metricity equivalent to that in African rhythm.

That there is this rather obvious cultural connection between African and African American religious ritual implies to me the potentiality of some Pan-African projects between us. We know, however, that Appiah contends that what Africans themselves hold in common is not race or culture but a common transition from traditional to modern life and loyalties caused by coloniza-tion and postcolonial interaction with the West; and that since this is the experience of Africans and not African Americans, the Pan-Africanist projects of Africa and the New World must remain separate. I wish to illustrate, contrariwise, that there are in fact intelligent reasons for common Pan-Africanist projects between Africans and African Americans. I will do this by pointing out that the common experience of contending with "contamination" by the West is evident in the struggle of a minority of church lead-ers, theologians, and laity in both Africa and Afro-America to indigenize Christianity. The depth of this common experience between us became evident to me when I attended a conference on "The Worshipping Church in Africa" in Malawi, held in the city of Blantyre, November 9-19, 1992.

The Re-Africanization of Christianity

> And so most striking to me, as I approached the village and the little plain church perched aloft, was the air of intense excite-ment that possessed the mass of black folk.
> — Du Bois, "Of the Faith of Our Fathers"

Present for the deliberations of the conference on "The Worshipping Church in Africa" were an ecumenical group of Africans from various parts of the continent—Uganda, Kenya, Malawi, Mozambique, Madagascar, Zimbabwe, Zambia, Cameroon, and Sierra Leone. Also participating were three Americans (two African Americans) and three Canadians (two missionaries to Mauritius and one to Malawi). The approximately 50 participants gathered in Blantyre to examine the life of worship within the African churches, to identify obstacles preventing the cultural contextualization of Christianity in the churches, and to devise practical strategies for encouraging liturgical renewal. The objective was to have the Association of Christian Lay Centers in Africa (ACLCA), which sponsored the conference, be able to present our findings to their Lay Training Centers and to such organizations as the All Africa Conference of Churches (AACC), of which Archbishop Desmond Tutu is the president. We hoped that these findings would begin to answer the complex question of how Africans can worship God most meaningfully according to their indigenous traditions. The question, I knew from the very start, is also one needing good answers in the African-American community (which commonality I assume is the reason I was invited to speak at the conference). Here I was in Malawi, a "native stranger," and yet it became clear to me as the conference proceeded that the black church in America faced identical obstacles and needed similar strategies.

Jonah Katoneene, a priest in the Church of Uganda and director of the ACLCA since 1988, said in his introductory comments opening the conference that the ACLCA was sponsoring the meeting because it is first and foremost an agent for social transformation in society. This sounded very much like it was part of the social gospel tradition of Reverdy Ransom and Adam Clayton Powell, Sr. The church, he said, talks about "abundance of life" but there still exists an "abundance of poverty" and an "abundance of civil strife." Our worship is suspended in the air and lacks grounding in our life realities, he explained, because it does not reflect the cultural lives and situational needs of African people. The content of our worship must be geared toward preparing us for our work in the world, so that we gather for worship in order that we may be empowered to scatter for mission.

In the opening-day sermon, T. N. Maseya, a minister in the Blantyre Synod of the Church of Central Africa Presbyterian (CCAP), said the growth of the church is occurring so rapidly that there is now, more than ever before, a need for Christians in Africa to unite as one church and live harmoniously across regions and ethnic groups. Maseya suggested that this goal would be more attainable if we were able to succeed in contextualizing our biblical understanding in African churches. By interpreting the Bible contextually, the church would be able to speak authoritatively about the myriad problems of the continent. We cannot just read the Bible and pray, Maseya said; we must be involved in the problems and persecutions that surround us. We must "sow in tears" in order that we may "reap in joy."

An example of shedding tears with those who are suffering was heard during one of the morning devotions of the first week, when intercessory prayers were being offered. One prayer indicated that Africans need to remember their continent—its drought, famine, poverty, war, and refugees. Here, the "agony of Africa" was not being used (as it was in *Time* magazine) to negate the sense of African kinship that was articulated with reference to "our continent." A Ugandan woman mournfully prayed, "I've never come across a clan called 'street children.' How can the light shine when we live in a world without justice, when these children live in our midst? How can the light shine? I think someone has blown it out." As Maseya said in his sermon, we cannot sing only joyful songs but must also sing sorrowful ones that reflect our concern for the problems that prevent our people from living an abundant life. There is, it should be noted, no hint of "racial fatigue" in these words—in the sermon or the prayers.

Following Katoneene's opening remarks and Maseya's opening sermon, we heard the keynote address by Silas Ncozana, General Secretary (bishop) of the Blantyre Synod of the CCAP. The address was given to provide a fuller overview of the concerns the conference would address. While his presentation left us with a challenge that directed our efforts over the next ten days, Ncozana could just as well have delivered the same lecture to a group of black church leaders and pastors in the United States. Continuing the general thread of thought found in Maseya's opening sermon, Ncozana argued (as our social gospelers had previously) that worship must embrace the concerns of politics so it can contend with the abundance of poverty and civil strife. The perceived division between the religious and the political is not African but European, he claimed. In many traditional African societies the village chief was also a member of the priesthood, so there was no separation between worship and politics:

> As we speak today, the church in Africa has only begun to understand that worship cannot take place where politics is not involved. Here we are not speaking of party politics, which is a different thing altogether. We are speaking of the politicization of Christian worshippers so that they understand the political agenda of God among his own people, the political agenda of a God who is inherently a political God, a social God, and an

economic God. Therefore, the kind of worship we hold in our churches must respond to the day-to-day cries of our people.

To illustrate the effectiveness of the church when it does respond to the daily cries of the people, Ncozana told a story about Walter Elmslie, one of the nineteenth-century Scottish missionaries to Malawi. There was a drought in Malawi (just as there was during the conference and had been for over a year) and Elmslie was being viewed with suspicion by the Tumbuka people because he had an instrument in front of his house that measured rainfall: He was accused of using magical power to withhold the rain. Though he was finally able to explain that the instrument was not magical, the people asked him anyway to pray for rain since he had the capability of measuring it. Elmslie hesitated to do so, because he feared he would disappoint the people, but then agreed to. Refusing to go to the village to pray, in fear of being confused with the priests of the local gods, Elmslie instead invited the people to the church. When the word got around that he was going to pray for rain, thousands of villagers, most of whom had never been to a church, came to witness the event. The following morning it rained so heavily that the villagers wanted to make Elmslie chief rainmaker. Elmslie refused the honor but the church from that point onward gained an increasing number of members as word got around that Elmslie had successfully prayed for rain. The point of the story, explained Ncozana, is that the traditional African worldview perceives worship to be practical and situational. Worship should not lack cultural grounding in our life realities, but rather should reflect the lives and needs of African people. As we listen for and respond to the cries of the masses, said Ncozana, we must find ourselves involved in the entirety of social and political life—from our health needs to our education needs.

Ncozana's implication, that Christianity would have been more deeply rooted in Africa if Christian worship had involved itself in these matters from the beginning, was well stated during the conference's last vesper service. In a point equally applicable to the African-American church, it was said in the sermon that if Christianity had become an authentic part of African culture from the outset then Christendom in Africa probably would not be facing its current crisis of being on the decline in countries where Islam is on the incline. Thus, Ncozana finds it suitable for there to be a meaningful dialogue between worship and the lives of the people. As reflected in the biblical prophets and in Jesus who called the church to be involved in the concerns of the world, God is a political, social, and economic God who requires that worship respond to the daily cries of the people in the everydayness of life.

But what is it that has prevented Africans from doing what is required of them in worship? Similarly, what is it that has prevented African Americans from doing so? Ncozana identified the principal source of the dilemma when he said that most of the African churches are still replicas of the missionary churches. Our churches, he said, are still very much connected with these European churches to the degree that we often continue to refer to them as our "mother churches":

> The Church in Africa south of the Sahara has been here for as many as three hundred years. Its model of worship has not changed from that of the missionary church from the West. For this reason, there is nothing we would refer to as typical African worship. This is true too in the established churches that continue to relate closely to the founding churches or Christian organizations based in the West.... The form of theological education that church leaders receive, the clerical robes we wear, our style of preaching, the architecture of the churches we build, the music we sing, and so forth, are all replicas of the missionary church. It is true that the greatest challenge the church in Africa is facing today is to rediscover its identity by transforming the western form of worship adopted from the missionary churches and bringing in African ways of worship. This would lead to a new form of worship that would bring out sharply the Africanness of the church.

This is what V. Y. Mudimbe discusses in his pivotal book, *The Invention of Africa*, which I mentioned in the previous chapter. Mudimbe addresses the missionary discourse of otherness, the African response, and the mingling of the two to create an African ideology of otherness that alienates Africans from themselves. This is what is occurring in the African churches.

Many older Africans brought up under the missionary teachings help to perpetuate this connection with the missionaries and prevent the Africanization of the church. These older people (not unlike the older generation in African-American churches) still reject the liturgical use of the drum and dancing as being "pagan" and outright evil. So, while for African Americans the drum was deferred in the diaspora, for Africans it was also deferred, along with dancing, in their own homeland. Ncozana argued against this continued deferrment perpetuated by the older generation:

> There is no aspect of everyday living which, in the final analysis, can be said to fall outside worship. Yet the worshipping church in Africa has totally neglected the gift of dance in worship. Missionaries who were responsible for introducing Christianity in Africa came from a background where dance was not a part of worship. Therefore, when they came to Africa where dance was an integral part of worship they condemned it outright. They viewed it as heathen and a source of immorality. This attitude was ingrained into all the new converts so much that even today to talk about dancing in the church is to invite trouble leading to excommunication.

Music and dance complement one another, Ncozana continued, but if young people try to dance to music in the church, many of the ministers and elders would reprimand them. To the contrary, said Ncozana, those of us who have studied liturgical dance have found that there is a silent language in bodily movement that can convey one's praise of God in a way that no other mode of expression can.

> *June 6: Traveled to the village I will be staying overnight at, about 20 miles northeast of Mutoko (a town), about 30 miles southwest of Mozambique. It is a beautiful mountainous area....*
> *The church service began around 7:30. We came at 8:00.... When we first came in, the children, in this youth service, were singing and dancing, having a great time. The music was repetitive, but increased in vigor, and a ring had formed amidst the mass of youths. The drums and tambourine and rattle accompanied their singing.*

Regarding Ncozana's comment that missionaries came from a background where dance was not a part of worship, Phyllis Byrd—an African-American minister living in Nairobi who is Assistant to the General Secretary of the AACC—later made an interesting point at one of the plenary discussions. She said that Europeans have now accepted liturgical dance as legitimate but still have the tendency to try and impose on African churches their Western standards or styles of dancing. I responded to Byrd's point by saying that "our" African way of expressing praise was right all along. Prior to the export of European standards for religious expression and European theological interpretations of the Bible, we fulfilled the biblical mandate to worship God intensely through dancing and drumming (2 Samuel 6:1-5, Psalm 150:3-5).

Ncozana went on to explain that it was through the concern expressed by youths that some of the African churches managed to break with some of the traditions instituted by the missionaries. Little by little the youths pestered the older folks, saying that they wanted to worship God according to traditions that were meaningful to them. Today, things are slowly changing, but, Ncozana concluded, we still must struggle to convince many more people that the use of drums and other local instruments can indeed be Christian.

The struggle, in brief, is not to Christianize the African traditions but to Africanize the Christian faith so that Africans understand and appreciate Christianity within their African context. In this respect, explained Ncozana, we (a "we" I would say can be inclusive of African Americans) have much to learn from the African Independent Churches:

> Dance in worship is freely used in Independent African Churches. Worshippers there are not inhibited by western influences because their point of reference is their culture, tradition, and primal religion. I believe the freedom that the Independent Churches have exercised in dance, and its appeal to worshippers, is finally being recognized by the established churches. Consequently, today some young people and women in established churches may dance in worship without too much suspicion from their leaders or fellow Christians.

To enhance the liturgical setting in which dance comes naturally, the African Independent Churches also make use of drums and other local instruments, clapping, and the singing of African tunes. Therefore, concluded Ncozana, we in the established churches have many lessons to learn from African Independent Churches if we are serious about creating an African model of worship and liturgy. Andrew Muwowo, National Youth Director of the United Church of Zambia, agreed with Ncozana's point. His exact words were: "All we need to do is to make our act of worship rich in African culture, as is the case with African Independent Churches."

What prevents Africans in the established churches from learning this crucial lesson is that they tend to view the African

Independent Churches as less legitimate than their own churches that were founded by the missionaries. This is the same way African-American mainline Protestant churches have viewed the Holiness and Pentecostal churches, which, like the African Independent Churches, have better maintained indigenous African-rooted forms of worship. In defense of the Independent Churches, Ncozana drew a parallel with the early Christian church that evolved during the day of the apostles as a sect of Judaism. Many Africans underestimate the Independent Churches by claiming that they are only splinter groups, he said, but the Christian religion was itself a splinter group that evolved out of another religion. "In our African context," Ncozana said, "we can say that Christianity is actually an 'Independent Church' because it sprang up from the Jewish context." Ncozana concluded that just as the new religion of the Christ was contextualized in the Jewish culture, so must we incorporate those indigenous African traditions that will assist us in being true worshippers of God.

***

Our task at this conference was not simply to determine how to Africanize the Christian faith, so that Africans can understand and appreciate Christianity within their African context. Our task was to determine how to re-Africanize Christianity (the same effort in which many African-American church leaders are involved). Ncozana implied this when he stated that the greatest challenge of the church in Africa is to rediscover its identity by bringing in African ways of worship that would "bring out sharply the Africanness of the church." The implication of the comment is that the church *already* embodies "Africanness," traits that only need to be recognized and enhanced. Although there are scholars such as Appiah who will claim that an authentic continental "Africanness" or Africanism is probably unattainable if one takes into account the diversity and plurality of the African realities, I have already and will continue to argue to the contrary. Indeed, I believe Ncozana's comment is equally true of the African-American church; and this position is, of course, a continuation of my response to Jack White's criticism (discussed in Chapter 1) that African Americans romantically claim the whole of Africa because we are unable to identify the specific ethnic groups from which we have come.

The conferees (who gathered together from around the continent) support my contention that there is a degree of cultural unity amid Africa's diversity. In response to Eustice Rutiba's presentation later in the conference, a number of the smaller working groups began identifying elements of Christian worship that are in effect already "African." That is, the working groups identified aspects of Christian worship that can be interpreted through a traditional African perspective, such as dancing, playing instruments, worshipping intensely, and healing. What we began to realize as the working groups presented their ideas at the plenary sessions is that the reason certain African religious practices were condemned by the Western missionaries—dancing, healing, and so forth—is not because these practices were actually evil or even nonbiblical but because they were not culturally European. European cultural preferences and racial biases, rather than what was actually biblical or nonbiblical, was the measure by which African traditional religious practices were judged and condemned. It is by this same foreign measure that the African-American church has been viewed by Euro-American Christians and sociologists of religion as an aberration of "normal" Christian worship, views we internalized and used to condemn ourselves for being ourselves.

Taking these points to heart, the conference facilitators planned an exercise for the six working groups. In this exercise the groups were to search through the scriptures for traditions that were already African in nature. At the conclusion of the exercise we had collectively derived sufficient biblical justification for the use of certain African traditions in worship, the kinds of indigenous traditions Ncozana said would assist Africans in being true worshippers of God. The scriptures we shared with one another, when everyone gathered for a plenary session, reflected the Christian authenticity of such traditional African religious practices as dancing, drumming, honoring the ancestors, communing with the saints, and herbal healing. Regarding healing, one of the working groups asked why African Christians will go to their pastor when they are well but only to the herbalist when they are ill. The answer given was that African churches have shunned healing rituals because African Christians have not dared to apply a traditional African perspective to the many instances of healing in the Bible. One conferee illustrated that the

African tradition of herbal healing has some precedence in John 9:6-7. In this passage, according to the Revised Standard Version (RSV) of the Bible, we read that Jesus "spat on the ground and made clay of the spittle and anointed the man's eyes with clay." Jesus told the blind man to go wash in the pool of Siloam, which he did. The man came back having his sight.

We also discovered numerous passages that supported the use of various instruments, dancing, and intense worship. Exodus 15:19-21 has Miriam, the prophetess and sister of Moses and Aaron, along with all the other women, drumming upon timbrels, dancing, and singing in celebration of the Hebrews' escape from the Egyptian army. In 2 Samuel 6:1-5 and 1 Chronicles 13:5-8 (RSV), David and all the house of Israel were, as they were moving the ark of God, "making merry before the Lord with all their might." As they worshipped "with all their might," they sang songs to the accompaniment of lyres, harps, tambourines, castanets, and cymbals. In 1 Chronicles 15:15 it is recorded that David commanded the chiefs of the Levites to appoint singers who "should play loudly on musical instruments, on harps and lyres and cymbals, to raise sounds of joy." In Psalm 150:3-5, a well-known passage, the importance of dance and various instruments (percussions, winds, and strings) in worship is demonstrated:

> Praise him with trumpet sound;
>   praise him with the lute and harp!
> Praise him with timbrel and dance;
>   praise him with strings and pipe!
> Praise him with sounding cymbals;
>   praise him with loud clashing cymbals!

One of the working groups pointed out that the African tradition of anointing the head of a chief at the time of enthronement is reflected in 1 Samuel 10:1, which reads: "Then Samuel took a vial of oil and poured it on his [Saul's] head, and kissed him and said, 'Has not the Lord anointed you to be prince over his people Israel?'" In addition to this, there is also Psalm 23:5, which reads: "Thou anointest my head with oil, my cup overflows." Similarly, one source of possible theological justification for what has been called "ancestral veneration" was found in the passage that reads, "Honor your father and your mother" (Exodus 20:12, Deuteronomy 5:16, and Ephesians 6:1 RSV). This passage is slightly rephrased in Proverbs 23:22.

Another group pointed out that the traditional African notion that the ancestors are with us during worship is reflected in the idea of the communion of saints found in the entirety of Hebrews 11. In this chapter the writer is celebrating the faith of men and women, from the first created through the prophets. These are the saints who now, as verse 12:1 puts it, surround us as "so great a cloud of witness." The latter verse, it was said by the group that presented it, reflected the African idea that our ancestors are ever-present in spite of their having passed on to the spiritual realm.

Finally, the groups also pointed out that the Bible has innumerable instances of situational worship, where communities, as in traditional African societies, came together to worship for special occasions. These communities gathered upon occasions of deliverance (2 Samuel 22), for reasons of purification and dedication (Nehemiah 12:27-43), and for purposes of presentation, naming, and circumcision (Luke 2).

***

This exercise of searching through the scriptures for traditions that were already African revealed to us that under the Western missionaries Africans were wrongfully led to believe that their religious traditions of drumming, dancing, and worshipping intensely were heathenistic and that they worshipped gods and ancestors rather than the one Creator. In short, we realized that a de-Africanized version of Christianity had been taught by the European colonizers. The same holds true for African Americans who received their Christianity as a hand-me-down from white churches and missionaries during slavery.

The extent of this de-Africanization became all the more apparent when the conferees attended some of Malawi's local churches on a Sunday morning. We discovered that the style of worship in the churches in Blantyre, in reflecting a European interpretation of Christianity, was very similar to that of the churches in the various African countries from which the participants came. One of the churches visited had a number of religious depictions, including the fourteen stations of the cross, and in each depiction Jesus and Mary are portrayed as Europeans. The artwork and literature in the church's bookstore was also replete with European depictions of the biblical personages, even though it was a church comprised of and presided over by Africans. In this church, as in most of the others, the liturgy was essentially Western. In some of the churches the choirs sang authentically African songs but without the kind of bodily movement that Andrew Muwowo identified as authentically African. In some of the churches the dancing was done only outside the church, once the service was over, to welcome the visitors. There were a few churches that made small efforts to include some semblance of African culture, which was accomplished by holding services in the vernacular and allowing for some singing of religious texts to African tunes. In our conclusion that the Western liturgical tradition clearly dominated in each case, we could very well have been referring to the preponderant number of African-American churches.

One of the concerns raised in the plenary discussion following the opening sermon and the keynote address was that Africans spend too much time blaming the missionaries for their problems, and that this prevents them from realizing their own potential to change their circumstances. There was broad consensus on this point (which sounds similar to, but is not identical to, Shelby Steele's position that I discussed in the introduction). Certainly it is Africans themselves, as with African Americans ourselves, who have maintained the liturgical, architectural, and artistic trappings of the European churches. Additionally, both Africans and African Americans have maintained significant parts of the European worldview, such as the division between the religious and the non-religious. This European worldview, which divides the world into two opposing spheres, causes us, Africans and African Americans, to exclude our social, political, and economic concerns from the liturgy. Consequently, worship in "our" churches has generally neglected to speak and respond to the daily needs of "our" people, including the cries and aspirations of women, youths, and the poor for justice. Thus, the challenge before all of us, as "Africans" no longer under missionary control or under captivity in the New World, is to reconcile this problem by again embracing our traditional wholistic worldview where all of life is sacred. Unbeknownst to Appiah, this makes for a Pan-Africanist project that reaches beyond the continent into the diaspora.

The liturgical renewal that is being proposed has far-reaching impact for the entirety of African peoples. Contextualizing Christianity for African churches, by using traditional modes of expression to reflect the African worldview, is a crucial means of helping Africans regain their suppressed identities. Regaining these identities will, in turn, allow Africans to affirm that God created them *as Africans* in God's divine image, and that they have a divine responsibility to help bring about abundance of life for each and every one of God's African children, women, and men. Regaining African identity also means that liturgically Africans will be able to address their peoples with authenticity and reach them in the worldview where they are situated. Such worship, in helping them to see themselves reflected in God not as dark aberrations that need "enlightening" by the Livingstones and Stanleys of Europe and America but as God's created people, will allow Africans to depart worship knowing that they have celebrated their lives, their humanity. From this newly nurtured sense of self-identity Africans can then cultivate their capacity for self-determination, whereby they (we, too) can build the ability to overcome hurdles that are political, social, and economic. Self-determination produces empowered individuals and communities that can help lead "our" people to a new day of liberation. This is why attaining our own identities as Afro-Christians and reinforcing those identities liturgically is so important.

A Requisite Therapy of History

Leaving, then, the white world, I have stepped within the Veil, raising it that you may view faintly its deeper recesses,—the meaning of its religion, the passion of its human sorrow, and the struggle of its greater souls.
— Du Bois, "The Forethought"

In beginning to nurture African self-identity and nourish African self-determination, in lieu of continuing to blame the Western missionaries for the problems of Africa, Africans must cultivate the identities and empowerment of *all* people in African communities. I argued in my presentation at the conference that the hymns we sing in "our" African churches must reflect the lives and situational needs of African peoples of every gender, ethnicity, and class. Our hymns must do this, I insisted, in order to help reorient our thinking toward liberation in these areas. Otherwise, we may continue to be unaware that we are oppressing one another, particularly those who are women, those who (in Africa) are of different ethnic groups, and those who are poor.

The point I was making, which is a point that Du Bois makes as early as 1920 in *Darkwater: Voices from Within the Veil,* is that we need to begin to affirm the fact that God created all of us in God's divine image and that each of us has a responsibility to help bring about abundance of life for every African woman just as for every African man. Hymns that help African women see themselves reflected in God as God's equal creations (equal with men) will allow women to leave worship knowing that all of us have celebrated their lives, their humanity, their womanliness. From this newly nurtured sense of self-identity women can then cultivate their capacity for self-determination, whereby they can build the ability to overcome hurdles that are political, social, and economic. A strong sense of self-determination can produce empowered women and thereby empowered families and communities that can help lead all of us to a new day of liberation. This is why supporting and nurturing the identity of women liturgically in the hymns we sing is so important.

In "our" various Western-derived liturgies, I said in my lecture, God is not only of the male gender but is white and wealthy—the spitting image of the group of people who were in control of the imperialist systems that exploited Africa and oppressed Africans. The point is, I said, other people—women, African peoples, and the poor—should also be able to boast of being reflected images of God. For us to be able to understand the crucial meaning of symbolism that affirms the divinity of people who are women and who are black, for us to be able to understand this without feelings of repulsion, is for us to use worship as a means of coming to terms with the horrible history of gender and race oppression.

My discussion of race oppression led me to discuss a key issue connected with liturgical art, namely, the artistic portrayal of Jesus and the other biblical personages as being of European ancestry.

June 3: Left for Bulawayo this morning...by car.... Stopped at Denise's Kitchen at Tangehamo Safaris for breakfast, a white-owned farm, restaurant, and gift shop. The bathrooms were labeled "Jane" and "Tarzan."

One reason we should depict the biblical personages as Africans, I explained, is so that we begin to reverse and erase the psychological chains of colonialism that have made us believe that black skin is indicative of our inferiority to those who have white skin. What I was suggesting is somewhat akin to our project of creolizing European languages, revising racist theologies with respect to blackness, and reinterpreting the meaning of race: We need in our liturgies what I called a "therapy of history." For those of us who possibly might suffer subconscious feelings of inferiority—subconsciously believing that African cultures are inferior to European cultures—what is prescribed in this "therapy of history" is the portrayal of Jesus and the other biblical personages as African in our liturgical representations and the portrayal of God as black in our symbolic conceptualization of the unseen Creator. When we arrive at the point where we can love and worship a Jesus, a God, who is portrayed as black, and do so without any hesitation or repulsion, then we will have grown to cultivate our capacity to appreciate and love fully our own blackness and the myriad facets of our Africanness.

I made the same point regarding people of European descent being able to learn to appreciate and love fully our blackness and Africanness, particularly those missionaries of European descent who still work in Africa and still export to Africa the divine images that edify their own European race and cultures. I said that when people of European descent can accept, appreciate, love, and worship a Jesus who in his pictorial representation is black, then and only then will they have entered into the kind of therapy that alone can begin to alleviate their subconscious feelings of superiority and their inferiority claims against people of African ancestry. Until then I insist that we must maintain our creative concepts of race for the sake of our solidarity; we must maintain our mythologies and rhythmic mystifications in order to fight off the theologies of the powerful that rush at us from alien worlds.

There is a further rationale behind my therapeutic prescription of pictorially representing Jesus as black. Not only did we find during our conference deliberations that Christianity in its biblical representation is more African than European, but many of the biblical personages may have in fact been African or of closer African ancestry than European. This was figured according to geographical considerations as well as the genealogies of the patriarchs in the Old and New Testaments (an exercise that Marcus Garvey and George Alexander McGuire each carried out in their religious instruction). Given the biblical evidence that such personages as Moses and Jesus may have been of African ancestry, as well as the scientific evidence that the first human beings (Adam and Eve) were in fact Africans, and given our effort to indigenize Christianity, it is quite logical that our churches would display

African depictions of the biblical figures. White depictions in African churches, I am sure Appiah's reasoning would concur, is illogical and irrational. In fact, the only way to explain the use of white depictions of the biblical personages in European churches, short of accusing the members of these churches of outright racial and cultural imperialism, is to contend that Europeans have contextualized Christianity for themselves. At the very least, accepting this explanation warrants that we accede to the legitimacy of contextualizing Christianity for ourselves.

There actually are some European missionaries who implemented this kind of contextualization in African churches, even before Africans themselves did (something that, to my knowledge, whites never initiated in African-American churches). This can be seen at the famous Cyrene Chapel at the Cyrene Mission just outside of the city of Bulawayo in Zimbabwe. The Cyrene Mission was founded in 1940 by a Scottish-born Anglican priest named Edward George Patterson. Patterson had the inside and outside of the mission's chapel adorned with murals painted by the African boys who attended the school to study agriculture, crafts, and art. Most of the murals inside the chapel were completed between 1948 and 1951, the outside ones between 1953 and 1982. This indigenizing of the scriptures, through paintings that portray Jesus and other biblical personages as Africans, is what we at the conference had in mind for the liturgy in all Afro-Christian churches.

All of us witnessed this kind of artistic indigenizing of Christianity upon our visit to Nyungwe Catholic Church in the town of Nyungwe, about two hours outside of Blantyre. Although the crucifix over the front door of the church was a European-featured Jesus that was fashioned of white clay, an effort was made inside the church to portray Jesus and Mary as Africans. These attempts, comprising two large murals behind the pulpit, were painted in part by a Malawian named Tambala Mponyani and a white Canadian priest named Claude Boucher, both associated with the Ku Ngoni Art Craft Center in the town of Mua. At least the fourteen stations of the cross, situated around the periphery of the sanctuary, were authentic African wood carvings that depicted the biblical personages as Africans. I thought that the wood carvings depicting Jesus and Simon of Cyrene as Africans were appropriate but that the Romans could have been portrayed as Europeans so that the true source and nature of

Jesus' death would have been captured. This would have depicted the fact that it was the Romans and not the Jews who put Jesus to death—the same people who later remained silent in the face of the African and Jewish holocausts.

After leaving the Nyungwe Catholic Church we went to the town of Zomba, where we visited St. Peter's Major Seminary. In the seminary chapel, above the pulpit, we saw a carving by James Samikwa, also from the Ku Ngoni Art Craft Center in Mua. It was a large wood carving of a crucifix comprised of a Jesus who was depicted as African. Behind this Jesus, helping the crucified Christ in his ascent to heaven, was a black angel. A large carving on one side of the floor beneath the pulpit depicted Mary and on the other side Peter, both portrayed as Africans. Unlike some of the paintings in the Nyungwe Catholic Church, these carvings were done by Malawian artists. The painted artwork on either side of the crucifix was also done by Africans who were students at the seminary. This indigenizing of Christian art is, again, what we at the conference had in mind for the entire liturgy in African churches. It is what I had in mind for the black church in America.

***

Following my presentation, Phyllis Byrd, who concurred with my arguments, played a video of the African-American preacher Wyatt Tee Walker giving a sermonic lecture on black sacred music before his New York City congregation, Canaan Baptist Church. Walker's choir sang samples of the musical forms that Walker discussed in his lecture, including several spirituals and gospel songs. It was evident to the Africans watching the video that this church was very much in touch with its indigenous musical heritage, which is what they desired for their African churches. Walker's spirited preaching style, a style comprised of a musical rhythmicity, also demonstrated his cultural situatedness in a vocal style that has African roots. I was not surprised that the Africans felt very much in sync with these rhythms of black folk.

November 11: It has been said twice now, and has become thematic, that Phyllis Byrd and I, African Americans, "belong to the village of Africa" (that is, Africa as a whole). It was alluded that the African Americans (Africans of the diaspora in general) are at some advantage over Africans since we can float above the ethnic divisions and regionalism that confines them, allowing us to "belong to the village Africa."

Walker explained in the video, however, that African Americans had not always viewed their legacy of spirited African-influenced worship in a positive light. The Holiness and Pentecostal churches kept these rhythmic traditions alive—the singing of spirituals, dance, spirit-possession, and so forth—until the mainline black Baptist and Methodist churches (with the help of people like Dett and Maynor) started to reclaim some of this legacy. There are many black churches, particularly those congregations comprised of middle- and upper-income African Americans, that have not nurtured this tradition. In fact, it is because only a minority of mainline black churches have reclaimed our indigenous traditions that some African-American scholars and ministers are pushing just as hard for liturgical renewal in our churches as some in Africa are pushing for liturgical renewal in African churches. Byrd also explained that while there has been significant improvement in the African-American church since the late 1960s, when African Americans began to take pride in their creolized African culture and even began to look back to Africa, efforts are today still being made to turn the mainline black churches away from European models of worship.

I gave as an example the work begun by the African American priest Father George A. Stallings, Jr., who in 1989 broke away from the Roman Catholic Church in order to found the African American Catholic Congregation. Stallings' defense is almost identical to the statement made by Archbishop Robertson in his eulogy of George Alexander McGuire: "Because he knew that the Pope would always be Italian, the Archbishop of Canterbury an Englishman, the head of the Russian Orthodox Church a Russian, and the metropolitan of the Greek Church a Greek, regardless of ramifications in other countries, Archbishop [Stallings] decided to establish the [African-American Catholic Congregation] as an autonomous institution with a Negro at its head."

In the first of his churches, which was named Imani Temple after the Swahili word for *faith,* Stallings reached back into various West African traditions to develop a distinctly African-American liturgy and a liturgical setting comprised of African patterns and designs. His services commenced with the summoning of the ancestors and African saints to the place of worship and the pouring of libation over soil taken from sacred African-American sites. Music was provided by a corps of musicians who played African percussion instruments, which helped induce lively dance and other uninhibited physical movement. The music as well as the preaching were distinctly African-American, very rhythmic and dance-oriented.

As I was indicating at the beginning of this chapter, I do not think there is a parallel in traditional European culture for what happens when a black preacher delivers a sermon in a traditionally folk manner. The preacher's first utterances are generally rendered in a normal speaking voice. As the sermon picks up momentum and rhythm and the congregation becomes involved in the preaching by giving affirmative responses, an atmosphere of heightened spirituality is corporately generated. In order for the preached word to keep pace with that heightening atmosphere of spirituality and for the delivery to express the surplus of spiritual meaning in the word that cannot be communicated through the speaking voice alone, the preacher may begin to chant or sing the sermon. As worship becomes even more spiritually excited and there remains spiritual surplus in the message that cannot be communicated by singing alone, the preacher will sometimes stop articulating altogether and dance—we can call it "dancing the sermon." "Danced religion," the height of worship in the traditional black religious experience, reveals the kinship between African and African-American religious ritual. I have seen Stallings honor this kinship on several occasions, but not all preachers who continue to practice the traditional black folk style of preaching go so far as to "dance" the sermon. But it is very common today to hear even academically educated black preachers maintaining the tradition of sermonic chanting or singing.

We can see, then, that there are models of indigenization on both sides of the Atlantic for African and African-American churches to follow. For instance, just as it was suggested later in the conference by Andrew Muwowo that an African liturgy include the reading of traditional African poetry due to its prevalence in certain African cultures, so did Stallings add to the two scriptural readings in his liturgy a third reading taken from a text held sacred in African-American culture. At different times this third reading was taken from the writings of such spiritually estimable African Americans as the theologian Howard Thurman and the poet Maya Angelou. Also, just as it was stated by Eustice Rutiba that the tradition of omitting women from positions of spiritual leadership is not traditionally African but Western, so has Stallings allowed for the ordination of women, this being one of the theological disparities he had with the Roman Catholic Church that resulted in his excommunication. Stallings is also allowing for a married priesthood in his church, arguing that the European attempt to separate the spiritual part of our humanness from the biological or sexual part is antithetical to our wholistic African view of ourselves and of life. Thus, Stallings' African American Catholic Congregation, because of its efforts at a liturgical renewal that is African-centered, can serve as an example of what liturgical renewal might look like in African churches. Again we see that there are rational grounds for a common Pan-Africanist agenda between Africa and Afro-America.

November 13: Throughout I have always said "we" as I have spoken to Africans individually and collectively. I feel very much a part of the cross-cultural group of Africans, as much, perhaps, as any other African. In other words, the cultural distance between Cameroon and Malawi is to me no different from the cultural distance between Afro-America and Cameroon. I can also say "we" authentically because we are all concerned about the same thing—undoing what Europeans have imposed upon us and recapturing our African selves.

***

In summarizing the first lectures by Ncozana and myself, Katoneene said worship cannot be "isolationist" in the sense of isolating historical reality from Christian liturgy. Instead, worship must be "integrationist" in the sense of integrating the historical context and the liturgy. We must also concern ourselves with the images that dominate in our worship—particularly the problem of the white Jesus in the African church—and how this imagery influences the symbolic language in the hymns we sing. The reason we need to replace foreign liturgical language, symbols, and images is so we can better see ourselves reflected in God as divinely created African people.

By contextualizing the language, symbols, and images of Christianity in our churches, continued Katoneene, we can better communicate authentically with God and with one another about how God interacts with us in our African lives. So, the life situation of the people must be reflected in the liturgy, which means we should not maintain false barriers between the sacred and the profane. A wholistic perspective on the world is traditionally African, which is to say that worship must reflect our cultural, social, political, and economic aspects of life.

Liturgical Reformation of Western Tradition

Why did God make me an outcast and a stranger in my own house? The shades of the prison-house closed round about us all: walls strait and stubborn to the whitest, but relentlessly narrow, tall, and unscalable to sons of night...
—Du Bois, "Of Our Spiritual Strivings"

Eustice Rutiba, head of the Department of Religious Studies and Philosophy at Makerere University in Uganda, added to the many points of the earlier lectures in his presentation titled "Elements of Traditional African Worship Which Can Be Utilized and Developed for Contemporary Christian Worship." Rutiba claimed that Africans have been so cut off from their cultures that they now need to engage in research to recover their traditions. One thing we will find in doing that research, he said, is that the tradition of omitting women from positions of spiritual leadership is not typically African but Western.

We find, however, that there are many African women who suffer the consequences of this Western tradition. These include women who, as two of the women at the conference informed me (and themselves exemplify), hold theological credentials and yet cannot even be ordained in their particular denominations. This tradition remains firm, they said, even though many denominations suffer from a shortage of pastors. Not only that, but the African men in their denominations treat them as inferiors, saying such things as: "You cannot be ordained because you are only women," "You are here to take care of the babies," and "What will happen if you become pregnant?" The story was told of one minister who even said, "If they ordain you I will turn in my collars."

June 6: My sermon from Philemon lasted but about ten minutes. It was translated into Shona. I told the story of Onesimus running away and being sent back, and probably later becoming a bishop, "a great religious man." And this is the purpose of the story, I said; we must always treat one another as brothers and sisters, as equals, so we can rise up and become great people.

I might have been a "native stranger" to Malawi, but I certainly understood what these African women were saying, given the similar environment in the black church in America. The point for both the black church in Africa and America to hear is that, as Rutiba said: If excluding women from leadership positions in the church is a tradition that is European and not African then we should be more faithful to our own cultural inclinations and not impose these restrictions on African women.

Rutiba also initiated discussion on a concern that became a major issue throughout the remaining part of the conference. He said that Africans traditionally gathered to worship in order to address specific situations in the community. To this effect, Andrew Muwowo later related some of the deliberations of the AACC's Eastern African Church Music Workshop, which was held in Nairobi in January 1981. It was said at the workshop that when Africans worshipped it was to find a solution to the current circumstances, such as how to deal with hunger, sickness, or enemies. When worship took place, often under a large tree, on a hill, or near a big rock, it was generally led by a chief, councillor, or an outstanding elder in the village, with the intent of driving away the bad spirits that had caused some misfortune. The shouting, crying, ululating, and other forms of expression were done, Muwowo said, either to praise the ancestral spirits or to frighten away the bad spirits. Rutiba felt that this kind of traditional situational worship was more ideal than meeting regularly to go through a prewritten liturgy, which is the Western way of holding services. He also contended that as an extension of this situational worship, various traditional African rituals could be subsumed under the rubric of Christian worship. These traditional rituals could include harvest, puberty rites, weddings, and funerals. In addition, said Rutiba, we need to introduce traditional African poetic recitations into Christian worship (which is what Stallings did in using the poetry of Maya Angelou).

The discussants agreed with Rutiba that African worship is traditionally situational, such that the people of traditional African communities generally gathered together in response to certain eminent or tragic events. It was further recommended by the discussants that special ecumenical services could be encouraged, where Christians from different congregational communities would gather around situational concerns. These concerns, to which the songs, prayers, sermons, and poetic recitations would be geared, could range from the political to the environmental. Ecumenical gatherings that address such situational concerns as harvest time, drought, poverty, the refugee problem, and the

AIDS epidemic would be a positive way of beginning to heal the divisions caused by denominationalism, which is nearly as harmful as the regional, national, and ethnic divisiveness that plagues the continent.

Situational worship involves a certain spontaneity, since the community gathers when there is some eminent or tragic event to address. This same spontaneity that traditionally occurred on the community level needs also to occur on the liturgical level. In terms of the order of the liturgy, the discussants agreed that more spontaneity was needed and that certain parts of a liturgy could be used according to need rather than as an attempt to remain faithful to a liturgical formula. Ncozana made a point during his opening address that extends this notion of spontaneity. He said that movement to and from, during and within worship is traditionally African, but that today any movement at all is viewed as unbecoming. This is true, he said, whether it is dancing or simply moving around the church.

***

The extensiveness of needed change in African liturgies was implied by Solomon Mbabi-Katana, retired music professor of Makerere University, when he indicated that a "musical reformation" is needed in African churches. He detailed this reformation in his presentation titled "Elements of Traditional African Music Which Can Be Utilized and Developed for Contemporary African Christian Music." The premise of the professor's presentation was that the adaptation of Western hymn tunes to African translations of those hymns disregards the natural musical inclination of African languages. The problem is not one that affects the African-American church (since English is our national language), but his points do seem to have some parallel bearing on, for instance, the reduction of African-American music to European notation. Notation has always failed to capture the rhythms, inflections, and textural glosses of our music. Mbabi-Katana's points also seem to have some parallel bearing on the reduction of spirituals to standard four-part hymn form.

Mbabi-Katana said that in Uganda the Catholic Church has attempted to improve the rendering of African translations of Western hymns sung to the old tunes by allowing the accompaniment of the drum (once deferred in its own land) but that this has failed to alter the basic problem of the incompatibility of Western tunes and African languages. He went on to explain that there is a remarkably close relationship between speech and singing in African traditional music, where the pitch gradation of spoken words corresponds with that of a song's tune:

> A study of the musical accents in the words of several African traditional songs would reveal generally that it is the word that gives rise to the tune. In several instances, melodies are so totally word-conceived that it is the word that determines the timbre or voice quality, pitch or location of the voice in a tonal scale and rhythm including the dynamic and durational aspects of the notes of melodies.

Andrew Muwowo made the same point in his later lecture on composing. He said that certain African words have multiple meanings, so that textual meaning is dependent on the pitch, rhythm, and duration of the syllables. This means that preset Western tunes confuse the meaning of African translations. Using Western melodies to accompany African translations of Western hymns would be like speaking disjunct English with the stresses and syllable breaks in all the wrong places. The effect of what Muwowo described was witnessed by the group of conferees that visited the Zingwangwa Church (CCAP) in Malawi. They reported to the plenary group that the Zingwangwa congregation sang European hymns whose translation into the national language, Chichewa, did not fit the Western tunes well. Muwowo suggested in his lecture that this effect is so unideal that English translations of texts set to African tunes and rhythms is actually preferable to African translations set to Western tunes.

Mbabi-Katana insisted that the same holds true for the use of canticles of Western origin. When translated into African languages they too must have musical settings that reflect the rhythms, pitches, and accents of the African words. Mbabi-Katana concluded that the text shapes a melody tonally and rhythmically: "The primacy of the text is an indisputable factor for a successful and accurate rendition of the traditional African songs." The timbre and tone qualities are also important to composing African songs for worship and to teaching these songs: "Timbre and tone quality in traditional African song is partly conditioned by the pronunciation of both consonants and vowels in the song and partly by aesthetically accepted vocal production in a particular cultural group."

***

Muwowo gave two lectures during the conference, both of which raised points similar to those discussed by Mbabi-Katana. Muwowo's lectures were titled "How to Compose Christian Music" and "Coordination, Promotion, and Development of African Christian Liturgy, Music, and the Arts." In these lectures Muwowo criticized the course of history that led Africans away from their rich musical tradition. He illustrated that Africans in the villages could sing chants in Latin without even being able to speak and comprehend the language. He continued, "A long time ago before Christianity was introduced in Africa, our foreparents worshipped God through their ancestral spirits. Their approach to worship was very rich in African traditional elements.... Thus we have gathered here to retrace the true style of worship for an African Christian today." Muwowo went on to point to a resolution made by the liturgy group of the Africa Association of Liturgy and Music (AFALMA), which met in Kenya in July 1991. A part of AFALMA's report read:

> We believe in God who conceived our existence and from whom Africa earned its identity. The powers of darkness have disturbed it but nobody could eradicate it. We are in the process of going back through the stories in order to fully recapture our identity. It is not necessary to trace back exactly the origin of African religion but it is important to stress that our religious experience is part of our everyday life. We want to fully worship God with an African identity. We are what we are because God is who He is.

Muwowo believes that Africans were misled culturally and theologically, but he also believes Africans have now begun to realize the value of their indigenous music for Christian worship. Given the preponderance of music in the lives of Africans and the fact that most Africans are, it was said, natural composers, Africans need only concern themselves with the means by which they will create it. Muwowo said there are basically two choices available to those who decide to compose: We can create an original piece or we can adapt traditional tunes so they accommodate new words. In either case, Africans need to formalize the musical styles and skills that come naturally to each particular ethnic group. This means that the music Africans create or adapt should be, as Mbabi-Katana explained earlier, dependent on the pitch and rhythm of the words. African composers should also consciously and creatively utilize all of the traditional musical elements characteristic of the music of their particular ethnic group, rather than using the characteristic elements of European music. This means that creative use can be made of traditional African call and response, improvisation, repetition, and certain African rhythms, meters, and scales. All of these elements also distinguish the sacred music tradition of the black church in America (ranging from the spirituals to contemporary gospel).

As I said earlier, this is even true of the black preaching event, which derives from the genealogy of African rhythm in the New World. When the congregation participating in such a sermonic event gets involved in the rhythms of the preaching, the verbal responses coming from the congregation increasingly fall within the intervals where the preacher metrically pauses to take a breath. As a worship experience heightens in the responsorial setting, worshippers do more than simply acknowledge the preached word with "amen" and similar brief responses; they actually preach back to the speaker. As the inspiration continues to heighten, the intervallic exchange between a preacher and members in the congregation is often surpassed in musical intricacy by what is best described as a contrapuntal texture. This contrapuntal texture involves the preacher's intoned delivery rhythmically weaving its way through a context of congregational response, response that is often itself tonal, melodic, and rhythmic. The musical threads of the contrapuntal fabric may be so intricately interwoven that when a preacher dramatically breaks off the chant, a congregational response is sometimes right there to complete the musical phrase and cadence. The intertwining of a congregation's sung phrases and nonarticulated sounds (moaning and humming) establish a kind of symphonic musicality. Thus, traditionally black folk preaching, with its emphasis on African-rooted melodic, rhythmic, and textural patterns, can be best described as "sacred symphony."

***

In terms of musical instrumentation, Africans can be equally creative within their traditions. Under the influence of the Western missionaries there was a restriction on the use of local instruments, just as there were legal restrictions against the drum in the American slave system. But Africans are now free to use their traditional string, wind, and percussion instruments, just as African Americans are now free to use drums and other instruments. In the Western part of Zambia the xylophone is a very popular instrument outside the church, but no effort has been made to bring it into the church. Here is an opportunity, said Muwowo, to use a traditional instrument so that we may sing a new song unto the Lord. Muwowo, sounding much like Ngũgĩ, went on to identify continued European cultural imperialism as the greatest obstacle of all in the quest for liturgical renewal in African churches, in that this imperialism has many Africans still believing that their own music is inferior to Western music. All of us at the conference came to the conclusion that this view of our traditional music is a mistake.

When the working groups reported to the plenary group on their discussions of Muwowo's presentation, one of the groups said we must encourage hymnists to follow the example of the late Ugandan composer Joseph Kyagambiddwa, who documented his original hymns in his native Luganda language. Since Africans traditionally have not documented their hymns, it was said, their hymnbooks do not reflect African worldviews or what Africans think about life. They missed the opportunity, for instance, to record in their hymns what they as African Christians felt about the liberation struggles of the various African countries. By writing down the hymns they create Africans will be preserving their history.

Regarding some of the difficulties involved in composing African hymns, the working groups generally agreed that Africans are natural composers. In terms of the ability to compose characteristically African music, it was said that most Africans have the ability to maintain complex rhythms. There are only a few, as one Zimbabwean put it, "born with weak beats." On the other hand, it was also recognized that given the improvisational nature and rhythmic complexity of much of African music, there exists the difficulty of transcribing it into music notation.

There are other obstacles standing in the way of Africans reaching their ideal goal of composing and documenting their music. Ncozana had explained earlier during his address that the introduction of hymns from the West, along with the fact that African tunes were not encouraged by some missionaries, served to stifle local initiative in the area of composing hymns. One of the working groups pointed out that young Africans are sometimes unaware of or distant from their own traditional cultures, including their traditional ritual musics. This is primarily the case among urban youths. When these youths go on to receive education outside (as well as inside) Africa, they tend to be led even further away from past traditions toward modern Western ones. Thus, in many instances Africans are increasingly losing their capability to create music that is authentically traditional. Even if some Africans could create traditional music, many of the youths prefer the new waves of music to the old ways, particularly those youths influenced by black popular music coming from America on television and audio recordings.

There are some concerns, in addition to the few already mentioned, that African Americans do not have to contend with. For example, the conference working groups generally agreed that when Africans do compose hymns they should be created to be sung in the native languages (an aspect of so-called "nativism" Appiah might disagree with). The only problem that we could foresee was that of the language barriers within interethnic congregations. The suggestion that we agreed upon at the plenary session was for interethnic congregations to sing hymns in the languages of all of the ethnic groups comprising the congregation, so that no group (no matter how small) feels alienated. It was agreed that the members of such interethnic congregations could grow accustomed to singing in other African languages.

***

In his lecture on "Coordination, Promotion, and Development of African Christian Liturgy, Music, and the Arts," Muwowo discussed the status of art in and the architectural designs of African churches. Part of the difficulty with contextualizing Christianity for African churches, he suggested, is that the Africanized liturgy and music we desire would appear foreign to the architectural context. Like African music, our architecture must also be African-centered:

> Regarding construction of church buildings, let us also consider the architectural design that bears some African significance. I say this because most of our church buildings today are western, designed with arched windows, a high tower with a bell,

as in England or France or any other part of the western world. Let us design something that is meaningful to us as Africans. Traditionally Africans have associated themselves mostly with round objects, such as round huts, stools, and circular dance formations.

Muwowo suggested that African churches could be designed in a circular form with the pulpit in the middle. As regards his concern for an African-centered aesthetics that is fitting for such an architectural design, Muwowo felt that the liturgical environment should include African art and crafts and that the people should be attired in African dress. In fact, Muwowo insisted that if we are to promote Christian art in worship, then this must be accompanied by indigenous traditional dress.

Muwowo also felt that African churches should use traditional African baskets for the collecting of the offering, locally made containers for communion, pulpits decorated with African patterns, and art depicting African scenes. He said that the report on the music workshop sponsored by the Mindolo Ecumenical Foundation, held in Kitwe, Zambia, in January 1988, suggested that during the offertory the members should walk to the front to bring their gifts (a customary practice in many African-American churches). This, the report said, is recollective of the practice of Africans walking humbly to the chief or king to offer animals, food, and other gifts.

African churches should use African art in order to fulfill the principal religious function of art: to evoke in Africans a deep religious response. "For example," said Muwowo, "if we look at an African sculpture figure of Jesus Christ crucified on the cross, we should really feel it with compassion so as to become better people who are changed or renewed spiritually." Indeed, this is a means of doing "contextual theology," since religious art is a way of interpreting and teaching the biblical message in the specific context of African churches. As an instance of "contextual theology," African art helps to establish the identity of worshippers. This permits a greater depth of spirituality because the environment has been adapted to the identity of the worshippers.

Muwowo suggested that the national Christian councils and the churches should support Christian art in Africa and encourage African artists to continue their creativity. African artists should be especially encouraged to create using the kind of materials and mediums that are indigenous to their communities, be it wood or stone that is carved, clay that is molded, or leather that is painted. Muwowo suggested that if exhibitions were sponsored in the churches and community then Christian artists would be encouraged to be artistically creative. All of these suggestions are equally applicable to the African-American churches, as our contextual theologians well know.

***

During the course of the conference we came to understand that the renewing of "our" liturgies will involve a slow educational process. It will take decades, and probably generations, to make recognizable progress toward liturgical renewal in our churches, given the fact that Africans, like African Americans, were systematically steered away from nurturing our own cultural identities for centuries under colonization and slavery.

> *November 14: The General Secretary, Silas Ncozana, said to me at dinner that we need to return to the mind-set of the 1960s, with African Americans linking up with Africa. He said this can help Africa reach its potential.*

In fact, this reeducation process will involve the same strategy employed by the colonialists, who used their schools to help indoctrinate Africans to Western values. In just about the same way, we need to use theological schools, universities, churches, and other educational institutions as locations where we can help develop curriculums and offer workshops that aid "us" in reaching our objectives. In the United States this means "multicultural" and "Afrocentric" curriculums which, as I explained in Chapter 1, are chided by those who then hypocritically claim we are uninformed and overly romantic about Africa.

Muwowo addressed this educational process in his paper on "Coordination, Promotion, and Development of African Christian Liturgy, Music, and the Arts." He agreed that it will be difficult to change the minds of Africans who have been brought up worshipping in Western traditions. But this, he said, makes it all the more crucial that proper instructional resources are made available. In fact, all that Muwowo suggested is, as he himself recognized, no easy task. There are many obstacles that would impede any efforts among Africans (and African Americans) toward liturgical renewal: Education in Western schools and curriculums often results in our acceptance of European values; we often have grown attached to Western music, liturgies, and art through their popularity and dominance; there is a general conservatism in African churches that distrusts Africanization and liturgical renewal; and there is often an otherworldly emphasis in our churches that prevents us from making Christianity relevant to the specific social, political, and economic problems of the day, including the problems surrounding gender, ethnicity, and class. Because we have to undo that which took the colonial settlers and their missionary descendants at least a century to engrain in African societies, said Muwowo, we realize that we can only hope to contribute to what will be a historical movement. I suggest, of course, that this historical movement will gain its greatest impetus if it is a Pan-African movement inclusive of both continental and diasporan Afro-Christians.

As the missionaries continue to leave Africa and Africans begin to recover from their cultural exile and rediscover their own cultural heritage, it can only be hoped that subsequent generations will begin to recognize the artistic beauty and the theological and theoretical validity of African music and art and the place these creative entities deserve in our liturgies. As a means of pushing this process along, the conferees agreed that all of us must encourage and nurture the composition of African music, art, and other liturgical creations that can fulfill our quest for a renewed liturgy. It is a word of encouragement to America's black church leaders and laity as well.

***

When Muwowo suggested that the various national Christian councils be urged to set aside one Sunday a year to be called "African Worship Sunday" as a means of promoting African indigenous worship in the church, it occurred to us that perhaps the liturgy produced by the conferees at the close of our deliberations would serve as a sufficient model. It occurred to me that it would be a rejuvenating model for the American black church. In producing this liturgy the conferees divided into two groups— one on liturgy and one on music. These groups creatively applied many of the ideas for liturgical renewal that we discussed over the course of our ten days together. For instance, the procession was comprised of the choir singing and dancing to the accompani-

115

ment of the drums as they and the clergy entered the worship place. It reminded me of my several visits to Stallings' Imani Temple, which is the closest instance I have seen in the United States. During the "declaration of purpose," which informed us that the worship was situational, everyone in the congregation was welcomed to "this our village." Continuing this use of African-centered language, God was referred to as "the king of this village." The speaker said, "The king of this village will speak to you through his spokesman." Then everyone was invited to say "welcome" to one another, and the congregants moved about the "village" shaking hands, hugging, and dancing as the choir sang.

Just as God was referred to as the "king" and the church as "our village," so was the sermon referred to as "storytelling." When it was time for the storytelling the spokesman of the "king," Felix Chingota, a minister of the CCAP Blantyre Synod, was accompanied to the center of the congregation where he sat down (upon a throne) to speak. The language referents to cultural traditionalisms well-known to all of us, the original hymns sung to original African tunes, the drumming and dancing, the African art in the worship place, the traditional attire of many of the participants, and much more resulted in a worship experience that was spiritually very satisfying. Indeed, it was a worship experience we felt would be worthy of serving as a model for churches that have begun the journey toward the indigenizing of their liturgy and the re-Africanization of Christianity. As satisfying to me as to my African kindred, it was an experience unquestionably worthy of serving as a model for any African-American churches that have also embarked upon this journey.

In order to help African (and African American) churches along in this process, a document titled "The Blantyre Covenant" was produced during the course of the conference and signed by the approximately 50 persons in attendance. This document, which summarizes the substance of the deliberations (and was read during the closing liturgy), with slightly modified language could have been referring to the black church in America. With just such a project in mind, I offer it here as evidence of one potential, rational Pan-Africanist joint-project for Africa and Afro-America and ideally for all of Afro-Christendom:

The Blantyre Covenant

We, an ecumenical group of Africans and ecumenical partners, gathered from various parts of the continent—from Uganda, Kenya, Malawi, Mozambique, Madagascar, Mauritius, Zimbabwe, Zambia, Sierra Leone, and Cameroon—have deliberated together for a workshop on the theme "The Worshipping Church in Africa," under the sponsorship of the Association of Christian Lay Centers in Africa (ACLCA). We have met to examine our worship lives as Africans within our churches, to identify obstacles preventing the cultural contextualization of Christianity in our churches, and to devise a practical plan for encouraging liturgical renewal. After deliberating together, singing, praying, and worshipping together, we have arrived at the point where we pledge our commitment to this covenant named after the city in Malawi in which we convened from November 9-19, 1992.

We are aware that contextualizing Christianity for the African churches, by using our traditional modes of expression to reflect the African religious worldview, is a crucial means of helping us regain our African identity, and thereby affirm that God created us in the divine image long before the coming of western missionaries.

We understand that Christianity, in its biblical representation, is significantly African, and that under the western missionaries we were led to believe that our religious traditions of drumming, dancing, and worshipping intensely were heathenistic and that we worshipped gods and ancestors rather than the one Creator.

We also recognize that we adopted the European worldview which divides the religious from the secular, the sacred from the profane, and that we thus excluded our social, political, and economic concerns from the church's agenda; so that our worship has generally neglected to respond to the daily needs of our people, including the cries and aspirations of women, youth, and the poor for justice.

We see the need for the renewal of our liturgical language, symbols, and images that are foreign, in order that we may see ourselves as Africans reflected in God as God's created people.

We recognize the artistic beauty and the theological and theoretical validity of our music and art, and the place these creative entities, derived from situational worship, deserve in our liturgies; that newly created hymns, even favorite western hymns, can be set to African melodies that have been adapted in order to capture the rhythm, pitch, and stresses of African languages. We recognize the need to encourage and nurture the composition of African music, art, and other liturgical creations that can fulfil our need for a renewed liturgy; and for the written documentation of those creative entities for further liturgical and later historical use.

We realize that it will take decades, and probably generations, to make recognizable progress toward liturgical renewal in our churches, given the fact that Africans were systematically steered away from nurturing our own cultural identities for centuries under colonial rule.

We are also aware of many of the obstacles that would impede any efforts toward liturgical renewal: that education in western schools and curriculums often results in acceptance of European values; that we often have grown attached to western music, liturgies, and art through their popularity and dominance; that there is a general conservatism in African churches which distrusts Africanization and liturgical renewal; that there is often an otherworldly emphasis in our churches which prevents us from making Christianity relevant to the specific social, political, and economic problems of the day, including the problems surrounding gender, ethnicity, and class.

Having arrived at this point of awareness, we, the undersigned, pledge to help our churches evolve to the point where we can worship God naturally and meaningfully, according to African traditions; to use the Lay Training Centers, theological schools, universities, churches, and other educational institutions in Africa as locations where we, in our various positions of influence, can develop curriculums and offer workshops that help us reach our objectives; and we commit ourselves to encourage the liturgical renewal within the worship lives of our local congregations.

We affirm our commitment to the universal church and offer our contribution to liturgical renewal for the enrichment of worship worldwide, in the name of the triune God.

4

RACIAL STRUGGLE AND RHYTHMIC CONFIDENCE

The evening before my first visit to the township of Soweto in South Africa in the summer of 1992, I went to see the musical *Sarafina!* It was showing at Johannesburg's Market Theatre, the location of the musical's premiere five years earlier in 1987. I was uneasy about being black and in South Africa, but of course I feel that way much of the time in America. I must say, then, that I did not feel as Eddie Harris, writing in *Native Stranger*, said that he felt when visiting South Africa: that he seemed at times to have more in common with the Dutch Afrikaner, the Boer, than with black South Africans. But given that I was somewhat uneasy about being black and in South Africa, I was somewhat comforted, as I would have been in America, when I saw such an amiably integrated group of blacks and whites present to see this musical by a black South African. I would have felt the same way in America if I had walked into an amiably integrated theater where Spike Lee's *Malcolm X* was showing, or in Germany where I saw that Lee's movie was showing in downtown Hamburg.

The point is this: That Mbongeni Ngema, born in 1955 and

raised in various government townships, could emerge as one of the preeminent playwrights in South Africa, and that his musical about South Africa's troubled history could educate an amiably integrated audience, made me feel as though a "new South Africa" was a real possibility. On the other hand, after I visited Soweto during the next two days and saw that as many as three million blacks live in this distant so-called "suburb" of Johannesburg, I realized that the legal dismantling of apartheid in 1991 would neither quickly nor easily alter the country's social, political, and economic reality. The legal abolition of apartheid particularly would not alter the theological underpinning of white society and white supremacy.

The South African Dutch Reformed minister J. A. Loubser speaks to the theological underpinnings of South Africa's former apartheid society in his book *The Apartheid Bible* (1987). He discusses openly the racist myths that circulate among white South Africans, among which are the notions that blacks cannot go to heaven and that missionary work is valueless since blacks recede into sin subsequent to their conversion. Loubser also discusses the biblical Genesis story of the so-called "curse of Ham" (Gen. 9:18-26), the interpretation being that African peoples are cursed always to be slaves. While Loubser contends that this questionable interpretation of the story of Noah and his sons was historically used by Afrikaners to justify the enslavement of Africans, he also implies that the myth is currently latent in the white subconscious. As I explain in my book *Sing a New Song: Liberating Black Hymnody* (1995), this latent myth is repeatedly reactivated by the symbolism—white being positive and black being negative—in the Western hymns that dominate in Christendom.

This was my point in Chapter 1, in discussing the racialist European imaginary regarding black personality and sexuality, which myths R. Nathaniel Dett and Dorothy Maynor still had to face in the early twentieth century. I said of Maynor specifically that the *Life* magazine photographs that captured her breasts "jouncing" as she sang spirituals and that capture her from the posterior bowing with her buttocks protruding conveyed to the sexualized imaginary of racialist whites Maynor's likeness to the "Hottentot Venus." Finally, I argued that the connection of these images during Maynor's day was inescapable, since representations of the physiognomy of the Hottentot woman entered the twentieth century in such art as Pablo Picasso's *Olympia* (1901), and since the dissected buttocks and genitalia of Sarah Bartmann (the "Hottentot Venus") remain on display in a Paris museum.

There remains in South African society, then, some residue of similarly suppressed racial myths. This is the reason that, in Chapter 2, I argued against Anthony Appiah's edification of Truth and Rationality to the level where the oppressed would be left without mythologies and mystifications (including our rhythms) to fend off the theologies of the powerful. Part of the social and political residue of South Africa's suppressed racial myths is manifested in the previous government's system of inferiorized education which was intended to teach black youths to accept their subservient position in the white-ruled society. As I presented in Chapter 3, missionary Christianity participated in this conspiracy, and Africans were left with a worldview that divides reality into two opposing spheres—the religious and the unreligious. This caused Africans (as it has African Americans) to exclude our social, political, and economic concerns from the liturgy. This is the "agony of Africa" that I am concerned about, the agony about which few whites seem deeply concerned. Here again, then, I repeat what I said in Chapter 2, in challenge to Appiah's belief that decent whites can hold the thought that if they were black and in South Africa they too would be victims. I said that certainly the number of whites who have this thought are relatively few, and the number who have been led to struggle against racism because of this thought are even fewer. But I myself certainly had this thought: that I am black and if I were a South African in the former apartheid regime I would be oppressed and would have to struggle for the liberation of my people.

It is worth repeating, then: I did not feel even for a moment what Eddie Harris said he felt, that he had seemed at times to have more in common with the Boer than with black South Africans. The Boer no doubt found reason to rejoice over the assassination of Chris Hani and would no doubt rejoice over the assassination of Nelson Mandela. I, on the other hand, equate Hani's assassination with that of Malcolm X and would equate Mandela's with that of Martin Luther King, Jr. Unless Harris is masking some sympathy with the postmodern conspiracy to explode racial identity (which impression I did not get from his book), his thought seems to be inauthentic.

Apartheid and White Lies

> Feeling that his rights and his dearest ideals are being trampled
> upon, that the public conscience is ever more deaf to his right-
> eous appeal, and that all the reactionary forces of prejudice,
> greed, and revenge are daily gaining new strength and fresh
> allies, the Negro faces no enviable dilemma.
> — Du Bois, "Of the Faith of Our Fathers"

The consequence of the previous South African government's system of inferiorized education, which was propped up by its racial
mythologies and its otherworldly politics of evangelical
Christianity, is illustrated in the movie *Sarafina!* The history
teacher at a Soweto grade school, Mary Masembuko, asks her students to give the name and color of the first man. "Adam," they
answer, "white." This is not an unrealistic scenerio even today in
America. In either case, the South African poet Stanley Motjuwadi
appropriately identifies this as our being "brainwhitewashed" in
his poem "White Lies." We should not be surprised about this
phenomenon in South Africa or America, or anywhere else on the
African continent or its diaspora where there has been colonization or slavery under Europeans. Frantz Fanon explains in *Black
Skin, White Masks* (1952) that:

> *In Europe, the black man is the symbol of Evil.* One must move
> softly, I know, but it is not easy. The torturer is the black man,
> Satan is black, one talks of shadows, when one is dirty one is
> black—whether one is thinking of physical dirtiness or of moral
> dirtiness. It would be astonishing, if the trouble were taken to
> bring them all together, to see the vast number of expressions
> that make the black man the equivalent of sin. In Europe,
> whether concretely or symbolically, the black man stands for
> the bad side of the character. As long as one cannot understand
> this fact, one is doomed to talk in circles about the "black prob-
> lem." Blackness, darkness, shadow, shades, night, the
> labyrinths of the earth, abysmal depths, blacken someone's rep-
> utation; and, on the other side, the bright look of innocence, the
> white dove of peace, magical, heavenly light. A magnificent
> blond child—how much peace there is in that phrase, how
> much joy, and above all how much hope! There is no compari-
> son with a magnificent black child: literally, such a thing is
> unwonted. Just the same, I shall not go back into the stories of
> black angels. In Europe, that is to say, in every civilized and civ-

ilizing country, the Negro is the symbol of sin. The archetype of the lowest values is represented by the Negro.

Ngũgĩ wa Thiong'o speaks similarly in *Barrel of a Pen* (1983):

In religious art you'll find that colonialist paintings tend to depict Satan as a black man with two horns and a tail with one leg raised in a dance of savagery: God is a white man with rays of light radiating from his face. But to the African, the colonialist was a devil,...for he had no human skin.

It is the same story in cinematic arts and even in music: assault our consciousness by giving us certain images of social realities. The musical arts are even more direct in their impact on the consciousness.... Missionary Christian songs created a mood of passivity and acceptance—"*Ndi Mwihia o na wanyona*" ("I'm a sinner") or "Wash me redeemer and I shall be whiter than snow," cried the African convert to his Maker.

It is these "white lies" and the struggle against allowing these kinds of lies to whitewash black brains that led to the 1976 uprisings in Soweto, the event dramatized in the musical and movie *Sarafina!*

***

Though the students of Soweto are receiving an inferior education comprised of "white lies," there are leaders among them who understand and, with rhythmic confidence, take action against their oppression. Their struggle outside the church parallels the struggle that I said in the previous chapter needs to occur inside the church. In the movie version of *Sarafina!*, one Soweto student, in discussing with several others the specific actions they should take, says about their school: "You think they put us here for education? This isn't education. This is some way to keep us off the street." Sarafina herself makes such a comment to her mother upon a visit to the white home in which her mother works. Expressing her anger toward her for being a domestic servant for the Boers rather than being heroic like her father who died in armed struggle, her mother asks Sarafina, Who otherwise would buy her school books? Sarafina responds, "School books are full of lies."

Sarafina's rebellious character is significantly modeled after the rhythmic confidence of Winnie Mandela. Like Winnie, playwright Ngema explains, Sarafina is beautiful and charming yet also very self-assured, her spirit having been tempered by the fires of apartheid. In fact, the idea for the musical actually came to Ngema when he visited his close friend Winnie in 1985, during which they discussed the plight of the jailed and exiled political leaders whose void was being filled by the youths. Infused with the rhythmic confidence of Winnie Mandela, Sarafina represents the energy and resilience of all the Soweto youths. As Nelson Mandela said about them upon his release from 27 years of imprisonment, these youths kept the struggle alive. If Eddie Harris lived through the 1960s in America, which I am sure he did, and if he understands the beating of the black motorist Rodney King by Los Angeles police as the partial failure of the civil rights movement, then certainly he does not really feel that he sometimes has more in common with the Boers than with Sarafina or Winnie Mandela.

Contrary to how the Boers would feel, certainly Harris would agree that teachers such as Sarafina's Mary Masembuko are due great credit for instilling in these youths pride in themselves as Africans. There were in fact such teachers in South Africa, for Masembuko's character is based on that of a school teacher of Durban named Phumzile Mlambo. Mlambo frequently faced difficulties with the apartheid South African government because she refused to teach their "white lies." Just as Durban's Mlambo doubtless had a lasting influence on the students she taught, so does Soweto's Masembuko wield influence. The "Mistress" (as they call her) gives her students lessons not found in the "authorized" textbooks and she opposes the forced instruction of Afrikaans, the language of the racist Afrikaners. Most importantly, she teaches her students to take pride in their history, history that predates the coming of the Boers who dispossessed them of their land. Ours is a history, the teacher instructs, that is "beautiful" because it helps us to know who we are as a people. This, we should recognize, is exactly what was said in the Blantyre Covenant about Africans contextualizing Christianity as a means of facilitating the regaining of "our" cultural identities after centuries under colonial rule. Of course, while we took no risks under an oppressive regime in formulating the Blantyre Covenant, Masembuko risks great danger in teaching the way she does. She takes the risk because she recognizes the role the youths will play in South Africa's future. I can (as Harris certainly must) better relate to the heroism of

Masembuko than to that of, say, Cecil Rhodes.

The cost of Masembuko's protest is multifold in the movie version of the drama. Though perhaps unintentional, her teaching certainly leads a group of boys in her class to set fire to the school (which episode opens the movie). The school principal is angry about the arson and reprimands the student body prior to the morning devotion. He is perhaps the equivalent of today's postmodernists who wish to explode racial identity amidst institutionalized racism. Unlike the principal, however, Masembuko never utters a word of disapproval about the arson; after all, her husband is himself a freedom fighter who is off engaging in the armed element of the struggle. In fact, just before leading the students in the singing of the Lord's Prayer, Masembuko gives them a rather devious grin that implies a measure of consent. The impetus of insurgency, begun thus in the teacher's defiance, eventually leads to her death in detention. But her rebellious spirit, her rhythmic confidence, lives on: When the principal of the school substitutes for the detained Mistress and attempts to follow the "authorized curriculum," the students stone him with their "authorized" textbooks, shouting at him and chasing him out of the classroom into the courtyard. The riot has begun, rhythmic confidence has exploded into chaos. When the security guards arrive at the scene, they respond with gunfire, some of the students firing back with stones—firing back only to meet their death.

After Sarafina witnesses her friend and classmate Crocodile's killing, shot in the back while fleeing from the security guards, the scene switches to a funeral procession that moves through the streets of Soweto toward the outlying cemetery. The preacher giving the eulogy of the slain students removes all blame for evil from the divine, saying: "God has given and the police have taken away." He also blames the United States and the United Kingdom for selling too many weapons to the Boers, he says, "to kill our children." This is actually the playwright speaking through his characters; for Ngema makes a similar comment about the overall significance of the movie: "Racism is the problem of the whole world; the only difference is that in South Africa, until recently, it has been by law." South African poet Dennis Brutus puts it this way in his poem titled "Sharpeville":

what the world whispers
apartheid declares with snarling guns.

By teaching that "God has given and the police have taken away," the minister giving the eulogy in Soweto instinctively condemned racial oppression without positing any theodicy to exonerate God of the potential accusation of being a "white racist." In reproaching racial oppression, then, it appears that the conventional biblical theodicies of missionary Christianity gave way to a secular theodicy, a crisis where the means by which the South Africans distinguished between suffering that should be personally endured and that which should be divinely eliminated was reduced to a secular decision. This "secular theodicy" was what William R. Jones called "humanocentric theism" in his book *Is God a White Racist?* For these black South Africans to be secular theodicists or humanocentric theists was for them to believe that the created (rather than the Creator) were the ultimate arbiters of what was morally good or evil in the world. In humanocentric theism, God is exonerated of any moral evil because God's sovereignty is separated from human history. This invalidates "divine racism" and any theological attempts by those who adhere to the "apartheid Bible" to justify racism. Thus, the preacher's partial blaming of the United States and the United Kingdom constitutes one opportunity for westerners to leave the movie with an important political message.

Because apartheid with snarling guns declares "detention!" "torture!" "death!" then the spirited music and dance (carryovers from the musical) could be seen as eclipsing Ngema's message to the West. However, the playwright's intention is also to capture the irrepressible human spirit and rhythmic confidence of the black youths, and there is no better way to do so than through the rhythms of the music and dance. This is one reason both acts of the musical, and the correlative parts of the movie, conclude with Ngema's chorus, "Freedom Is Coming Tomorrow." This powerful song is a statement not just of the youths' hope to attain freedom but of their resolve to be free.

That the theme of hopefulness—in the face of depravity, in the face of this "agony of Africa"—is the intended theme of the movie is signaled by its subtitle, "The Sound of Freedom." The "sound of freedom" signals an ability to turn feelings of sorrow into a rhythmic impetus toward liberation. As I began to say in my introduction as a hint of what I am now beginning to characterize as a dialectic between rhythmicity (power) and arhythmicity (suppression), there would have been no Soweto uprisings if the oppressor had contrived of some method of de-rhythmizing the colonized Africans. Had they enacted with their apartheid laws certain policies that forbade Africans not only to drum but also to dance, sing, preach, pray, clap, stomp, sway, and even to cradle their infants in their bosoms to the rhythm of their heartbeats, then after a generation or two the Boers would have succeeded in squelching the rhythmic confidence of their subjects: no black churches, no Blantyre Covenant, no African National Congress (ANC), no ANC Youth League "Freedom Charter." But in fact there are few black South Africans "born with weak beats": Rhythmic confidence abounds, and liberation was won.

The ability to turn feelings of sorrow into rhythmic sounds of freedom, signaled by the song "Freedom Is Coming Tomorrow," is in fact the hallmark of black music-making throughout the world. This is illustrated in the African-American spirituals that Dett and Maynor so loved. One of the well-known spirituals of this proclivity begins, "Nobody knows the trouble I see/ Nobody knows my sorrow/ Nobody knows the trouble I see"; and it ends, "Glory hallelujah!" The "glory hallelujah" is akin to "Freedom is coming tomorrow": Both are declarations of intended liberation. "Freedom is coming tomorrow" is a statement also akin to the intention behind the famous civil rights song, "We Shall Overcome." However, the "tomorrow" of "Freedom is coming..." is a more assured statement of intention than the "some day" of "We shall overcome..." "Some day," like "glory hallelujah," is of an indefinite eschatology or futurity, even implying the possibility that the resolution of the problem will come in that glorious day of the "other" world. "Tomorrow," conversely, indicates not only greater determinative resolve but implies a deadline, an ultimatum, and urgency.

There is one song in the movie that is even more radical and resolute than the resplendent and rhythmic "Freedom Is Coming Tomorrow," mainly because it hints strongly at the possibility of using violence if the ultimatum is not met. As Sarafina is nursing the wound of Crocodile, who was interrogated by security guards and bitten badly by one of their dogs, she confidently promises him that things will not always be as they presently are. She then imagines herself and her friends marching in the night with torches, singing with rhythmic confidence, "Nkonyane Kandabe": "You can't wound us, stop us, kill us.... We are coming." The song continues, "The war is at your door; we are coming." That the dispossessed are "coming" to repossess their birthrights and that a liberated Nelson Mandela will "tomorrow" play a leading part in the procuring of that freedom is quite in line with the general nature of human hopefulness. The spirited music may interrupt the tragic drama, causing Western audiences to forget the role their governments play in the tragedy, but hope in tragic life is always a dramatic aside.

***

Throughout the movie, Sarafina prayerfully speaks to "Nelson" (Mandela) with a faith that parallels a Christian's faith in Jesus. Indeed, it seems intentional on the part of the writers of the filmscript that Mandela be portrayed as a "suffering servant" who displaces the "white" and corrupt Christ of the apartheid Bible. This is depicted most clearly in the movie's scene where the students, supervised by their beloved teacher, are trying to agree on what kind of drama to present as the school play. Of the suggestions the students make, one is "Jesus comes back," an idea that receives only heckles. The next idea, Sarafina's "Mandela comes back," is received with great excitement. The teacher, overjoyed by the idea herself, names the play "The Day of Liberation." Later, in a moment of solitude and dejection, the Mistress admits to Sarafina that the play cannot be staged without provoking further problems with the security guards, who were still looking for the "troublemakers" who set the school ablaze. Anyone who shouted "Viva Mandela!" would, she says, become suspect.

What the movie reflects in this respect is that whites, threatened by the symbolism for which Mandela stands, go to extremes to contest the faith blacks have in this "suffering servant." The same conspiracy was being played out in America by those who were promoting Mangosuthu Buthelezi's Inkatha Freedom Party on the bogus grounds that Mandela was a Communist and Buthelezi a democratic capitalist who would work amiably with the West.

That white South Africans, like many white Americans, will go to significant lengths to subvert this faith is also illustrated in a small Christian tract I picked up in a white-run multiracial "mission" church in Johannesburg. The tract is titled "What Is the Answer?" and was released by the Gospel Publishing House in Roodepoort. Accompanying the title on the cover page are photographs of Nelson Mandela (top left), Mikhail Gorbachev (top right), George Bush (bottom left), and John Major (bottom right). Inside the tract is a list of South Africa's societal ills, among which is the statement most relevant to the movie: "Racism divides our country." Ensuing is the statement that the answer to the country's problems cannot be found in politicians (no doubt those on the cover of the tract) but only in Jesus Christ. This should strike our ear as comprising echoes of the apartheid Bible, for Mandela is out of place in the group of presidents and prime ministers who are participants in the Western ideology of white supremacy; not to mention that Mandela is no doubt intentionally (but wrongly) placed beside one who was a Communist. Only those Christian evangelicals who adhere to the ethos of the apartheid Bible would print such a tract that allows the oppressive colonial regime of P. W. Botha and F. W. DeKlerk to escape any criticism.

To the momentary advantage of the West's anti-Mandela faction, there is a point at which Sarafina's faith in the black "suffering servant" actually wanes. It is the point at which Sarafina questions whether "Nelson" can really hear her petitions. What happens is that after the rioting, the students suspected of murdering the black informant and security guard (Constable Sabela) are rounded up and held in detention. Sarafina, having been cruelly interrogated and thrown into a cell, and perhaps anticipating the torture she later receives, speaks silently to "Nelson," as she has throughout the movie. Acknowledging that she is full of hatred, she says: "Make me numb, Nelson. Make me numb." When she continues to feel the hatred as well as the fear and pain, Sarafina says: "You are not there, are you? You cannot hear us." This is the beginning of a conversion in Sarafina, a major turning point in the movie. We know for certain that her rhythmic confidence has been broken when she visits her mother at the home of the Boers, showing her mother her scars and confessing that previously she had been too rebellious and wrong about her. "You are a hero," Sarafina says to her mother. "You survived."

***

What is the answer? The movie's message that simply surviving is heroic is preposterous. The fact that Miriam Makeba, the black South African singer and activist, plays a character who turns out to be essentially a mammy is an act of political cliteridectomy. Known as the "Empress of African Song" and "Mama Africa," Makeba was born in Johannesburg and began singing songs of protest at an early age. When in 1960 she gained wide attention in the United States for her activism against apartheid, she was not permitted to return to South Africa even to attend her own mother's funeral. In 1963 when she testified before the United Nations Special Committee Against Apartheid, her recordings (which carried the rhythms of her forebears) were subsequently banned in South Africa. In 1968 she again found herself in exile, this time from the United States, when she married the radical Stokely Carmichael. The role Makeba plays in the movie is thus unbecoming to her real-life character. What is equally tragic is that the teacher, the real hero, who jeopardized her life in order to teach a nonwhitewashed history that would empower her students, is so eclipsed by the mother's alleged heroism that she, Mary Masembuko, appears to have been the "troublemaker."

Evidently the movie, unlike the musical, was made to be palatable to the taste of the white Western mentality, which has always edified the black mammy as the ideal example of acceptable black female disposition. The idea of erecting a monument to the Christian black mammy as a reward for her faithfulness to whites was actually being politically discussed among whites in the early 1920s. The black response then is the same as our response should be today. As put in an editorial in the March 21, 1923, issue of *The New York Amsterdam News:* "A monument to 'black mammies' is a mockery, a farce, and a disgrace to the intelligence of the United States Senate.... These men would erect a monument to commemorate, what? A position of humility, subserviency, meniality, servility is the idea they desire branded and scorched into the brain and heart of every American who happens to be of African lineage." The writer continues, "Does it not seem strange that white folk are always praising us for the virtue of humility, a characteristic they refuse to possess? Their history is full of oppression and tyranny. They praise and glory in the achievements of their warriors and heroic women who were willing to die rather than suffer affronts of their enemies." The writer concludes, "We have had enough of this humble spirit...crammed down our system, we don't appreciate a monument to that part of our life."

Sarafina's mother is undoubtedly dead today, ascended to the "kitchen heaven," the "kaffir heaven." She passed, say, in 1990, a year before Mandela's release. Unfortunately, we know nothing of what she thought of white South Africans because she hardly speaks in the movie. But it is imaginable that if she were to speak to the whites wanting to erect this cinematic monument *(Sarafina!)* in her memory, she might speak like the fictitious mammy in a short story created by Maude Nooks Howard. Howard's story, which first appeared in the *New York Times* as a response to the political move to erect a monument to the black mammy, was reprinted in *The New York Amsterdam News* on January 31, 1923. A fictitious mistress ascends to heaven and, locating her old mammy, says: "We the Daughters of the American Revolution are going to erect a beautiful and costly monument to your memory, because you were faithful, good and true." The mammy replies, "Chile, doan yo'll go 'n' spen' all dat money 'cause we wuz good 'n' faithful 'n' true. Dat wan't nuthin'; Jesus jes' teached us to be lak dat, da's all, Honey. But Missy, ef yo'all wunt de 'pinion of yo' Mammy 'bout yo'all showin' 'preciation, tell all dem Missys back dah to jes' treat dem we lef' behin' fa'r.... Honey, dey's folks lak you'alls." This is a mammy who is a master of the "mastery of form" that I discussed in Chapter 1: She wears an outer Europeanism (in this case arhythmicity or the mark of slavery) in order to conceal an inner Africanism (in this case rhythmic confidence and a will toward freedom). In the movie, Sarafina's mother is deprived of this hidden quality of the so-called mammy. In other words, the mammy is portrayed in the movie as a real type of character rather than as a real type of mask.

On the other hand, the musical version of *Sarafina!*, which was produced without the input of a white cowriter, director, and producers in America and Europe, was far more rhythmically confident and potent. In Ngema's musical there is no fake mother and thus no fake mammy as hero. Furthermore, because the teacher is not murdered in the musical, thus becoming a martyr, it is Sarafina herself who is resolute, resilient, and heroic to the end—traits that the Sarafina of the movie lacks at the conclusion. The movie fails the integrity of the oppressed and the rhythmic confidence conveyed in the music, not by developing the character of the teacher into a martyr but by setting her up only to be knocked down by a fake mammy figure.

***

The close of the movie has Sarafina leaving her mother and going to discard the gun the murdered teacher had been storing for her revolutionary husband. Sarafina then returns to her school and imagines what could have occurred had her classmates, many now dead, been able to present their school play. The school had been closed because of the rioting, but Sarafina imagines the students dramatizing "The Day of Liberation." Attired in a suit like Nelson Mandela and occasionally waving her fist like him, Sarafina portrays the return of the "suffering servant" to the people of Soweto. After some stirring words, promising everyone that they can look forward to the day the killing will be over and a new South Africa will be fashioned through reconciliation, the rhythmically resplendent reprise, "Freedom Is Coming Tomorrow," closes the movie.

In the musical this song is sung at the end of both acts. It is a declaration of resoluteness that captures the unbroken rhythmic confidence of Sarafina's rebelliousness—the *real* spirit of Winnie Mandela and Miriam Makeba. But in the movie, given the heroism attributed to the mother's quietistic survival, the "tomorrow" of "Freedom is coming..." has lost its potency and credibility. I declare, we have had enough of this spirit of humility forced down our system. We do not appreciate such a cinematic monument idealizing that portrayal of our history.

Rhythmicity and Arhythmicity

"But what is this group; and how do you differentiate it; and how can you call it 'black' when you admit it is not black?" I recognize it quite easily...; the black man is a person who must ride "Jim Crow" in Georgia.
— Du Bois, *Dusk of Dawn*

The reason we do not appreciate such a cinematic monument that heroizes a fake mammy figure is that it is the oppressors who always have the luxury of being concerned about their self-image while the oppressed must be concerned about our self-visibility. As Fanon says in *Black Skin, White Masks,* "A feeling of inferiority? No, a feeling of nonexistence." Thus, when invisible, particularly to ourselves, we are essentially slaves. Whites in South Africa and America seem bent on relegating us to a position where we might not see ourselves and therefore recognize our human worth. At the conference on "The Worshipping Church in Africa" we recognized this phenomenon and documented it in the Blantyre

Covenant (Chapter 3).

This colonialistic relegation of black people to invisibility is what Ralph Ellison was getting at in the prologue to his novel *Invisible Man* (1952) when pondering the problem of being unseen—worse, bumped into—by white people. The narrator of the prologue (partly Ellison's deepest invisible self) speaks as an unnamed, fictional figure: "I am invisible, understand, simply because people refuse to see me.... When they approach me they see only my surroundings, themselves, or figments of their imagination—indeed, everything and anything except me." The narrator muses further: "Or again, you often doubt if you really exist. You wonder whether you aren't simply a phantom in other people's minds. Say, a figure in a nightmare which the sleeper tries with all his strength to destroy." These passages from *Invisible Man* point to a basic psychology in G. W. F. Hegel's master-slave dialectic in *The Phenomenology of Mind* (1807). This psychology is with respect to the consciousness of a master existing for itself while a situation is created by the master where the consciousness of his slave is dependent upon and exists solely for him. With the systemic tools of power and control at their disposal, those who are masters strive to maintain the kind of situation that will deplete the enslaved of our rhythmic confidence and keep us viewing ourselves through our oppressor's eyes—as mammies, invisible men, as rhythmless.

This dialectic between rhythmicity and arhythmicity, power and poverty, is perfectly illustrated in a well-known anthology of poetry by Edgar Lee Masters, *Spoon River Anthology* (1915). As a privileged, visible white male, Masters (who is a master in the master-slave dialectic, a casual reader of the apartheid Bible) all but relegates the black citizenry of Spoon River to invisibility. Of the 214 real and fictionalized persons he brings to life from his home town in Illinois, the only black characters he poeticizes are perhaps Shack *Dye* the *black*smith, who is portrayed as a fool; perhaps Eugene Carmen, the so-called "slave" of banker and businessman Thomas Rhodes; and, no doubt, Benjamin Pantier's dog *Nig*. There are no black women poeticized, for they are all mammies. Masters' *Spoon River* therefore embodies the unconscious (if not conscious) drive of the master to relegate black people to the invisible, the arhythmic underside of the master-slave dialectic. This is why we do not appreciate a cinematic monument—the movie *Sarafina!*—that heroizes a fake mammy figure.

Let us understand that invisibility, here, does not mean to be invisible beneath our appearance, that is, to be invisible in the being-behind-our-appearance of blackness. It means to be invisible in and because of our phenotype. As Jean-Paul Sartre posits in *Being and Nothingness* (1956), there simply is no essence behind appearance; appearance reveals essence. To be sure, I am not positing the reverse of Senghor's rhythmic essentialism by suggesting that there is an arhythmicity that is the archetype of a vital nothingness. Invisibility is not an interior "something" that is hidden underneath an exterior of blackness; invisibility is concretely the totality of perceived nobodiness and of decimated self-image, self-respect, self-confidence, and self-determination, resulting from our viewing ourselves through mainstream eyes: forgetting our rhythms. The notion of simply surviving, then, is preposterous. To be an invisible man is insane; to be a mammy is mad.

In speaking to what I am describing as black arhythmicity, Ellison's *Invisible Man*—since it is fundamentally about the moral poverty of human invisibility—is a redress to the ethnocentrism, if not racialism, of America's privileged whose sacred literary canon comprises works such as Masters' *Spoon River*. H. G. Wells's novel *The Invisible Man* also deals with the problem of achieving social identity, but Ellison's experience as the truly invisible on the utter underside of Western civilization allows him to surpass Wells's novel not only in depth and ingenuity but in disclosing the deeper meaning of what it means to be unseen and ultimately what it means to have one's drum deferred and one's rhythmic confidence dashed.

***

It is because cultural imbalances perpetrated by Europeanist biases have had oppressive hegemony over African peoples throughout the world that today's rappers find radical spaces in the interstices of the establishment, in the liminal margins of mainstream society. Many rappers—like Sista Souljah and Malcolm X's daughter, Amila Shabazz—thus see themselves on a sacred mission to alleviate the syndrome of black invisibility and arhythmicity maintained by white control over the master-slave dialectic. These youthful speakers (who see themselves well and have astounding rhythmic confidence) articulate rhythms of hope, rhythms that transport their black listeners beyond repressive invisibilities and historical concealments. They articulate rhythms that move metrically against the stream of imperialistic sagas and the pernicious perjuries of America and South Africa as they have been traditionally told and retold in the western scholastic canon (including *Spoon River*) almost to everyone's believing. Rap, then, is the equivalent of Ngema's "Freedom Is Coming Tomorrow": It critiques the passivist ethos of the movie *Sarafina!* Sista Souljah, Amila Shabazz, Queen Latifah, MC Lyte, and many more are mammies who have come from behind the mask.

Here again, Ellison's novel is insightful as regards this rhythmic insurgency, for Ellison understood well the dynamics of Hegel's master-slave dialectic. He understood the idea of bondage being "a consciousness repressed within itself" and the bond being capable of entering into their own consciousness and of fixing it so as to be truly self-dependent and self-existent. The narrator in Ellison's prologue reflects this as regards his feeling of being a phantom in other peoples' minds: "It's when you feel like this that, out of resentment, you begin to bump people back. And, let me confess, you feel that way most of the time. You ache with the need to convince yourself that you do exist in the real world, that you're a part of all the sound and anguish, and you strike out with your fists, you curse and you swear to make them recognize you."

This feeling of being a phantom is the systemic problem of arhythmicity. It is, for instance, the problem that James Baldwin assays in his essay "Nobody Knows My Name." Written upon his first visit to the South, Baldwin informs us that a black poet who remembered the old South instructed him to recollect periodically the sins of those early days as a means of "steadying his soul," of sobering him up to reality. In this poignant piece, Baldwin does think soberly on the problems of the old South—the violent arhythmicity imposed upon black children, women, and men. Thus, the mood of this "Letter from the South" (the essay's subtitle) is akin to that of a letter being written from prison, the prison of invisibility, namelessness, and mamminess. Baldwin also knew that Malcolm X was correct in claiming that anything south of Canada is "the South." In his letter from Harlem titled "Fifth Avenue, Uptown," Baldwin says that black people in the North (like those in the South) only wish to be treated with respect—as visible human beings with names.

***

In order to maintain self-respect within this perpetually impinging dialectic between rhythmicity and arhythmicity, it is necessary for the oppressed to challenge—in some "form"—the imposing disposition of mastership. Contrary to what we see in the fake mammy figure in the movie *Sarafina!*, white supremacist discourse and demeanor do not generally go unreproached by black people; though our responses sometimes go unnoticed because of the tendency of the master class to relegate us to invisibility. Our retorts and liberational intentions often go unnoticed when masked behind discourse and demeanor that appear unthreatening—assimilative or even accommodative. Conversely, our retorts and liberational intentions are generally alarming to whites when we speak or act explicitly against their supremacist intentions and inventions.

In Houston Baker's words, these two types of African-American response to white supremacist discourse and demeanor are the "mastery of form" and the "deformation of mastery." The "mastery of form" involves the masterful manipulation of the minstrel mask where in actuality African Americans are confronting and critiquing the guardians of our oppression. The "deformation of mastery" is outright insurgency where black speakers and actors explicitly attack white supremacist ideology. I will put this differently in terms of Fanon's statement in *Black Skin, White Masks* that the black person is "a slave who has been allowed to assume the attitude of a master" and the white person "a master who has allowed his slaves to eat at his table." In this respect, the one who has mastered the form is one who will assume the attitude but not the disposition of a master, one who will eat at the master's table but not enjoy the meal.

May 22: Tea time, possibly a British tradition, is a tradition here in South Africa. We stopped for tea at a tea shop—I had coffee.

On the other hand, the one who deforms the master is the one who not only refuses the meal but critiques it because she or he prefers, as it were, soul food to crackers.

I first discussed the "mastery of form" in Chapter 1 with reference to R. Nathaniel Dett and Dorothy Maynor. I said that both of them, musically and personally, masked an inner Africanism behind an outer Europeanism. Musically speaking, they mastered the form in such a way that the inner religious and rhythmic substance of the spirituals they performed was maintained but encased within European musical forms. Personally, they mastered the extrinsic qualities of the trained European musician—academic credentials—having been trained at some of the country's best academic institutions. With this musical and personal "mastery of form," Dett and Maynor were able to transgress the essentialist color-line in their national and international travels.

I also explained that Dett quietly developed his own ideas about the purpose and value of his choir's 1930 tour of Europe, ideas which differed from those of the tour's sponsor, philanthropist George Foster Peabody. Peabody, we recall, wanted to demonstrate to Europeans, particularly those with colonial "possessions" in Africa, that the Negro's natural musical skills could be developed with the kind of opportunity whites in America were affording them. What happened instead was rather radical due to Dett's ability to preserve the best of the spirituals while encasing them in sophisticated arrangements. As an editorialist wrote after Dett's choir sang before Livingstone's tomb, "they were in a sense paying off an old and bloody score, but in a coin such as revenge rarely employs." The writer, we recall, was speaking of the spirituals, which were being deemed superior to the hymns created by Anglo-Saxons. The editorialist's words are worth repeating verbatim: "What these colored choristers were offering before the altar of the white master...were flowers plucked from the Gethsemane he imposed, flowers so exquisite that he must now bow his head in their presence and acknowledge his inability to gather their equal." As I concluded in Chapter 1, the "mastery of form" is a magnificient maneuver if "slaves" are able (as Dett and Maynor were) to garner the currency to compete against the odds with the "masters" who impose their Gethsemane.

The "mastery of form" is a viable strategy for some African Americans because what the guardians of our invisibility and our mammyism hear and see in our discourse and demeanor is not what they get. They hear certain stereotypic sounds that they anticipate coming from unenlightened or passivistic black mouths, sounds ranging from blues-like complaintiveness to rap-like playfulness. But what they get—what really sounds from behind the mask of the minstrel or the mammy when the "form" of buffoonery, quietism, or Europeanism is mastered—is *noise*. Noise is comprised of those dissonant sounds that begin to confront and disrupt white "mastery." In an essay in Gerald Early's *Lure and Loathing*, titled "Off-Timing: Stepping to the Different Drummer," novelist and English professor Kirstin Hunter Lattany defines this "mastery of form" through a rhythmic hermeneutic derived from reference to jazz:

> I use off-timing as a metaphor for subversion, for code, for ironic attitudes toward mainstream beliefs and behavior, for choosing a vantage point of distance from the majority, for coolness, for sly commentary on the master race, for riffing and improvising off the man's tune and making fun of it.
>
> The cakewalk was off-timing, mocking the airs of Massa and Missy, and making the antics of Philadelphia's New Year's mummers doubly, deliciously funny to blacks in the know. Louis Armstrong's mockery of minstrelsy was definitely off-timing, shored up by his strong talent, as it had to be; one needs a strong sense of self to play off the master and his stereotypes. Those Hampton students who cooly ignored George Bush's commencement speech in 1991 were off-timing. Haitians who adapt Catholic saints to voodoo rites are off-timing. No matter what she says, when Marian Anderson appeared on the Lincoln Memorial stage as a substitute for the DAR's—and opened her concert with "My Country 'Tis of Thee"—she was making dramatic and effective use of off-timing. The sister in Washington, D.C., who said, when asked her reaction to the Queen of England's visit, "Well, she's fascinating. But so am I," was definitely off-timing. Bill ("Bojangles") Robinson's tap routine to "Me and My Shadow" was a superbly elegant bit of off-timing, a mockery of the mocker that made a suave, ironic comment on racism.
>
> Off-timing, I learned in my youth, was the subversive attitude we had to maintain if we were to survive in the man's society. It was Uncle Julius's sly devaluation of European values in *The Conjure Woman*, and Larnie Bell's knowing jazz renderings of Bach fugues in *God Bless the Child*, and was more a skewed, but single, ironic consciousness than a double one.

In the early part of the century during the era of ragtime, to "rag" a piece of classical music was synonymous with what Lattany has termed "off-timing." For instance, it was also off-timing when ragtime pianists ragged Mendelssohn's "Wedding March," turning it into a honky-tonk, tin-pan-alley turkey trot. The point is that the mammy is really a masked "rag" woman.

***

The television show *In Living Color* (which was produced and hosted by Keenan Ivory Wayans until the Fox television network forced it to be less subversive) is an excellent example of off-timing, ragging, the "mastery of form." The actors on the comedic variety show, which premiered in 1989, articulate the familiar stereotypic sounds of minstrelsy; but they are actually, to use another synonym, "signifyin'" by sounding deeply critical critiques of white culture. The paradigm of the show's "mastery of form" appears in one of the show's earlier subversive characters, Homey the Clown. Homey (played by Damon Wayans) is a black parolee forced by "the system" to wear a clown getup and entertain children, but his appearing as a clown actually allows him to go unnoticed when his discourse and demeanor are critical of the system of "the man."

The epitome of the Homey the Clown skits is when Homey "makes it" and, still in clown-face, dons a three-piece suit because he is advertising a children's cereal. Sitting at dinner at Chez Whitey with two white men, Homey indicates that he would like to meet "the man." One of the two white men responds, "You got to be a complete sell-out to meet the man." Homey says, "What you talkin' about Mr. Charlie? Did I show you my new look." Homey shows them a picture of himself with his kinky clown hair straightened and combed down to his shoulders in imitation of white hair. Responding to the hesitance of the white men, Homey then says: "I denounce Farrakhan." "Jesse Jackson did that," one of the men responds. "Did I mention," says Homey, "Rodney King was way out of line."

Suddenly the door to the office of "the man" opens and bright "heavenly" light shines through. Homey walks through the light where he comes into the presence of "the man." The man says, "Well, well, well, Homey the Clown." Homey retorts, eager now to unmask himself: "Well, well, well, if it ain't the man, Mr. Establishment, Whitey himself, Ofay, White Devil, Cracker." Homey wants to continue but the man interrupts him, eager for him to prove his allegiance by kissing his ring. With a glare of disbelief and disdain in his eyes, Homey winds up his baseball sock and hones in on the man's head and bops him, just as he had always bopped the children who disrespected him when expecting self-demeaning clownish behavior. Homey says, "It was all a part of Homey's master plan just to bop the man." The man calls him a fool, says Homey does not know what he is doing. "Oh yes I do," retorts Homey, "I just got even with your ass."

That the "mastery of form" is (at least was) the strategy behind *In Living Color* was implied in the show's portrayal of Supreme Court Justice Clarence Thomas. In a skit on the newly appointed justice, Thomas, once he becomes certain that his lifetime appointment is secure, removes his minstrel whiteface. In fact, there were some African Americans, based on numerous discussions I heard during the Clarence Thomas/Anita Hill hearings, who conjectured that perhaps Thomas was in fact posing as an Uncle Tom until his golden opportunity to bop "the man" had been secured. At least there was this hope; or perhaps the hope was that Thomas might be converted, given his emotional cry that the hearings were a "hi-tech lynching." It is certainly true that oppressed people have the capacity to master the form so well that we can actually leave one another uncertain as to where we really stand—uncertain until some hint, some signification is given. When Thomas cried out about being lynched, there were those among us who read this as the hint that he did and would remember the horrible past that has shaped our present. Nelson George exemplifies this optimism in an essay titled "Race Loyalty," written for *Village Voice* in 1991 and published in his *Buppies, B-Boys, Baps and Bohos:*

> Thomas's shrewd, impassioned cries of "high-tech lynching" were...predictable.... Some see this ploy as pure hypocrisy, and I think there's something to that view. Yet to totally discount Thomas's protestations on this point is to overlook the contours of the man's nature....
> Looking for a silver lining in Thomas's 52-48 confirmation vote? Well, maybe his tortuous journey to America's most prestigious retirement home will grant him an insight into the vulnerability of the disenfranchised that hanging with Bush's crowd had dulled. It is a long shot, but a lifetime gives a man a lot of time to evolve.

So, I do not think Thomas was supported by blacks always out of the racial guilt of opposing a black person for the highest court and therefore that this racial reasoning was so utterly narrow. I think the "mastery of form," ragging on the man, is such a tricky maneuver that we ourselves are sometimes tricked by those who, knowing that we believe in this strategy, are able to throw out signifiers that confuse us. In his "mastery of form," Thomas was a double-agent in fact working for the Republican government. So, we can understand now that there was this hope—hope that sometimes interferes with rationality because it rises like smoke (free-form) within the interstices of oppression and alienation. It was a hope that Thomas might have been a master of the "mastery of form." But when we discover that the Uncle Tom or the black mammy is not just for the moment engaged in the "mastery of form," or that the one who has mastered the form is a double-agent, we should be very angry at having been tricked. The character of Sarafina's mother, like Clarence Thomas, has tricked us, due to the proclivity of the movie scriptwriters.

The point is that whenever an outer "form" is worn to mask what is really reproach to white supremacist discourse and demeanor, the result is the "mastery of form." This is a viable strategy for existence and catharsis that has its roots in the era of slavery in the behavior we called "puttin' on ole master." It too requires a certain rhythm—"off-timing"—which is part of our culture of rhythmic confidence.

Mastery in Music or Murder

> This meaning is not without interest to you, Gentle Reader; for the problem of the Twentieth Century is the problem of the color line.
> — Du Bois, "The Forethought"

The attempt to call out and unmask someone suspected of the "mastery of form" can leave the white thief vulnerable to the unbalancing rhythmic verbiage and gesture of "off-timing," which is intended to reestablish the stolen equilibrium. Such thieves are destined to learn that "off-timing" or signifyin' is worse than lying—worse, because one can never prove that another has signified.

An example of a failed attempt of a white "master" to steal a black man's mask and unbalance his rhythmic confidence is illustrated in an article on filmmaker Spike Lee, published in the October 1992 issue of *Esquire* magazine. The title of the article, written by a Jewish woman named Barbara Grizzuti Harrison, is "Spike Lee Hates Your Cracker Ass." The magazine cover, a photo of Lee with closed fists and crossed arms forming an X, has the caption "Spike Lee strikes a pose behind Malcolm." The title and caption of the article hint of the intent of the author to unmask Lee, behind which facade she presumes to see a little black man who "hates your cracker ass" and is using the larger persona of Malcolm, the mystique of the X, and the powerful medium of film as his mouthpiece for articulating black nationalist "noise" rather than integrationist "harmony." Lee's pose and the magazine's caption, both signaling the release of his movie *Malcolm X* (which was then forthcoming), together inferred that the article would comprise a dialectic between "master" and masked man. Lee, however, maintains his poise—his "mastery of form," his rhythmic confidence—which unhinges his interviewer, Barbara Harrison, just as it unhinges Lula in LeRoi Jones's (Amiri Baraka's) pertinent play of 1964, *Dutchman*.

Baraka's Lula is a thirty-year-old white woman (somewhat younger than Barbara Harrison). While riding on a city train, Lula makes an insane but intellectualized advance on a younger black man named Clay, a twenty-year-old (somewhat younger than Spike Lee). So it is with Barbara's advance on Spike, Barbara writing in her *Esquire* article: "For five minutes or so I felt as if we were connecting. I felt a reciprocal absence of self-consciousness. We were like those characters in Forties and Fifties movies—prisoner on one side, visitor on the other, hands touching, palms and fingers meeting, establishing corresponding prints on either side of the glass divide." But when the dialogue between Clay and Lula fails to go as Lula wishes, she falls into a harangue, flinging indecent epithets and calling Clay an "Uncle Tom" because he was raised in a well-to-do part of town and is attired in a three-piece suit. Barbara, equally as frustrated with Spike, writes in her article: "He rebuffs me at every turn. And my anger leads me directly into stupidity...into racism, he would say...he did say. How dare he accuse me of assuming superiority? His great-grandfather went to Tuskegee; I don't know my great-grandfather's name; my maternal grandfather, a shepherd, was an indentured servant. Until my children's generation, nobody in my family went to college." Like Lula, Barbara continues her harangue, not just describing Spike as so fragile that his wrists look as if they could be "snapped like a sapless twig" or concluding that she liked Spike's work "so much more than he allowed me to like him," but titling her article "Spike Lee Hates Your Cracker Ass."

In his "deforming" retort to Lula, Clay informs the older white woman that she cannot possibly understand black people simply because she is sexually familiar with black men. Clay just as well could have been speaking to Barbara, who finds it necessary to confess in her article that she had been "crazy about" one black man in her life. Still "deforming" Lula for her presumed knowledge of black people and for her calling him "Uncle Tom," Clay says: "Let me be who I feel like being. Uncle Tom. Thomas. Whoever. It's none of your business. You don't know anything except what's there for you to see. An act. Lies. Device. Not the pure heart, the pumping black heart. You don't ever know that. And I sit here, in this buttoned-up suit, to keep myself from cutting all your throats." Many of us had hoped that Clarence Thomas and Sarafina's mother had turned out to be acting—lies, device.

***

That black music is also an act, a device, an instance of the "mastery of form," is not understood by Lula's kind. Barbara Harrison, who wishes it not to be so, recalls the time Billie Holiday had been a "sister" to her when a black man in Minton's jazz club accused her of being a "white devil-woman." "'She's a nigger,' Billie Holiday said. 'She can be raped. Anybody who can be raped is a nigger.' I loved her forever." But Clay does not buy it, considering whites who pop their fingers to the music of Bessie Smith and Charlie Parker, expressing their love for them, to be blinded to the fact that Bessie and Bird were, in masked form, cursing them to their faces. We are deprived of this side of Sarafina's mother in the movie.

The reason white folks cannot comprehend or imitate bop is explained by Langston Hughes's fictitious cultural critic, Jesse B. Simple (a cousin to Clay in the tradition of "off-timing"). The reason is that whites do not know the experience of getting their heads beaten (like Rodney King). Bebop, the comical cultural critic continues, is the product of police brutality—wop! bop! be-bop! That percussive head-beating moves down from the crown of the head and right out the bell of the horn. "And they sit there talking about the tortured genius of Charlie Parker," says Clay. "Bird would've played not a note of music if he just walked up to East Sixty-seventh Street and killed the first ten white people he saw. Not a note!... If Bessie Smith had killed some white people she wouldn't have needed that music. She could have talked very straight and plain about the world. No metaphors. No grunts." The country blues singers used to say they laugh in order to keep from crying, but Clay is suggesting that they laughed in order to keep from killing. "Crazy niggers turning their backs on sanity," figures Clay. "When all it needs is that simple act. Murder. Just murder!"

Suddenly (say the stage directions) Clay is weary from his outburst—weary, as it were, from his having partially unmasked himself. But prior to his transgressing the threshold of murder, beyond which there would have been no return—Lula's funeral and Clay's trial—Clay commences his retreat, buttoning himself back up behind his three-piece suit. "But who needs it?" he resolves. "I'd rather be a fool. Insane. Safe with my words, and no deaths, and clean, hard thoughts, urging me to new conquests." But upon his retreat to calm himself, to remask himself, Lula stabs him to death. He is unmasked in death; he is nothing but a black man who bleeds like all the "deformers" known all along for their insurgency. Spike, on the other hand, did not uncover any violence or threat of violence against Barbara, as Clay had against Lula. Spike chose to remain safe with his words, his clean, hard thoughts urging him onto new conquests, new films. Thus, there are no deaths—only Spike's genealogy of cinematic ritual murder and Barbara's rhetorical "stab in the back" ("Spike Lee Hates Your Cracker Ass").

***

This is the way I propose that we understand black music. In addition to Houston Baker's suggestion that the spirituals and the blues are instances of the "deformation of mastery," I contend that all forms of black music, from the spirituals to rap, can also be understood as instances of the "mastery of form." I am not speaking of the kind of "mastery" or "masking" that we have come to understand as typifying the character of the spirituals. To be clear about the matter, Dett writes about the latter form of "mastery" in the introduction to his edition of *Religious Folk-Songs of the Negro: As Sung at Hampton Institute* (1927):

> for in striving to give voice to his experience the slave found in the Testaments, in the story of the children of Israel, for instance, much in the way of a text that was ready made; all of which was quite to his liking though, of course, unconsciously, for he could thus sing of one thing and mean another. This indirect mode of

expression, it is well known, is one of the most characteristic earmarks by which the art of the East is distinguished from that of the West; it is characteristic of Negro music, often hiding, masklike, its fundamental mood and not a little of its real meaning.

This is a closely related kind of "mastery of form," but it is not the only kind, not the kind I am speaking of at present. I am speaking of a mastery that masks a tendency toward murder. This is "mastery of form" not at the intellectual level but at the visceral level.

Bebop, for instance, is not simply the musical expression of the bopping of black heads; it is "the riot," the whomping back of white heads—wop! bop! be-bop!—by which I mean it is the exorcising of violence. Rap, in its "mastery of form," similarly exorcises violence, in that it makes one too weary to murder. Rap, like bop, may provoke "the riot" (as many whites fear) but it simultaneously exorcises violence by exhausting the body.

> *June 8: Lectured at Seke Teacher's College, in the town of Seke about 15 miles outside of Harare.... I talked about the sacredness of black secular music, especially the blues and rap. Discussed rap as prophetic, warning of racial, political, and economic injustices.... The two professors who hosted me...said that in my lectures I have "that touch." They said I could easily "incite a mob."*

Despite its aspect of intellectual insurgency, rap is first and foremost exhausting to the body; for it is the body, not the rational understanding, that is the absorber of rap's rhythms. I think Nelson George unknowingly alludes to this in *Buppies, B-Boys, Baps and Bohos* when he says, "Rap records aren't primarily about the rap. They're about the intensification of rhythm, about how much beat you can stand before your mind explodes into angel dust and your legs crumble to the dance floor."

Violent aggressivity—the "scratching" of rap DJs giving sound to blades slitting throats—is physiologically canalized, transformed, and exorcised. As Fanon says in *The Wretched of the Earth* with respect to the dance and spirit possession among Africa's colonized:

> The native's relaxation takes precisely the form of a muscular orgy in which the most acute aggressivity and the most impelling violence are canalized, transformed, and conjured away.... There are no limits—for in reality your purpose in com-

ing together is to allow the accumulated libido, the hampered aggressivity, to dissolve as in volcanic eruption. Symbolical killings, fantastic rides, imaginary mass murders—all must be brought out.

Jean-Paul Sartre's interpretation of this passage, written in his preface to Fanon's book, is also worth hearing: "They dance; that keeps them busy; it relaxes their painfully contracted muscles; and then the dance mimes secretly, often without their knowing, the refusal they cannot utter and the murders they dare not commit."

Symbolic murders, such as Public Enemy's "By the Time I Get to Arizona," Ice T's "Cop Killer," Johne Battle's "Ultimate Drive By," and Paris's "Bush Killa" are brought out into the open, so that the accumulated libido can be dissolved on the very border that crosses over into outright violence. Paris's "Bush Killa" is recorded on his second album, *Sleeping with the Enemy*, which has a liner photo of the rapper standing behind a tree with a gun in his hand stalking President George Bush. The assassination attempt, the lyric reveals, is prompted by Bush's alleged genocidal policies against blacks.

Television news anchorman Dan Rather did a piece on the kindred rap by Public Enemy, "By the Time I Get to Arizona." The journalistic piece was titled "Rap Goes Violent" and appeared on the CBS Evening News of January 9, 1992. Dan Rather labeled as "unsettling news from the street" the fact that Public Enemy had, in enacting assassinations against Arizona officials for not approving a national King holiday, labeled a whole state violent.

These allegedly violent rap songs are what rappers have termed "revenge fantasies," but it is the fantasy that permits the relaxation of the most acute aggressivity and the most impelling violence. Rap is not connected to the fantasy in any way other than being its vehicle. Like writers of fiction, cultural critics have also engaged in this fantasy. In his poignant and powerful essay "To Be a Black Man," first published in *Village Voice* in 1991 and subsequently in *Buppies, B-Boys, Baps and Bohos*, Nelson George hints at having a "revenge fantasy" himself:

To be a black man is to enter an elevator and have a white woman shift her bags away from you. It's to see the white man next to her push out his chest and try to stare you down. It's watching them pirouette to avoid brushing against you. It's to laugh at their timidity and then want to pull out a nine-millimeter automatic and mow down every white mother-fucker in sight.

A phenomenon similar to the "revenge fantasy" is what the late African-American historian Earl E. Thorpe called the "rescue fantasy" in his book *The Old South: A Psychohistory* (1972). Fanon illustrates the rescue fantasy in *Black Skin, White Masks*. He says, "The soul of the white man was corrupted, and, as I was told by a friend who was a teacher in the United States, 'The presence of the Negroes beside the whites is in a way an insurance policy on humanness. When the whites feel that they have become too mechanized, they turn to the men of color and ask them for a little human sustenance.'" Regarding the rescue fantasy being a phenomenon similar to the revenge fantasy, Thorpe says that African Americans have often believed that our race would rescue whites from their decadence but that this desire to rescue is often merely a substitute for the desire to murder. Those who criticize rap for its violence should therefore understand that rap appears to be violent only insofar as it exorcises violence, murder. These critics should, furthermore, heed the final warning Clay gave Lula and her kind just prior to his murder:

> But listen, though, one more thing. And you tell this to your father, who's probably the kind of man who needs to know at once. So he can plan ahead. Tell him not to preach so much rationalism and cold logic to these niggers. Let them alone. Let them sing curses at you in code and see your filth as simple lack of style. Don't make the mistake...of talking too much about the advantages of Western rationalism, or the great intellectual legacy of the white man, or maybe they'll begin to listen. And then, maybe one day, you'll find they actually do understand exactly what you are talking about, all these fantasy people.... They'll murder you, and have very rational explanations. Very much like your own.

***

That rap and other forms of black music are in the foregoing respect more physiological than rational, are really instances of the "mastery of form" rather than of the "deformation of mastery," suggests that the Lulas and Barbaras of the master's discourse and demeanor ought not attempt to unmask the Clays, Spike Lees, and Public Enemies of America. Again, Fanon says in *Black Skin,*

White Masks: "In every society, in every collectivity, exists—must exist—a channel, an outlet through which the forces accumulated in the form of aggression can be released."

French economist Jacques Attali argues similarly in his book *Noise: The Political Economy of Music* (1977). Noise, as Attali defines it somewhat symbolically, is any audible means of disturbance and propaganda by which control is exercised. Music is the organization and channelization of this noise within the social arena as a means of maintaining societal balance. In this respect, music is a strategy that runs parallel to religion, which also channels power via its reconciling of people with the social order. Thus, the appropriation, monopolization, and comodification of music comprises a harnessing of power that occurs by means of three strategies: music being used to make people forget the fear of violence, to make people believe in order and harmony, or to make people be silent (by repeating monotonously music that has been mass-produced in order to drown out all other noises). We should be able to see where music created for religious ritual functions in all three respects. "The game of music," says Attali, "thus resembles the game of power: monopolize the right to violence; provoke anxiety and then provide a feeling of security; provoke disorder and then propose order; create a problem in order to solve it." Attali continues:

> The musical ideal then almost becomes an ideal of health: quality, purity, the elimination of noises; silencing drives, deodorizing the body, emptying it of its needs, and reducing it to silence. Make no mistake: if all of society agrees to address itself so loudly through music, it is because it has nothing more to say, because it no longer has a meaningful discourse to hold.... In this sense, music is meaningless, liquidating, the prelude to a cold social silence in which man will reach his culmination in repetition. Unless it is the herald of the birth of a relation never yet seen.

When music (or rhythm) is meant to make people forget, explains Attali, it is being used as a form of ritual sacrifice. "Noise is a weapon and music, primordially, is the formation, domestication, and ritualization of that weapon as a simulacrum of ritual murder." Music (particularly rhythm) symbolically signifies the channeling of violence, and it ritualizes the murder as a substitute for general violence, thereby signifying that the social order is possible. So music—inscribed, as Attali says, between noise and silence—is itself a kind of "mastery of form." As he has said, music is a strategy that runs parallel to religion.

"Civilization," esteemed in the master's discourse about the advantages of Western rationalism (Anthony Appiah's discourse), is itself but a mask. One of its false faces is religion, which, if unmasked, would reveal the possibility of murder, or at least police brutality. "You say you believe in the necessity of religion," says Nietzsche. "Be sincere! You believe in the necessity of police!" Similarly, the popular culture industry says it believes in the cultural and economic necessity of black music, television, and film, of Public Enemy, Homey the Clown, and Spike Lee, promoting them and capitalizing upon them despite warnings that they unmask these alleged Malcolm-X types. Be for real! The industry believes in the necessity of ritual violence!

5

AFRICAN RHYTHM IN
PERSONIFICATION

In the previous chapter I explained an aspect of African-American culture through the paradigm I adapted from the thought of Houston Baker—the "mastery of form" and the "deformation of mastery." The former I had discussed earlier, in Chapter 1, where I explained that R. Nathaniel Dett and Dorothy Maynor mastered in their renditions of the spirituals the form of an outer Europeanism while savoring the substance of an inner Africanism (the religious and rhythmic substance). In the last chapter I explained that that which is the "deformation of mastery," with respect to debunking language carried by an apparent rhythmic insurgency, is in another respect the "mastery of form," since music (particularly its rhythm) tends to mask what is otherwise a tendency toward murder. In both instances, the rhythms of black folk find expression: In the "mastery" it is the Africanism subtly carried within the outer Europeanism, while in the "deformation" it is rhythmic insurgency (that is, an extrinsic black rhythmicity that can convey the impression of being equivalent to riot). However, both ways of being and of discoursing are not in themselves carriers of our rhythmic traditions; they are only vehicles for the expression of our rhythmic traditions. In this chapter I present what I think is the paradigmic African personality responsible for the perpetuation of our rhythmic traditions. I am not speaking of an essentialist quality in the sense that Senghor was with his "African personality," and I am still not thinking of rhythm as being that which represents some kind of racial "character of abandon." I am thinking, still, that African rhythm, even diasporized and creolized, gives rise to recurrent themes and traits in Afro-cultures.

What I am positing with respect to a paradigmatic African personality responsible for the perpetuation of our rhythmic traditions is this: When we depersonify the personage of the African trickster-god—Eshu-Elegbra of the Yoruba, Legba of the Fon of Dahomey, Papa Lebas of the voodooists of New Orleans—and then culturalize the trickster's personality, what we have is in fact a core theme in Afro-cultures. This core theme is a synchronous duplicity that does not, like the European dualistic view of reality, divide the sacred from the secular or the spiritual from the physical. Despite what Africans and African Americans have declared doctrinally, we have always had a view of life that was more wholistic than dualistic. But even within this African cosmology (the personage of the African trickster-god depersonified), we find the trickster personality actually alive; and I believe that those who personify this paradigm of personality in African-American cultural reality are in fact core cultural carriers of the rhythms of black folk. The tricksters comprise the personified genealogy of African rhythm in the New World. So, the trickster as rhythmic carrier is, to borrow Dett's language, the one who reincarnates and re-christens rhythm in each new generation.

I suggest that the African trickster-god—who is both female and male, sacred and profane, benevolent and malevolent, reconciler and disrupter, loved and feared—is not only a symbol of the synchronous duplicity of much of African-American culture; the trickster is also a paradigm of personality that can be found in myriad mythic and real personages of African-American culture—the legendary Stackolee, the voodoo queen Marie Laveau, Pan-Africanist Marcus Garvey, blues singer Memphis Minnie, cult leader Father Divine, Baptist preacher C. L. Franklin, radical linguist H. Rap Brown, gospel composer Thomas Dorsey, folklorist Zora Neale Hurston, hip hop rapper Queen Latifah, and the intellectual and Malcolm X lookalike Cornel West (who is the rhythmic activist and academic that Malcolm would have been had he ever received the education he desired). In the dialectic between rhythmicity and arhythmicity, all of the above individuals are replete with rhythmic confidence; none of them were "born with weak beats": None of the women are fake mammy figures; none of the men are invisible men. Some are masters of the "mastery of form" and others of the "deformation of mastery." Still, all of them can be understood through the trickster paradigm to be carriers of the rhythms of black folk.

In an essay titled "Niggas With Attitude," in his book *Buppies, B-Boys, Baps and Bohos*, Nelson George places this rap group and the constituency it represents in the lineage of the aforementioned Stackolee. "Like George Jackson embracing the metaphor of the mythic black stud Stagger Lee, young people—women and men— celebrate the hardest parts of their imaginations and invent themselves as niggas-for-life with no apologies and incredible pride." The Stagger Lee or Stackolee mythic type is, in today's post-soul era, what is called a B-boy. But there are three other African-American character types that George says began germinating in the 1970s and burgeoning in the 1980s. I believe that each of the characters he defines can be understood as a part of the trickster's manifold personality, and that it is perhaps the postmodern age of fragmentation that has spawned the four types. George says:

> There is the Buppie, ambitious and acquisitive, determined to savor the fruits of integration by any means necessary; the B-boy, molded by hip hop aesthetics and the tragedies of underclass life; the Black American Princess or Prince a/k/a Bap, who, whether by family heritage or personal will, enjoys an expectation of mainstream success and acceptance that borders on arrogance; and the Boho, a thoughtful, self-conscious figure...whose range of interest and taste challenges both black and white stereotypes of African American behavior.

The Trickster as Core Cultural Carrier

> The people moaned and fluttered, and then the gaunt-cheeked brown woman beside me suddenly leaped straight into the air and shrieked like a lost soul, while round about came wail and groan and outcry...
> — Du Bois, "Of the Faith of Our Fathers"

This synchronous duplicity in the trickster-based personality, which is ripe for the carrying of our African-based rhythmic traditions, can be seen most explicity in our urban gods of the twentieth century. With the arrival of black culture from the South during the great black migration, cities like Harlem saw an influx of black tricksters that ranged from the southern root doctor and the creole card-reader to pastors and scholars such as Reverdy Ransom. But the creole card reader and the pastoral scholar are extremes; betwixt and between we find the likes of Father Divine. Divine, like Marcus Garvey before him, was a trickster personality insofar as he meshed the serious with its antithesis. Although I do not use the words *trickster, trick,* or *trickiness* in a pejorative sense, there sometimes exists a sarcastic element to discourse about tricksters because of the comic side to their seriousness, the destructive side to their constructiveness, and so forth. One wants to contemplate and congratulate tricksters, but one also wants sometimes to laugh and dance or even deconstruct and demean.

What most distinguished Divine's cult from both the mainline Protestant and the Holiness and Pentecostal churches was that Divine was believed to be God, Christ reincarnated. It is quite a trick, but with some divinely beneficial social consequences that should be understood in the light of the biblical Christ feeding the multitudes with fish and bread. In an article in *The New York Amsterdam News* titled "Divine Feeds 600," the black messiah is reported to have said: "I preach Christ not only in word, but in deed and in action. What I have to offer is only the outward expression of a per cent of the limitless blessings I have in the storehouse for you."

Divine certainly sounded as though he believed himself to be God, but upon direct inquiry he was known to have given tricky answers. One instance was reported in the same newspaper, under the headline "Bail Doubled as Cult Head Flashes Roll." On this occasion Divine had been summoned to court for maintaining a children's boarding house without a permit from the health department, and the judge pointedly asked him if he believed himself to be God. Divine answered with the undaunted rhythmic confidence of a god who knew how to contend with all who come by way of the crossroads: "I do not say I am God and I do not say I am the devil, but I will bring God to the consciousness of the people, and I will command men to deal justly with the people or else I will move them out of office." "Who?" asked the judge. "Every judge and ruler that will not deal justly with the people," answered Divine. When indirectly asked the original question—whether he believed he had the authority to direct the lives of his followers—Divine answered: "I believe that they have a right to be governed by their highest intuition and believe that I am God if they wish to." "Do you tell them that you are God?" the judge prodded. Divine began rhythmically, as he had before: "I do not tell them that I am God. I do not tell them that I am the devil. Many say I am the devil and millions say I am God, but I will prove to the world that God rules in the affairs of men and none can hinder him." The judge actually should have been inquiring as to whether Divine were (to make my point) Papa Labas, a descendant of Legba and Eshu Elegbra.

Whether or not Divine really believed himself to be God, he spoke and carried himself with the kind of rhythmic confidence that led others to believe he was. But as of the later half of 1931, only a few thousand people had succumbed to his divine trickiness, his rhythmic confidence. Not long afterwards, however, he conjured almost overnight notoriety. The story of this rapid ascent began on December 2, when he and his followers were first brought before the judicial courts, indicted for disorderly conduct (being too noisy in their worship) at Divine's Sayville, Long Island, headquarters. Being the man of confidence that he was, Divine would appeal his conviction for disorderly conduct. His attorney filed the appeal based on what he perceived to be the judge's unwarranted hostility toward his client. When his appeal was eventually heard, the judge, after hearing his attorney, agreed that freedom of religious expression was guaranteed under the United States Constitution. Divine and his followers were acquitted of the charges.

While he was awaiting the appeal of that court case, Divine relinquished his headquarters on Long Island and moved to Harlem in early 1932. It was there that he gained overnight celebrity status when the judge who had sentenced him to prison for disorderly conduct expired unexpectedly. The top headline of the June 9, 1932, issue of *The New York Amsterdam News* read, "Judge Who Sent Divine to Jail Dies Suddenly." The article began:

> The fanatical followers of the Rev. Major J. Divine, convicted "God" of a Long Island religious cult, claimed the fulfillment of a weird prophecy this morning. For, in less than four days after they had sworn it would come to pass, Supreme Court Justice Lewis J. Smith, the stern jurist who sentenced their

leader to a one-year term in Suffolk County jail at Riverhead Saturday for maintaining a public nuisance, died suddenly at his home in Hempstead.

The article continued, "Followers of the Sayville 'Messiah' have contended since his conviction on May 25 that any sentence given Divine would result in the death of the jurist, who, they charged, was openly hostile to their leader during the whole of the trial." Indeed, the judge, as reported in the local paper under the headline "Attorney to Seek Bail," was eager to discredit Divine upon cross-examination. Among other things, he said: "I am informed that his name is not Divine but George Baker, and that he was born in some Southern State or on an island off Georgia." He continued, "I am informed that he is not an ordained minister, that the woman they call 'Mother Divine' is not related to him, but that he has another woman as his wife and has children."

When Divine won his release from prison on bail pending an appeal, he was greeted by about 7,000 followers. Mother Divine (who was a white woman) led the singing of "The Lord Has Come," and the trickster himself sang "I'm the Light of the World." According to an article titled "Cult Head Acclaimed by Throng," the divine one then spoke to his throng of worshippers: "You may not have seen my flesh with you for a few weeks but I was with you all the time. I am just as operative in the spirit as I am with the body." Like the transformation of William Bunch of Ripley, Tennessee, into the infamous blues singer Peetie Wheatstraw of East St. Louis (known as "the Devil's Son-in-Law"), George Baker, born in some southern state, was transformed into the infamous cult leader Father Divine of Harlem.

Divine's transformation involved a trick on the man who claimed to have taught Divine everything he knew, an Ethiopian who went by the name Rev. St. Bishop the Vine. The trick, quite simply, is that Divine took some of what St. Bishop began to teach him and used it (or misused it) to surpass the size and significance of his teacher's own ministry. St. Bishop, who had his own religious following in Harlem, was not amused by the trickiness of his former understudy. A few months after Divine's indictment, the local press printed some criticisms that were made against the cult leader by St. Bishop. He said in an article titled "'I Taught Father Divine'" that it was he who taught Divine about the "God-Within-Man Gospel" but Divine had abandoned his tutelage before completely grasping the ideas:

He goes around here teaching that married members of the race must sever their marital relationships, thereby causing dissensions among married couples with consequently a demolition of their morals. This teaching is dangerous and wrong and therefore should not be permitted, for such, if indulged in, will eventually lead many into a false conception of their social responsibilities.
This is not right. I taught Divine, but he, not having remained long enough under my tutelage, failed to realize the complete idea whereby a clear conception plus the ability to teach unerringly would have been attained.

Divine the preacher was, as a trickster figure of the lineage of St. Bishop, a carrier of black rhythms, the rhythms of preaching that I discussed in Chapter 3. A local journalist who had observed his worship services wrote about it under the caption "Sayville Cult Head Undaunted by Cops":

One of the most remarkable things about "Father" Divine is his inexhaustible energy. Almost daily he preaches in one place or another, and when "Father" Divine preaches, he puts into it something more than reading the "Word." He goes through gymnastic feats that would have won an Olympic championship for him had he been competing in the Olympics. He is agile, wiry, and resilient. In the course of a sermon he leaps, twists, contorts, and wobbles. But he never appears to be tired.

One observer of a Divine worship service commented in a newspaper article titled "Challenge for Divine," "As I sat in the midst of a hysterical congregation...and listened attentively to the various remarks emanating from the lips of an insignificant individual whom his followers herald as the true and living God, I wondered why we continue to send missionaries to various parts of the uncivilized world, when they are very much needed here." But with thousands of followers now proclaiming this preacher of inexhaustible energy to be God, Divine had "one up" on those who were his detractors.

***

When the local papers were not busy following Divine's legal proceedings and uncovering whatever scandals they could by interviewing people like St. Bishop, they did give some space to recognizing the other side of the trickster's synchronous duplicity: the social ministry for which his followers worshipped him. There should be little doubt that Divine's ministering to the material, social, political, and economic needs of the common people was a by-product of the Harlem social gospelers I discussed in Chapter 2: Reverdy Ransom, Adam Clayton Powell, Sr., and the others. It became widely known, in part due to the press, that rooming accommodations at Divine's boarding homes were very inexpensive and that his restaurants provided wholesome meals at insubstantial costs, in fact at no cost for the poorest of the poor. Through his Peace Mission he also engaged in activism against racial discrimination, war, and, in general, fascism.

Divine also began sponsoring large classes in politics, in which his followers were taught by experts about the structure of city, state, and national governments and how to cast their vote. Those who were aliens were prepared to acquire citizenship so they too could cast their ballot. In the article titled "Bail Doubled as Cult Leader Flashes Roll," it was reported that hundreds of Divine's followers were attending the school three nights a week because their leader had instructed them to keep abreast of local, state, and national events and to keep watch over their political representatives. In terms of his own spiritual influence over the country's and the world's political affairs, Divine made some rhythmically confident remarks at one of his mass meetings, which were reported in a newspaper piece titled "Divine Takes Vote Battle into Court":

> I shall make the laws through aldermen and congressmen and senators, just the same as I make the laws in this peace mission of mine. I will accomplish the world over, just as I have accomplished in my personal jurisdiction. Even if I am not living in the flesh, I shall remain eternally and reign.
> We are going to clean the city of sin and corruption with the help of ballots and politicians or without them. If we don't get what we want with ballots, we will get it through mental telepathy, through the transmission of thought forces.

Divine also said, "Recent miraculous changes in politics have come not so much from what administrations have done as from what God has done through administrations."

In the same newspaper piece Divine's chief attorney announced that the number of Divine's "sub-heavens" in the eastern part of the country had been increased to thirty-one and that the number of his followers in New York and New Jersey alone was far in excess of 20,000. The divine trickster, a man of rhythmic confidence, carrier of African-American rhythmic culture (in both the priestly and prophetic traditions), had become a social and political power deserving respect—but respect with an occasional smirk. To this effect, even some rationally minded people who did not agree with Divine's claim of divinity were beginning to respect his work.

***

This synchronous duplicity seen in the trickster personality of Father Divine is all the more evident in the country blues tradition, as I hinted in my earlier reference to Peetie Wheatstraw. The synchronous duplicity is implied in Son House's famous "Preachin' Blues," which was written at a time in the life of this famous Mississippi Delta bluesman when he was both preaching and playing the blues, entrenched in both the so-called sacred and profane, the priestly and prophetic. In my book titled *Blues and Evil* (1993) I cover at length this synchronous duplicity in the blues. But what I did not say in that book and what is not so evident is that when Son House in "Preachin' Blues" crooned the words "I swear to God, I got to preach these gospel blues," he was essentially referring to the same gospel-blues synchronous duplicity that Michael Harris is referring to in his book *The Rise of Gospel Blues: The Music of Thomas Andrew Dorsey in the Urban Church* (1992). Harris is writing about the gospel music created by the late Dorsey, music traditionally viewed as the religious antithesis of the blues. To Harris, however, gospel is "sacred blues," just as to James Cone, writing in *The Spirituals and the Blues* (1972), the blues are "secular spirituals."

Again, I contend that the trickster-god, who is a paradigm of personality for the black musician of African rhythm, is what black music is when personified. So, Harris's pairing of the terms "gospel" and "blues" is quite appropriate, for it is akin to the tradition of adjoining the terms "preaching" and "blues" in the songs that Bessie Smith, Robert Johnson, Son House, and Big Bill Broonzy each entitled "Preaching the Blues." In both instances, the syntactic synthesis depicts the sacred-secular and priestly-prophetic dialectic, the theological tension, that characterized the lives of these great musicians, just as it characterized the life of

Father Divine. In fact, Harris carefully portrays Dorsey as the personification of the tension between the assimilationist and indigenous African-American traditions. This "double consciousness," as Du Bois would say, reveals itself in the "twoness" of the music Dorsey helped fashion, a music in which the two warring traditions of *gospel* and *blues* find themselves in a hybrid synthesis. I might point out that in a similar way Divine singing "I'm the Light of the World" is such a synthesis, both sacred and profane. It is in this sphere of tension that duplicity resolves into synthesis—into synchronous duplicity—that the rhythms of black folk are free to be what they were in African societies: syncopated, multimetric, percussive, and typically concretized in dance.

That the traditions of gospel and blues are generally perceived as being antithetical is likely the reason Dorsey is viewed as having reneged several times on his Christian conversion: The sacred-secular dichotomizing resulting from Christian dualism does not permit the option of integrating a church upbringing with blues strivings. The influence of this doctrinaire impermissibility is revealed after the death of Dorsey's wife during childbirth and his infant son shortly afterwards. Dorsey's first inclination was to return wholeheartedly to singing the blues, which, musically and textually, is a vehicle for both the expression of mourning and the expulsion of acrimony. Since Dorsey was also needful of the spiritual and emotional solace gospel music provided, he was uncertain as to which way to turn—toward the blues or toward gospel. It was not until he wrote "Precious Lord, Take My Hand" in response to the deaths of his wife and child, that he was able to articulate textually that bottomless utterance, the "blues cry," which arises in the interstices of the soul and spirit and permits not only the soothing of the spirit but the purging of the physiological pain. "Precious Lord" is therefore analyzed by Harris as the prototype of the music he calls the "gospel blues," a music that provides closure to the sacred-secular dissection for which Christian dualism is responsible, a music that is the carrier of the rhythms of black folk by virtue of its traditional syncronous duplicity.

On the one hand, accepting the terminology "gospel blues" may require other styles of gospel to be defined as "gospel rhythm and blues," "gospel jazz," or "gospel rap." These designations would in fact reveal more information about what gospel has been at the stages its texts have been rhythmically contextualized in jazz and rhythm and blues and rhythmically texturized in rap. On the other hand, "gospel blues" could be the preferred designation for gospel music altogether, since the "blues" element is more than certain harmonies, melodies, and rhythms that set blues apart from jazz, rhythm and blues, and rap. The "blues" element is fundamentally the primal cry and guttural moan (rhythmic drone) which, being African retentions, are repeatedly "reincarnated and rechristened" in the musical offspring of the blues as an indication of a gospel singer's capacity to get "lowdown." Thus, what Dorsey described as a typical "lowdown" performance of blues singer Ma Rainey, during the days he accompanied her under the name "Georgia Tom," is what he pursued and captured for the expressive aesthetic of his gospels: The blues mother rhythmically possessed her listeners, Dorsey recalled, and they swayed, rocked, moaned, and groaned.

What is implied in this rhythmic possession that makes people sway, rock, moan, and groan is that our rhythms are inextricably tied to our sexuality. I will explain this more fully in a moment but at present need only to say that Dorsey's "gospel blues," now imbued with the Skip-James cry and the Robert-Johnson moan of the blues, attained this Ma-Rainey capacity to "possess" rhythmically (and sexually), which is the reason his songs were often shunned by the mainline black churches. The cry and moan shattered the formalism of the assimilationist liturgies, leaving the mainline ministers unraveled by the fact that their antitype—the blues singer, tricksters of another type—were amidst them, worse, engaging their protected congregations in "lowdown" dialogue. The blues cry and moan, virulent and authentic, rhythmic and sexual drone par excellence, also revealed the whooping of these ministers to be rather counterfeit, contends Harris, mere mockery of the true downhome moan. There are some black churches, particularly of the Pentecostal tradition, where the whooping is not counterfeit, where the sexual is as unrestrained as it is in Robert Johnson's protracted moans; but Harris is right. This early attempt to bring "the blues" back into the religious universe of Americans of African descent, from which indigenous universe it had been expunged via the assimilationist influences, was a revolutionary act. It was, perhaps, an instance of the "mastery of form"—an outer Europeanism (the orthodox Christian doctrines which were a master-slave hand-me-down from the antebellum white church) and an inner

Africanism (the cry and the moan). What Dorsey accomplished, then, is not unlike what Dett accomplished in his "mastery of form," by which he helped bring the spirituals back into the cultural universe of the New Negro.

Part of the difficulty involved in bringing "the blues" back into the religious universe of not only African Americans but all Afro-Christians side-tracked by assimilationist influences, is that the blues is inextricably linked with our sexuality. This is a tacit part of the preceding claim that the cry and the moan shattered the formalism of the assimilationist liturgies, leaving preachers unraveled by the fact that their antitype were in their midst, worse, engaging their congregations in "lowdown" dialogue. Our rhythms have always been tied to our sexuality and are in fact a representation of it. So, not only is there an implied connection between one's ability to dance and one's ability to "rock and roll" (in bed), but one's sexuality, one's rhythmic capability, is observable even in the way one walks. To this effect, Blind Boy Fuller, in his "Good Feeling Blues" (1940), says about his "little woman": "When she walks, she reels and rocks behind."

***

If it is true that we examine each other's sexuality based on the way we walk, then we can imagine how dance is an even greater indicator for measuring our sexual rhythms. In Blind Clyde Church's "Number Nine Blues" (1929), we should notice that the idea of dance is intertwined with sex in such a way that doing the "bedspring pop" also conveys the image of a dance step: "Do that dance they call the bedspring pop; you can shut your eyes, begin to reel and rock." The same juxtaposition of dance and sex is evident in Huddie Ledbetter's "Kansas City Papa" (1935). Leadbelly (as he is known) says that the women in Kansas City are doing the "turkey trot" while the women in Louisiana are doing the "eagle rock." Given this juxtaposition of dance and sex, it is difficult to say whether Walter Davis, in "I Can Tell By the Way You Smell" (1935), is watching someone dancing or rocking and rolling: "He got the motion and she got the swing; just look at papa out there on that thing." On the other hand, perhaps the distinction between dancing and loving is merely semantic, since the trickster (the sweet talker) can always transform one into the other. After all, there is a symbiotic relationship in the dance and sexual "steps" used to choreograph one's rhythmic confidence. All of this is the explicit cultural baggage of the blues that Dorsey, though perhaps unknowingly, was painstakingly bringing into the church through his gospel blues.

When women stopped singing the blues and returned to the church to sing gospel, they too brought the tricky cultural baggage of the blues into the church. As blues women, they, like the blues men, were also concerned about having a lover with good rhythm. In her recording titled "Baby Doll" (1926), Bessie Smith, whom Dorsey said could possess her listeners so that they moaned and rocked, went to the doctor who said she was perfectly well, which led her to conclude that what she really needed was a "babydoll" who could provide her with all her loving. He can be ugly and he can be black, she sings, "so long as he can eagle rock and ball the jack." Furry Lewis, singing about his woman in his "Black Gypsy Blues" (1929), used the same language, which sounds more like a dance step than a way of loving. "Ain't nobody in town can eagle rock like you," he sang.

The blues singer is often perceived to be a divine lover and he often portrays himself in this way as akin to the sexually gluttonous trickster always wearing a prodigiously erect phallus. Willie Baker, in his "No No Blues" (1929), portrays himself in just this way—Legba or Papa Lebas on the loose. He says he is no gambler and plays no pool but is a "rambling roller jelly-baking jelly-baking fool." Louie Lasky similarly displays the rhythmic confidence of a trickster ready to roll a woman's lemon better than any other man. In his blues boast titled "How You Want Your Rollin' Done" (1935), he claims to be able to deliver the goods according to the specifics of a woman's request: "Now tell me mama just how you want your rolling done; and just as long as you like it [even] if it takes the whole night long." Frank Stokes, in his "Frank Stokes' Dream" (1929), was evidently dreaming of having an everlasting effect on whatever woman he made orgasmic. He sang, "Take me in your arms, rock me good and slow; know you hear them Frank Stokes blues anywhere on earth you go." Bobby Grant, in his "Nappy Head Blues" (1927), said he was going to buy himself a bed and shine it like the morning sun, for when he gets in bed "it rock like a Cadillac car." Leroy Carr, in his "Bread Baker" (1934), did a variation on this verse. It was his woman who had a magnificent bed in her home that "shines like a morning star." Sang Carr, "When it starts to rocking, it looks just like a Cadillac car." A "slow" or "easy" rock was divinely desired, as Rubin Lacy certainly knew (even after he became a preacher). Lacy sang in his blues "Ham Hound Crave" (1928), "Let me be you[r] rocker till your straight chair comes; and I rock you easier [than] you[r] straight chair ever done." Clifford Gibson's woman is what blues singers called an "easy-roller." In his blues "She Rolls It Slow" (1931), he sang: "Oh she mix up her jelly, she rolls it over slow; gets it all together, then she mix it in her dough."

This sexuality, bound up as it is with dance, can potentially and often does spill over into the church, where it is often indistinguishable from what is generally understood to be religious spirituality. James Cone's explanation in *The Spirituals and the Blues* is that those who do not express or release their sexuality in dance on Saturday night may find themselves doing so in dance on Sunday morning. In fact, the blues singers were often quick to point this out in their own way, generally by depicting the preacher as nothing but a sexual trickster himself. Kid Wesley Wilson, in his "The Gin Done Done It" (1929), recalled the time he went to church to do the holy roll and ended up grabbing a sister to "convert her soul." He continued on to explain that two minutes later the preacher came in: "She stopped rolling with me, started rolling with him."

But I am only partly in agreement with Cone, for my attempt at understanding black culture through the lens of the trickster is that both Sunday morning churchin' like Saturday night jookin' are replete with the kind of rhythmicity that merges spirituality and sexuality. Except in churches where there may be severe repression of sexuality, such as in the missionary-influenced African churches I spoke of in Chapter 3, the Afro-Christian church is most naturally and healthfully a place of synchronous duplicity. If sexuality is repressed as completely as possible during worship, if the blues element that Dorsey brought into gospel is repressed, then sexuality is likely to be found exploding after worship in sexual encounter (even among teenagers). As I explained in the previous chapter, dancing allows the conjuring away of myriad physical tensions. So, given my claim in Chapter 3 that there is a common Pan-African agenda for the black church in Africa and America, one crucial project would be to allow the expression of "the blues" back into black worship.

Sexuality and Seduction in the Gospel-Blues Continuum

> The mass of "gospel" hymns which has swept through American churches and well-nigh ruined our sense of song consists largely of debased imitations of Negro melodies made by ears that caught the jingle but not the music, the body but not the soul, of the jubilee songs.
> — Du Bois, "Of the Faith of Our Fathers"

My foregoing comments suggest that as blues was becoming popular during the early decades of the twentieth century, black churchgoers and preachers wrongly denounced it as music "taken up from the devil." It was really, despite its sexually explicit lyrics, a kindred music of the gospel-blues continuum. When jazz rose to popularity in the 1920s, it too was misunderstood by blacks as antithetical to gospel music rather than understood as a kindred part of the gospel-blues continuum. But with jazz crossing over the color-line in a way that the blues initially did not, whites began debating whether this music could intoxicate them and seduce them into sexual promiscuity and interracial mixing. In this respect, given the fear of miscegenation, there were those writing in Harlem's local press who felt that Father Divine's legal problems stemmed from the fact that he had about as many white followers as black followers, not to mention that Mother Divine was white.

This fear whites had of sexual seduction through black culture is reminiscent of the theory of Joseph Arthur de Gobineau, whose *Essay on the Inequality of the Human Races* I mentioned in Chapter 1. Gobineau claimed that the black "female" races have historically been the seducers and corrupters of the white "male" races. However, the reaction that jazz once engendered and that rap now engenders among whites suggests that there is a terror greater than the threat of racial seduction: the utter dread that the white "female" races will be *raped* by the black "male" races. Frantz Fanon, writing in *Black Skin, White Masks,* claimed that for most white people the black man represents "sexual instinct in its raw state" and is "the incarnation of a genital potency beyond all moralities and prohibitions." A close examination of the reactions rap causes in certain elements of American society, like the reactions to jazz before it, reveals a terror that rap may lead to racial insurrection. The dread is not of the sort of social unrest witnessed during the 1960s but of chaotic gang warfare and rampant rape:

165

tricksters with their undaunted rhythmic confidence and their ever-prominent and prodigious phalluses gone wild.

The frequent juxtaposition of *rap* and *rape* in the media justifies my contention. Tipper Gore's editorial in the January 8, 1990, issue of *The Washington Post,* titled "Hate, Rape, and Rap," is the first instance of this linkage. The juxtaposition occurs again in an editorial in the July 30, 1990, issue of *Newsweek* titled "American's Slide into the Sewer." Here, journalist George Will juxtaposes the rap lyrics of 2 Live Crew and the explicit testimony of the legal defendants regarding their attack of a jogger in New York's Central Park in April 1990. In another newspaper, the September 12, 1990, issue of *USA Today,* it was reported that during sentencing one of the males convicted in this case "swaggered through a rambling, rap-styled poem he had composed in jail." Far worse was the piece on serial killers on the CBS Evening News with Dan Rather on August 22, 1991. The journalist who authored this piece had brief clips on serial killers ranging from Son of Sam to Jeffrey Dahmer—all white males. But by an amazing hermeneutical maneuver the journalist mentioned rap music in the context of America's problems of hate and violence. This was accompanied by a film-clip of rapper Ice T, who is neither a white male nor a serial killer.

Is the attack on rap, then, not a consequence of this connection: that when certain whites see *rap* they read *rape*? Fanon had long contended, again writing in *Black Skin, White Masks,* that when whites say "rape" they mean "black." The 1990's extension of the conjecture holds that when certain whites say "rap" they mean "rape." This is the confusion that the legal defender of 2 Live Crew's album, *As Nasty as They Wanna Be,* was fighting to untangle when he stated to an all-white Florida jury, on October 3, 1990, that "rape is not a black artistic event." Nelson George was commenting likewise in his essay "To Be a Black Man," when he said: "To be a black man is to be...Nat Turner and Willie Horton and Luther Campbell in the dreams of people you've never met." The title and the substance of Public Enemy's third album, *Fear of a Black Planet,* points directly to the fear among whites of the ghetto's allegedly "illegitimate sexualities" penetrating their neighborhoods and their bodies, not to mention their fear of the "spiritual peril" of what C. G. Jung called "going black under the skin." As I explain further on in the chapter, this is the reason there has been a misunderstanding of black culture in general, a misunderstanding comprised of the fear of being tricked into falling out of the white light into "darkness."

The reality of rap has been overshadowed by the ominousness of these feelings and fears, as well as by debates regarding rap's legitimacy. Tricksters, who are cultural carriers of our rhythmic traditions, will always be questioned in this regard because there is, as with Father Divine, always two sides of the personality that merge in raucous harmony. However, when rap is considered in its authentic context—the gospel-blues continuum—there is no question that the musicality, rhythmicity, unique expressivity, creative sexuality, and ideology of rap have historical, social, political, and cultural continuity, as well as legitimacy. The vocal style, for instance, has its beginnings in African orature. This mode of orature first resurfaced in North America as "pattin' juba," a patting and rapping good-time enjoyed by the enslaved in the mid-nineteenth century; and it continues to the present day in the myriad manifestations of black religion and black street ritual. In an essay of 1980, titled "Rapping Deejays," published in *Buppies, B-Boys, Baps and Bohos*, Nelson George says:

> The deejay raps over the instrumental section or breaks of popular dance records reminiscent of Jamaican deejays talk over the heavy dub instrumentation of reggae. Most of the youngsters who do this in America are ignorant of the Jamaican precedent, yet the raps serve the same purpose in both these African-derived cultures. Whether it's heard in a park in Brooklyn or a junkyard in Kingston, it is rhythmic music and the spoken voice unconsciously creating a potent echo of Africa.

> *June 4: On the way back to Harare, we stopped off at the town of Gweru for lunch.... As we ate in the Chicken Inn (a chain) we heard the rap group Public Enemy blasting away.*

On the political side, today's hard-core rappers follow a tradition dating back to the liberation spirituals and antislavery songs of the nineteenth century. Instead of calling the tradition the gospel-blues continuum we might call it, after Cornel West, the "spiritual-blues impulse." They are the same thing: a tradition which includes more recent expressions such as Gil Scott-Heron's political poem "The Revolution Will Not Be Televised," Len Chandler's mid-1960s radical freedom song "Move on Over or We'll Move on Over You," James Brown's late-1960s soul song "Say It Loud, I'm Black and I'm Proud," Louis Farrakhan's first composed song for the Nation of Islam, "A White Man's Heaven Is a Black Man's Hell," and Mbongeni Ngema's "Freedom Is Coming Tomorrow."

June 8: My lecture in the afternoon (at Seke Teacher's College) went from 2:00-4:00 in a large auditorium (the theater). I discussed a broad range of topics, essentially encouraging these future primary school teachers to encourage the self-identity and empowerment of black children.... We chanted...James Brown's chorus to "Say It Loud, I'm Black and I'm Proud." There were about 100 people present.

The revolutionary ethos and *rapsodic* expressionism found in the musical poetry of today's hard-core rappers shows the same attitude of rhythmic confidence as the black-power black nationalism of Marcus Garvey, George Alexander McGuire, Elijah Muhammad, Malcolm X, Muhammad Ali, Stokely Carmichael, H. Rap Brown, Angela Davis, Elaine Brown, Louis Farrakhan, Spike Lee, and such fictional yet real apostles of liberation as Sarafina (Winnie Mandela) and Mary Masembuko (Phumzile Mlambo). These are people who refuse to be invisible men and mammies.

This attitude of rhythmic confidence, causative of what philosopher Michel Foucault called the "insurrection of subjugated knowledges," is certainly similar to the celebration and glorification of Senghor's negritude. Fanon foresaw that this attitude was to penetrate every reach of the African diaspora. He writes in *The Wretched of the Earth*, "The poets of [negritude] will not stop at the limits of the [African] continent. From America, black voices will take up the hymn with fuller unison." Even today, the problems of Afro-America—capitalist exploitation, state repression, selective prosecution, civil terrorism, personal and systemic racism—are not fundamentally different from the problems caused by apartheid in South Africa. In fact, Mandela has become a symbol of resistance to America's rapping sidewalk prophets, just as Malcolm X is a hero to the young freedom fighters of the ANC Youth League. As the self-proclaimed oracles of God's wrath, rappers declare (with the same rhythmic confidence that Father Divine displayed before prosecuting judges) that those who sow the wind shall—by whatever means necessary—reap the whirlwind. Divine's words to the judge are worth recalling: "I do not say I am God and I do not say I am the devil, but I will bring

God to the consciousness of the people, and I will command men to deal justly with the people or else I will move them out of office." In a moment I will discuss rap's attempt to "bring God to the consciousness of the people" under the theological notion of "rap gnosticism"—knowledge deified to the degree that it is believed to be salvational.

Thus, it is not rapping per se—its style of vocalization, its syncopation, or its driving percussive rhythms—that is dreaded by the protected white world. What threatens is the cultural and attitudinal blackness of the music, the verbal brashness of its performers, their rhythmic irruption of speech, their confident insurrection of subjugated knowledges. In the dialectic between rhythmicity and arhythmicity, the rhythmic insurgency wins out. Whites had witnessed with great discomfort the earlier manifestations of this discursive explosion in the 1960s. Now the discursive explosion is reemerging with redoubled force, and it is declaring that simply surviving is preposterous. For instance, MC Supreme's rap and video, "Black in America," reveals the believed reality of attempted racial genocide, which implies that simply surviving is death. NWA (Niggas With Attitude) open their album *Straight Outta Compton* with the declaration: "You are now about to witness the strength of street knowledge." It is this strength of street knowledge, the triumph of the street ethic, that rapper Ice T (on *The Oprah Winfrey Show*) accused the critics of rap of fearing. But, to quote one of the opening lines of Jean-Paul Sartre's *Black Orpheus:* "What then did you expect when you unbound the gag that had muted those black mouths? That they would chant your praises?"

***

This insurrection of subjugated knowledges—the ungagged black mouth and the power of street knowledge—was feared by certain whites in the 1960s and is feared by certain whites today. This is particularly the case since currently the "insurrection of subjugated knowledges" is coupled with an insurrection of subjugated sexualities. Male rappers, flaunting with rhythmic confidence exaggerated perceptions of their sexual capacities, tease white fears of alleged black illicit sexualities. Andrew Hacker, a white male himself, says in *Two Nations:* "Certainly, among the capacities that make for manhood, sexual potency continues to rank high even in our modern times. Compounding the ordinary insecurities most men have in this sphere, white men face the mythic fear that black men may outrival them in virility and competence." Thus, male rappers, by flaunting with rhythmic confidence exaggerated perceptions of their sexual capacities, fuel the fantasy of the black penis and the illusion of the black rapist. In this respect, as is perhaps most clearly signified by 2 Live Crew's "Dick Almighty," on the pornographic album *As Nasty as They Wanna Be*, white fear has made rap, more than any other form of black music today, into a phallic symbol. This supports Fanon's longtime contention that whites view the black male as a "terrifying penis." In this respect, Father Divine, with his thousands of white female followers, which included Mother Divine, must have terrorized the white male imagination: a black trickster who has conjured white women to follow him! "Still," admits Hacker, "fantasies persist that black men and women are less burdened by inhibitions, and can delight in primal pleasures beyond the capacities of whites." Hacker adds parenthetically with Gobineauan language, "The erotic abandon displayed in black dancing has no white counterpart."

For oppressed black males aware of this white terror of black male sexuality, it is gratifying to wield such power. It feeds their rhythmic confidence. In his book *Race Matters*, Cornel West explains:

> Black sexuality is a taboo subject in America principally because it is a form of black power over which whites have little control—yet its visible manifestations evoke the most visceral of white responses, be it one of seductive obsession or downright disgust. On the one hand, black sexuality among blacks simply does not include whites, nor does it make them a central point of reference. It proceeds as if whites do not exist, as if whites are invisible and simply don't matter. This form of black sexuality puts black agency center stage with no white presence at all. This can be uncomfortable for white people accustomed to being the custodians of power.
>
> On the other hand, black sexuality between blacks and whites proceeds based on underground desires that Americans deny or ignore in public and over which laws have no effective control. In fact, the dominant sexual myths of black women and men portray whites as being "out of control"—seduced, tempted, overcome, overpowered by black bodies. This form of

black sexuality makes white passivity the norm—hardly an acceptable self-image for a white-run society.

Blacks who are aware of this dynamic also hold power for the reason Foucault gives in his first volume of *The History of Sexuality:* "If sex is repressed, that is, condemned to prohibition, nonexistence, and silence, then the mere fact that one is speaking about it has the appearance of a deliberate transgression. A person who holds forth in such language places himself to a certain extent outside the reach of power; he upsets established law; he somehow anticipates the coming freedom." While modern society speaks of sexuality only within the repressive enclave of secrecy, and while the confession remains the customary standard for sexual discourse, rap's insurgence of subjugated sexualities is tricky: There is no secret, no confession, no self-interrogation; the emphasis on sexuality is intentional. It is the rhythmical forcefulness of rap's insurrection that allows it to penetrate white defenses.

Of course, not all rap is a protest music of insurrectionary knowledges or sexualities; some of it is simply pop or, as some rappers call it, "candy rap." Nonetheless, rap, whether "candy" or hard-core, attracts youths who are protest listeners—those who listen to rap as a means of protesting against the establishment. For black youths who embrace rap as a symbol of protest, it is an expression of black pride and black power. For white youths— who may despise black pride and black power but emulate soul, despise blackness of mind but have gone "black under the skin"— rap is an icon of the resentment they feel toward the "square" white status quo. Nonetheless, for whites who fear the ghetto's "illegitimate sexualities" penetrating their neighborhoods and their bodies, even "candy rap" is threatening because its African rhythm—the rhythms of black folk—are sexual and seductive. Andrew Hacker admits:

> Even if all one's black neighbors were vouchsafed to be middle class or better, there may still be misgivings about their teenaged children. To start, there is the well-known wariness of white parents that their children—especially their daughters— could begin to make black friends. Plus the fear that even less intimate contacts will influence the vocabulary and diction, even the academic commitments, of their own offspring. And if white parents are already uneasy over the kinds of music their children enjoy, imagine their anxieties at hearing an even greater black resonance.

***

This is why rap is attacked. But there is a price to pay for suppressing black rhythmicity in the ongoing dialectic with those who would have rap become arhythmic. As in any situation where an icon is attacked, the assault upon rap has imbued it with even further symbolic meaning and potency for resentment listeners, and has increased the population of listeners who subscribe to its newly broadened symbolism of protest. Perhaps worse of all for the Gobineaus of the world is that the iconoclasm has given rappers greater rhythmic confidence, so that the trickster's phallus has become all the more prodigious and the discomfort of social intercourse all the more intense.

Who is to blame for the increased population of resentment listeners and the multiplied rhythmic confidence of rappers? First to be blamed are those who have overreacted in their sense of dread, which results from erroneous characterizations of the African or the black person from an essentialist perspective—today's Joseph Arthur Gobineaus, Carl Sandburgs, and Olin Downeses. These are they who lynched, mutilated, and castrated rap seemingly as sexual revenge (white males such as George Will) and as a rite of purification (white females such as Tipper Gore). It is as though this population of rap iconoclasts, volleying to win in the dialectic of rhythmicity and arhythmicity, believe that if they can subjugate "lower-class sexualities" and expunge the language that makes these sexualities a "discursive fact" then their own sexuality (and especially their children's) could be repressed and controlled. After all, the connection between rhythm and sexuality in the white world does not take on nearly the intensity that it does in the genealogy of African rhythm in the gospel-blues continuum. As Hacker was quoted earlier (though I would have used different words), "The erotic abandon displayed in black dancing has no white counterpart." Many white youths who understand this parental motivation to suppress "erotic abandon" often join the ranks of rap's resentment listeners out of their own needs to engage in insurrection.

Also to be blamed for the increased population of resentment listeners and the multiplied rhythmic confidence of rappers is the federal government, as illustrated in the selective prosecution of 2 Live Crew. During the summer of 1990, their album *As Nasty as They Wanna Be* was ruled obscene by a federal district court judge in Florida, and two of the group's members (including its leader Luther Campbell) were arrested on obscenity charges for performing raps from the album in a Florida nightclub. Although the group also recorded a "nice" version of the album, titled *As Nice as They Wanna Be*, the attempted suppression fueled the sale of the "nasty" version and, for some black-pride and white protest-listening constituencies, elevated the group's leader to the status of a traditional "badman" hero. In a long-playing single titled "Banned in the USA," Campbell (a trickster truly to be feared) responded in a role with a "badman" assault upon the "white-collar people trying to cramp our style, saying we're too nasty and we're too loud." He concludes, "*Too live* is what we are." Because of the suppressors of black rhythms—the government "feds" and the religious "fundis" (fundamentalists)—the rhythmic voice of rap has become increasingly confident.

Another instance of the federal government's attempt to suppress black rhythms has been their monitoring of the insurrectionary knowledges of rap. Just as they monitored the insurrectionary voice of Malcolm X and presumably monitor the insurgent "noise" of Farrakhan, so did the FBI send a warning letter to the record company of NWA regarding a rap they recorded titled "F--- tha Police." While NWA maintains that this rap is simply a "revenge fantasy" that responds to the civil terrorism long perpetrated against the black ghetto poor, the FBI contends that it encourages violence against police.

As I said in the previous chapter, symbolic murders—such as Public Enemy's "By the Time I Get to Arizona," Ice T's "Cop Killer," Johne Battle's "Ultimate Drive By," and Paris's "Bush Killa"—are brought out into the open, so that the accumulated libido is dissolved on the very border that crosses over into outright violence. In other words, that rap and other forms of black music are more physiological than rational, are really instances of the "mastery of form" rather than of the "deformation of mastery," suggests that those who attack rap as sexual revenge and as a rite of purification ought not attempt to unmask the NWAs of America. Rap, like bop, may provoke "the riot," as many whites fear, but it simultaneously absorbs violence by exhausting the body. So, despite its aspect of intellectual insurgency, rap is first and foremost exhausting to the body; for it is the body, not the rational understanding, that is the absorber of rap's rhythms. Violent aggressivity—the "scratching" of rap DJs giving sound to blades ready to slit throats—is physiologically canalized, transformed, and exorcised. In this respect, we remember, in Leroi Jones' *Dutchman,* Clay's final warning to Lula and her kind prior to his murder. He warned whites not to preach so much rationalism to "these niggers," to leave them alone and let them sing their curses at whites in code and see their filth as simple lack of style. "Don't make the mistake...of talking too much about the advantages of Western rationalism, or the great intellectual legacy of the white man, or maybe they'll begin to listen. And then, maybe one day, you'll find they actually do understand exactly what you are talking about, all these fantasy people.... They'll murder you, and have very rational explanations. Very much like your own."

***

The least threatening form of hip hop is Christian rap, the newest form of gospel music. Akin to contemporary gospel, Christian rap has its beginnings as concert rather than liturgical music, and it too will likely find its way into those black churches that finally decide that it is time to speak to the masses of today's black youths. Among the rap evangelists who have sung unto the Lord this new song are PID (Preachers in Disguise), ETW (End of Time Warriors), SFC (Soldiers for Christ), DC Talk, Witness, D-Boy Rodriguez, Helen Baylor, Michael Peace, and Fresh Fish. Even secular pop star MC Hammer has done a Christian rap (and video) titled "Pray."

Christian hip hop is, like the sacred and secular black music before it, a part of the gospel-blues continuum and a carrier of the rhythms of black folk. Just as the hard-core rap of Public Enemy makes Michael Jackson's "Man in the Mirror" seem otherworldly, so does the experientially oriented hard-core style of PID makes the messages of earlier forms of gospel seem drastically archaic and irrelevant. The difference is attitude. When PID addresses such issues as homelessness, sexually transmitted disease, and racism, and does so in a language that today's inner-city youths understand, the group succeeds where modern gospel has virtually failed; the group's disposition succeeds where the church's Christian tradition falls short of the mark. These rappers get positive messages across to secular inner-city constituencies that have lost faith in a savior they have never seen and who, by all pictorial accounts, is a "white boy."

Therefore, in contrast to the older forms of gospel, the rap gospelers have begun to redefine what ministry to the "sick and shut-in" should entail. They perceive the "sick" to be those who lack unity with and self-actualization within the black community because they are politically held down, socially split up, and psychologically cut off from the rhythms of black folk. Not just the "least of us" but the postmodern conspirators who are terroristically trying to explode our racial identity would fit into this group—Stephen Carter, Shelby Steele, Glenn Loury, Stanley Crouch, Anthony Appiah. The "shut-in" are those whom the postmodern conspirators, burdened by "racial fatigue," blame for their own victimization: those who are held captive on the modern plantations of America's neocolonialist slavocracy, namely, the victims of economic exploitation, selective criminal prosecution, covert government harassment, civil terrorism, and personal and institutional racism.

While the precursors of Christian rap (the gospel music of Carter, Steele, and Loury) have had almost nothing to say about the life-and-death problems that the "ghetto poor" daily face (issues considered "worldly" by old-style gospel), Christian rap may turn out to be the single prophetically pragmatic voice in Afro-Christianity. Despite the threat of this music entering the church, the same threat Dorsey's music first posed because it embodied the blues cry and moan, this new song must be embraced and encouraged by the black church if the historical institution is ever to reclaim its relevance among the "least of us" who too often and for too long have been neglected by the church's otherworldly politics.

***

Gospel rap is tricky, though. Its Christian externals allow one radical factor to be overlooked: Not only does it make its gospel precursors appear otherworldly, but the Jesus of gospel rap makes the Jesus of old-style gospel appear increasingly "white" like the Jesus of the apartheid Bible. While the Jesus of the old-style gospel clearly is the "white Jesus"—the ideological icon with lily-white complexion, long flowing blond or brunet hair, and Nordic facial features—the Jesus of gospel rap is black, owing to the tradition of black Christian nationalism that I spoke of in Chapter 3 (namely, Albert Cleage). In the era in which old-style gospel evolved, black churches customarily carried images of the "white Jesus" in portraits, murals, and stained-glass windows, reflecting that Jesus was "white" in black parishioners' minds. Furthermore, the Jesus portrayed in old-style gospel is "white" because this music characteristically calls for a complete turn toward Jesus by means of fanatical self-effacement of individual identity and human personhood. In old-style gospel Jesus is, according to its lyrics, "everything" and "all" and human beings and human life are nothing. But this is antithetical to the attitude of rhythmic confidence, particularly the radical rhythmic confidence we find in rap. Perhaps it is naturally religious for religious human beings to perceive themselves as nothing in order to edify and worship God as everything, but what is lacking in old-style gospel is the idea that in and through God black people can become if not everything then at least something. The Jesus of old-style gospel is "white" because the message that black people are nothing coincides with what long has been told us by the missionaries, anthropologists, critics, and artistic benefactors who created and nurtured the artifact of the black personality. In gospel hip hop, however, this tradition is being radically overturned with rhythmic confidence.

This practice is, as I said in Chapter 3, an instance of the "therapy of history," which allows us to begin to reverse the psychological chains of colonization (a Pan-African project as the Blantyre Covenant suggests). I said in that chapter that for those of us who might suffer subconscious feelings of inferiority—subconsciously believing that African cultures are inferior to European cultures—what is prescribed in this "therapy of history" is the portrayal of Jesus and the other biblical personages as African in our liturgical representations and the portrayal of God as black in our symbolic conceptualization of the unseen Creator. I believe the hard-core gospel rappers are helping us in this therapy through their representation of God as being black by virtue of God being a God of the oppressed. I believe they could engage in an even more important "therapy of history" by symbolically and characteristically portraying God as a black female.

In this respect, the hard-core gospel rap of PID clearly differs from that segment of secular rap that mutes or eliminates what Cornel West calls "utopian aspirations"—aspirations seeking transcendence from or opposition to evil. But hard-core gospel rap is not fundamentally different from the equally prevalent secular corpus of rap that does embody utopian aspirations. Kool Moe Dee has, for instance, a rap titled "God Made Me Funke." Like the God of gospel rap, his is black, for only a black God would, after God's own image, make a brother or a sister "funke." Kool Moe Dee is therefore taking us through a "therapy of history." Similarly, Public Enemy, in a piece titled "Welcome to the Terrordome" on their *Fear of a Black Planet* album, relates Jesus Christ's crucifixion to their own persecution by those who fear their brash blackness. Their statement that "crucifixion ain't no fiction"—that crucifixion is the living reality of the black oppressed—brings down to the experiential level that which for today's black youths is an archaic biblicism: the crucifixion of an incarnate "white" God.

Finally, rap is, in a tricky way, theological. Utopian aspirations in rap are epitomized in the idea of salvational knowledge or what I call "rap gnosticism." This deifying of knowledge is signified by the names of such rap groups as the Poor Righteous Teachers (PRT), the Intellectual Hoodlum, and KRS-One (Knowledge Reigns Supreme Over Nearly Everyone), and by myriad rap songs such as "Knowledge Is King" by Kool Moe Dee, and "Holy Intellect" by PRT. Thus, when the various writers on rap speak of the "message rappers," the "political rappers," or the "teachers," they are essentially alluding to the "utopian aspirations" inherent in rap gnosticism, as opposed to those "candy" rappers who mute "utopian aspirations."

Integration on the Black Side of the Color Line

> The world-old phenomenon of the contact of diverse races...is to have new exemplification during the new century.... Whatever we may say of the results of such contact in the past, it certainly forms a chapter in human action not pleasant to look back upon.
> — Du Bois, "Of the Sons of Master and Man"

All that I have discussed in this chapter—the gospel-blues continuum as personified by the trickster-god personality which threatens the protected white world—explains why there is a general misunderstanding among whites in this country as to what is meant by black culture. For instance, in an October 23, 1992, letter to the editor of the Durham, North Carolina, *Herald-Sun,* a local resident named David Shauber revealed the extremes to which this misunderstanding can go. What precipitated his letter was the controversy at the University of North Carolina at Chapel Hill (UNC) as to whether or not the university should build a free-standing black cultural center. The university's chancellor, Paul Hardin, initially argued that there should be no such center that is "free-standing" in that this would promote segregation. But following the rhythmic irruption of speech and the confident insurrection of subjugated knowledges led by black students, which led to some clarification of the validity and purpose of such a center, the chancellor reconsidered his position. The decision to pursue the possibility of erecting a free-standing black cultural center is what instigated David Shauber to write his letter to the editor. Sounding much like Arthur Schlesinger, Jr. and Linda Chavez, in lectures they gave at UNC on March 29 and 31, respectively, Shauber said: "The concept of black culture is a myth perpetuated by groups who want to feel good about themselves rather than enter into mainstream American culture." Concluding his assessment of black culture, Shauber, in the crackpot style of Dinesh D'Souza, threw out some exaggerated statistics: "What are its attributes? Some 65% of babies born out of wedlock; 70% of males ages 18-35 in trouble with the law; 75% of children living in poverty and supported by the taxpayer. If that's black culture, who needs it?" No doubt Shauber, like many other critics of a free-standing black center, views this potential cultural location as nothing more than a continuation of what Katrina Hazzard-Gordon (cited in Chapter 1) called the "jook continuum": a tricky place of rhythmic insurgency, ranging from blues moods to rap "illegitimate sexualities."

Initially the controversy that led to Shauber's letter was mere local news. It was reported that late in the evening of September 3 approximately 300 students converged on the chancellor's home in Chapel Hill, rhythmically chanting "No justice, no peace!" and calling for a free-standing black cultural center. On September 10, hundreds of students held a demonstration in the university's administration building, where again there was this irruption of speech and confident insurrection of subjugated knowledges. A day later, *The New York Times* reported on the event. The article, which appeared in the sports pages, included a photograph of two of the university's football players, Timothy Smith and John Bradley, presenting the chancellor with a notification of a deadline to approve the building of a free-standing center. The letter presented to the chancellor said that failure to meet the deadline would lead to "direct action," which some athletes speculated meant the boycott of sports events.

Film director Spike Lee, a trickster himself (as shown in the previous chapter), saw the news piece and decided to make a call on the university. On September 18, he, along with the tricky Khalid Muhammed of the Nation of Islam, spoke to approximately 7,000 students at the university's Dean Smith Center. Their celebrity brought even more national attention to the project, which was reported on by National Public Radio, the ABC Evening News, *The Wall Street Journal*, *Newsweek*, and *Jet* magazine. In the September 29 issue of *The Wall Street Journal*, in a piece sarcastically titled "They Call It 'Diversity,'" the writer reported that the chancellor was worried that a free-standing black cultural center would violate the advances of the civil rights movement and resurrect the "separate but equal" standard of *Plessy v. Ferguson*.

The controversy (and this very same rhetoric) found its way into the state's 1992 gubernatorial campaign. Republican candidate Jim Gardner, during the last weeks of his failing campaign, similarly criticized the plans to build a free-standing black cultural center, claiming that it would undo twenty years of work toward racial integration. Speaking to about fifty supporters gathered at his Republican headquarters in Chapel Hill, Gardner's exact words were reported in the the October 27, 1992, issue of the university's student newspaper, *The Daily Tarheel*, under the caption "Gardner Blasts BCC Plans": "Imagine, we spent 20 years trying to bring the races together in North Carolina. Why do we want to go back and destroy 20 years of hard work? If we do that, what are we going to do, have an Indian center next year, an Asian center the next year?" He went on to say that if he were elected (which he was not) he would use his influence to convince the university's trustees to vote against the proposal. Similarly, when Dinesh D'Souza spoke at UNC in a debate on March 30, 1993, he said of the idea to build such a center that it would be an act of black separatism and black supremacy.

This view that a free-standing black cultural center would be segregative is not only held by the likes of Jim Gardner and Dinesh D'Souza but also by such postmodern co-conspirators against black racial identity as Shelby Steele. In *The Content of Our Character*, Steele calls the phenomenon of the black cultural center (along with the black student union, the black studies curriculum, and the like) an instance of "neo-separtism." He says, "There is a geopolitics involved in this activity, where race is tied to territory in a way that mimics the whites only/colored only designations of the past. Only now these race spaces are staked out in the name of pride." Steele went on to claim that this "impulse to self-segregate" and thereby avoid whites reveals the fear blacks have that they do not measure up to whites; that to integrate and become mainstream is to face the threatening possibility of actual freedom and potential failure. This is the very same thing David Shauber was saying in his letter to the editor: "The concept of black culture is a myth perpetuated by groups who want to feel good about themselves rather than enter into mainstream American culture."

Contrary to the claims of Steele, Gardner, and D'Souza, and the initial claim of the university chancellor, black culture has never been segregative. More than any other culture found in this country, it has been integrative. As Hazzard-Gordon shows in *Jookin'*, which I discussed at length in Chapter 1, whites have always been drawn to dance with blacks (let us not forget the connection it has with our sexuality). Even during the middle passage, when the enslaved were made to "dance" for exercise, the crewmen would sometimes strip down and dance with the naked women. Similarly, at the urban slave balls held in such cities as New Orleans, Mobile, Louisville, and Charleston, whites were not just onlookers, they were often participants.

Unlike such prestigious white institutions like UNC, which would not even permit blacks to attend undergraduate school until the 1960s, the black colleges (places of black culture) were the locations of racial integration. In 1925 the wife of Walter Scott Copeland, editor for the Hampton, Virginia, *Daily Press,* went to a show at Hampton Institute and found to her dismay that blacks and whites were allowed to sit together. The incident led her husband to campaign successfully for the state legislature to pass a law, which they did in 1926, requiring segregation in public places throughout the state. But since Hampton was a private institution, the integration, on our side of the color line, continued up to and beyond 1963 when the law was ruled unconstitutional by the Virginia Supreme Court. Thus, for the greater part of the twentieth century, Hampton was an oasis of integration in a desert of segregation. This is one of the factors that resulted in Hampton having done more than any white institution in the South in the undermining of racism.

This very point was made about the tenor Roland Hayes in a newspaper article of 1929 titled "Collapsible Color Line." The idea is similar to what was said about Dett's choir by journalists that I documented in Chapter 1. The author writing on Hayes, going by the pseudonym Uncle Dudley, commented: "At the recitals of Mr. Roland Hayes the color line dissolves. White and black sit elbow to elbow. And there will be more of this before there is less. What is the meaning of it? Just what has happened here? Something quite simple and very profound.... This people that we have wronged has found a way to conquer us; not by violence, but by melody. In the face of a cultural triumph in this magnitude by the negro the pretense of white superiority will become more difficult to maintain." Indeed, African-American culture has always had an ethical impulse for creating community, which has always tended to include whites who were willing to integrate on the black side of the color line (the color line that was always enforced by whites).

In a *Time* magazine article titled "What America Would Be Like Without Blacks," Ralph Ellison identified black culture, in the foregoing respect, as the silent conquerer of those who have wronged us. He said that despite the harsh reality visited upon us, these injustices have failed to keep us from being one of the major tributaries to mainstream American culture. "On this level the melting pot did indeed melt," Ellison wrote, "creating such deceptive metamorphoses and blending of identities, values and lifestyles that most American whites are culturally part Negro American without even realizing it." According to Cornel West, writing in *Race Matters,* there was a new wave of the Afro-Americanization of white youths beginning in the 1960s:

> The major cultural impact of the 1960s was not to demystify black sexuality but rather to make black bodies more accessible to white bodies *on an equal basis.* The history of such access up to that time was primarily one of brutal white rape and ugly white abuse. The Afro-Americanization of white youth—given the disproportionate black role in popular music and athletics—has put white kids in closer contact with their own bodies and facilitated more humane interaction with black people. Listening to Motown records in the sixties or dancing to hip hop music in the nineties may not lead one to question the sex-

ual myths of black women and men, but when white and black kids buy the same billboard hits and laud the same athletic heroes the result is often a shared cultural space where some humane interaction takes place.

Morever, African rhythm, disseminated worldwide through African-American popular music, has been a unifying factor globally—cross-cultural common ground for which our rhythms are largely responsible.

***

The proof that black culture has always been integrative is especially evident in its influence on mainstream American culture. America is not, as C. G. Jung said, a culturally white nation so much as it is a black one. As a black journalist wrote in response to Jung's idea, "The white people of this country may be startled by such talk; to Negroes it is an old story." This comment, a response to an article by Jung titled "Your Negroid and Indian Behavior," published in the April 1930 issue of *The Forum,* was made in an editorial titled "Negroid America," published in the April 16, 1930, issue of *The New York Amsterdam News.* The journalist interpreted Jung to have said that America is not really a white nation but partly a colored one.

In his article, Jung explained that he made his first visit to the United States in 1909, which was when he received his initial impression of Americans as a whole. His impression was that there was "a subtle difference" that distinguished white Americans from white Europeans. He said that if he used the theory of heredity he would certainly be at a loss to explain how Americans of European origin arrived at their "striking peculiarities." A better hypothesis to explain these peculiarities, he figured, was to consider the influence of the Negro, given the fact that America is not demographically a completely white nation but is partly "colored." He determined that these differences were behavioral ones that encompass the language, gestures, mentality, and movements of Americans. In terms of the latter, he said that the "loose joints and swaying hips" of "primitive Negro women" are frequently seen in white American women. "Now what is more contagious than to live side by side with a rather primitive people? Go to Africa and see what happens. When the effect is so very obvious that you stumble over it, then you call it 'going black.'" This "going black," a reality that Jung says whites hate to admit, results insofar as the behaviors of allegedly inferior people are generally able to fascinate and seduce the inferior psychic levels of the white race's bygone youth. It is akin to a foreign country getting under the skin of those born in it, Jung says: "Below the threshold of consciousness the contagion meets little resistance. Since the Negro lives within your cities and even within your houses, he also lives within your skin, subconsciously."

The notion of the Negro getting under white skin has been explored before, for instance in Charles Reade's *A Simpleton* (1873). In this novel the Boers, because of their closeness to the "kaffirs" of South Africa, are depicted as having degenerated into savages. This degeneration was in fact a longtime fear among white missionaries in Africa—the likes of Livingstone and Stanley even in fairly modern days. These missionaries feared the possibility of, in Freudian and Jungian terms, regressing into the repressed psychic phase of savagery. They feared "going native" or, as Jung put it, "going black under the skin."

What is it that Jung believed was getting beneath white skin? I believe it was the rhythms of black folk, which have always given rise to certain dominant traits in our culture. Jung himself says that American music is most obviously pervaded by African rhythm and melody, which are most insinuating and can obsess listeners for days. What we are alleged by Jung to have contributed to the degeneracy of American culture, then, are "illegitimate sexualities." I will explain by way of reference to the blues, which should recall some of the things I said about the connection between rhythmicity and sexuality earlier in this chapter.

According to white blues scholars who maintain another form of the myth of the "Negro soul," this "evil"—the seduction of white people—commenced with the blues before it was inherited by jazz. Symbolic of this influence and transfer is the fact that the words "rock" and "roll" (the words that whites derived to name rhythm and blues when they began imitating our rhythm), originally meant to do the "shake, rattle, and roll," as Joe McCoy put it in his blues titled "Shake Mattie" (1931). The same holds true for the word "jazz," as Trixie Smith alludes in her blues titled "The World's Jazz Crazy and So Am I" (1925). Smith equates "real good jazz," which she says everyone likes, with "the motion" that her "daddy" has. It is this acquisition through music of our alleged "illegitimate sexualities" that Jung was identifying as the source of America "going black."

The aforementioned editorialist who reviewed Jung's article for *The New York Amsterdam News* listed a number of aspects of African-American popular culture as having "crept into" mainstream American culture. Specifically regarding Jung's comment that the Negro not only lives in America's cities but under white Americans' skins, the reviewer said:

> It is not surprising...to hear that the Negro has influenced American character and customs, that he has crept into American speech and art. Any close observer of the American stage can recognize songs, jokes and dances derived, if not stolen outright, from the Negro.... Often when Negro performers are accused of imitating white ones they are only taking back what was originally theirs. It is a sure bet that whenever a Negro performer devises an outstanding sketch or trick it will not be long before white performers are making reputations by imitating him, and some are nervy enough to call him the copier and themselves the originators.

The writer concludes, "The Negro has gone deeper into American life than is realized, and he will go deeper still."

***

While the reason given to deny the legitimacy of a black cultural center at UNC is that it will be segregative, the fact is that Americans are not simply denying that black culture has always been integrative; they are denying the fact that black culture is the basis of a significant segment of American culture, that the rhythms of black folk beat within the cultural world of white folk. In this denial there seems to be manifested a significant amount of the fear that I have been discussing, fear that is particularly evident in David Shauber's letter to the editor. The fear is not that a free-standing black cultural center will be segregative but that it will become a black and white bohemia where the black trickster and his prodigious phallus are let loose to avenge black oppression. The fear is not that a black cultural center will be a place of separatism but that it will be a place of interracial mixing on the black side of the color line, like Father Divine's cult. We have forgotten that this has been a long-standing source of anxiety and dread among whites dating back to the harangues against the dangers of jazz and Theodore Bilbo's preachments on the floor of the United States Senate about the threat of mass miscegenation. I illustrated earlier in this chapter, with reference to Andrew Hacker, that this fear is the basis of certain whites' rejection of rap. To this Hacker adds that whites may laud the originality of black musicians but they feel more comfortable when white musicians adapt black creativity to white sensibilities. In other words, whites feel more comfortable when the "integration" is on their side of the color line where they can police the social intercourse and better prevent the sexual.

R. Nathaniel Dett and Dorothy Maynor, whom I discussed in Chapter 1, were safe Negroes: In their travels and concert performances they engaged in integration on the white side of the color line. There was no effort on their part to insist that whites meet them on our terms on our turf. As can be gathered from Chapter 1, I think the kind of "mastery of form" that we found in Dett and Maynor—their bringing an inner Africanism to whites in the form of sophisticated renditions of the spirituals—was immensely important at that time in history: They challenged the racialist notion of the (inferior) Negro soul. But what is occurring now at UNC is a far more radical black expression of rhythmic confidence: African Americans "drawing the line" and bidding the "other" come. The issue of African Americans daring to "draw the line" has something to do with those in control not wanting to relinquish hegemony, but it is also very frightening. The frightening component derives from the suspicion that on the black side of the color line the "deformation of mastery" is much more likely to occur, the mask is more likely to fall, a fight with knives or a rape is much more likely to occur, the trickster is more likely to drop his drawers.

Journalist J. A. Rogers addressed this fear around the time that it was an acknowledged issue among whites. He did so in an article titled "The French Harlem," published in the April 4, 1928, issue of *The New York Amsterdam News*. The setting is the Bal Negre in Paris, which Rogers visited on one of his trips abroad, but it is very much the "American dilemma" that he has on his mind:

> Paris now has a miniature Harlem and all within the space of three months. It is the Bal Negre on the Rue Blomet.
> Prior to this the ballroom had a rather small clientele. One could see what is rare in Paris, a dance hall where nearly all the couples on the floor were Negroes. A mixed couple, white man dancing with colored woman, or the opposite, was rare. Then

two of the leading newspapers suddenly discovered the place and carried long articles about it, with the result that the white clientele has grown to such proportions that the place is overcrowded now.

Just such a thing happened some years ago in Chicago. A few white people had been in the habit of visiting the cabarets on the South Side. Then one day a paper...in its vice crusade announced that white people were attending Negro cabarets, and that there was no color line. The result was that white people simply poured into these places, making a fortune for their owners. Harlem and other Negro neighborhoods in the North and parts of the South have all had a similar experience.

The simple fact is that in spite of what our American sociologists and legislators may say, the Negro will have, in no matter what part of the world, no easy task preserving his isolation...once the white people get on his track. The American Negro was brought from over 3,000 miles away, and were he taken "back" to Africa, it is safe to say that an equal number of boats would have to be provided for the white people who would want to go along. Excerpting an account of the Bal Negre appearing in one of the local dailies, we learn that whites attending the cabaret began to feel at home. One said, "the contagion works. We allow ourselves to be converted, to chat and to enjoy ourselves at this strange carnival." And later: "Little by little we learn that we have been deceived in our preconceptions, and finish by not regretting not having seen a fight with knives or a rape."

The simple fact is that in spite of what the likes of Jim Gardner, Shelby Steele, and Dinesh D'Souza may say, African Americans will have, in no matter what part of the world, no easy task of preserving our isolation, no possibility of separatism or neo-segregationism once whites get on our track; for our culture of the gospel-blues continuum has gotten under their skin. The real problem is that black cultural centers at white universities across the country are places of conversion where, once the contagion takes hold, whites enjoy themselves and thereby affirm what is a significant part of what is culturally American. The real problem is that the rhythms of black folk are sexual and seductive, the spirit of the gospel-blues continuum is the African trickster-god.

CONCLUSION

I have been arguing that there is a genealogy of African rhythm in the New World. It is rhythm which, carried especially by the African trickster personality in personification, has been "reincarnated and rechristened" in Afro-cultures with each new generation. It is African rhythm that first left its imprint in the soil in which plantation archaeologists dig. It is the rhythms of black folk that have since given rise to certain identifiable, though sometimes subtle, traits in our music, dance, art, athletics, clothing trends, hair styles, talk, gait, gesture, possibly our intellectual life (our "soul of method"), and certainly our way of being in the world (our rhythmic confidence); and there is unlimited potential for even more cultural reassertion.

If we can imagine there being any validity to the slogan that began appearing on T-shirts on black college campuses in 1987— "It's a Black Thing, You Wouldn't Understand"—then that "black thing," if an attempt were to be made to reduce it to its cultural pith, would have to be the rhythms of black folk. What I wish for us to understand is that we ought to permit this "black thing" to persist among those of us who need our racial identity—need one another, need Africa, and need Africa's rhythm—for all of us may one day need that identity. I am basing my logic on a ternary pattern in our history: the black middle-class rejecting black core culture—> the folk maintaining our rhythmic genealogy—> and the black middle-class returning to these traditions (in part because of white middle-class interest and commodification).

This ternary model outlining our cultural history typifies, for instance, the way we behaved with regard to our spirituals and the blues. Upwardly mobile blacks of the late nineteenth and early twentieth century abandoned the "slave songs" and their first-born progeny (the blues) because these forms of music were too reflective of the supposedly inferior "slave culture" of our captive forebears. The sentiment expressed in 1938 by Lucius Harper, a black columnist for *The Chicago Defender*, is not unlike the intolerance we hear today regarding things "racial" (particularly "racial identity"). Writing on October 16 in a piece titled "We Prefer the 'Blues' to Our Essential Causes," Harper said: "While we have failed in these fundamental instances [of gleaning political recognition from whites], we have succeeded in winning favor and almost unanimous popularity in our 'blues' songs, spirituals and 'jitterbug' accomplishments. Why?" He answered, "Our blue melodies have been made popular because they are different, humorous and silly. The sillier the better. They excite the primitive emotion in man and arouse his bestiality. He begins to hum, moan and jump usually when they are put into action. They stir up the emotions and fit in handily with bootleg liquor. They break the serious strain of life and inspire the 'on with the dance' philosophy. They are popular because the American people, both white and black, relish nonsense."

Were it not for the folk who preserved the spirituals and the blues and our "jitterbug accomplishments," because they still needed to hum and moan and jump, then the black middle-class would not have been able to recapture this wonderful rhythmic tradition that later gave momentum to the civil rights movement. Martin Luther King, at the forefront of innumerable mass meetings and freedom marches, confirmed the accuracy of this claim when he explained in his book, *Why We Can't Wait* (1964), that the freedom songs were in a sense the "the soul of the movement." "I have heard people talk of their beat and rhythm," he writes, "but we in the movement are as inspired by their words."

It is probably natural for a theologian to perceive the text as just as important inspirationally as the rhythm, given that it is the text that conveys explicit religious meaning; but psychologists of music can help us see that it is rhythm that especially gives us the feeling of power. Carl Seashore says of rhythm in his book *Psychology of Music* (1938), "The pattern once grasped, there is an assurance of ability to cope with the future. This results in...a motor attitude, or a projection of the self in action; for rhythm is never rhythm unless one feels that he himself is acting it, or, what may seem contradictory, that he is even carried by his own action." The "motor attitude" or "projection of the self in action" is the essential component of what I have been calling "rhythmic confidence." Since black people have not had raw political and economic power, we have been dependent on gleaning our psychological empowerment by theological means and from cultural resources—respectively, text (ethical righteousness) and rhythm (rhythmic confidence). Each of these two components upheld the other, so that King's equal emphasis on both the words and the rhythm is correct. Were it not for our "jitterbug accomplishments," then, we would not have had the cultural resources that during the civil rights movement helped nurture our courage.

The argument I am making can be restated with reference to the preservation of the African drum and the subsequent creation of jazz, if we accept a thought-provoking hypothesis of Leonard Barrett. Barrett says in *Soul-Force* that wherever the drum was suppressed in puritan America the Africans' "soul" suffered, while in America's Latin slave system the "soul" of Africa was preserved; which is why jazz was created in New Orleans where Africans had access to the drum, and not in Boston or Philadelphia where Africans did not have such access. My point is that had we voluntarily relinquished the drum under the pressure of America's mainstream suppressive and assimilative forces, we would not today have jazz, one of the world's greatest cultural creations for which African Americans are responsible.

If one approves of French economist Jacques Attali's use of music as a prophetic lens through which future political and economic arrangements can be seen, then without jazz we also would have been deprived of significant prophecy. "Music is prophecy," says Attali in his book titled *Noise* (1977). "Its styles and economic organization are ahead of the rest of society because it explores, much faster than material reality can, the entire range of possibilities in a given code. It makes audible the new world that will gradually become visible, that will impose itself and regulate the order of things. " What jazz (our rhythm) also prophesies in economic, political, and social respects is that if we do not claim ("it is ours"), name ("Afro"), and maintain (via racialism) our rhythmic traditions then there will be others who will claim ("it is theirs"), name ("Euro"), and maintain (via racism) our traditions while concurrently depriving us of any moral claim of having contributed significantly to world culture. Jazz prophesies that if we begin to relinquish our "racial identity" it may very well be stolen from us, and it will then be said that it was never ours to begin with .

Scholars such as Anthony Appiah, who argue that black racialism is no longer an intelligent response to white racism, ought to consider the prophecy of our rhythm: The postmodernists ought to leave our racial identity alone, for our history (which runs parallel to our genealogy of African rhythm) has taught us that one day we all may need to be racially African. The point is that if Derrick Bell is correct in *Faces at the Bottom of the Well* (1992) that racism is intractable, then the day when we will be judged by the content of our character rather than by the color of our skin is far from being realized.

At the very least, we should heed the prophecy of historian John Hope Franklin who tells us in his book, *The Color Line* (1993), that the problem of the 21st century will be the same problem that Du Bois said in 1903 would be the problem of the 20th. Manning Marable, in an essay titled "The New International Racism" in his book *Crisis of Color Democracy* (1992), says of global racism: "The fundamental political reality of the twenty-first century will be the struggle for equality and democracy between the white 'North' and the impoverished, exploited, nonwhite 'South.'" So given this prophecy, we must maintain our rhythmic mystifications—our genealogy of African rhythm and our resultant "racial identity"in order to better fend off theologies and policies of the powerful. In this respect, to reject race and Pan-Africanism is to reject religion.

There is one more prophecy (for the time being) that our rhythmic genealogy/racial identity gives us. This prophecy has to do with the African trickster-god, the personage that I have already explained to be both superhuman and subhuman, female and male, sacred and profane, benevolent and malevolent, and who walks with a limp because one foot moves in the realm of the mundane and the other in the realm of the divine. This trickster figure is not only symbolic of what our rhythm (our music) is when personified but prototypal of a paradigm of personality and morality in Afro-cultural history. The moral dichotomy of good and evil is too restrictive. Restoring wholeness and balance in our lives, in the lives of all Afro-peoples whose cultures and world-

190

views have been impinged upon by the West, is a worthy Pan-Africanist project for black religion. This project of adhering to the prophecy of our rhythmic genealogy and of restoring wholeness and balance in our lives should ideally include the obliteration of that dichotomy that still remains between being culturally black and theologically black, for the rhythms that have sustained and saved us are the same that should be used to help the downtrodden become upbeat. Those who enjoy culturally personifying the African trickster with our rhythms must know that the privilege of standing at the crossroads (which is the trickster's location before the door opening toward synthesis) involves opening the gates to the gods for the sake of the "least of us."

BIBLIOGRAPHY

Abbott, Robert S. "Refinement Sadly Lacking in Modern Youth." *The Chicago Defender*, 10 March 1934, 11.

"Abyssinian Church Holds Services in New Community Edifice." *The New York Amsterdam News*, 28 Feb. 1923, 9.

"Abyssinian Pastor Says Ministers Should Give Jobless Aid, or Quit." *The New York Amsterdam News*, 17 Dec. 1930, 2.

African Art and Motion: An Illustrated Guide to the Exhibition. Washington: National Gallery of Art, 1974.

Appiah, Kwame Anthony. *In My Father's House: Africa in the Philosophy of Culture.* New York: Oxford University Press, 1992.

Asante, Molefi Kete. *The Afrocentric Idea.* Philadelphia: Temple University Press, 1987.

_____. *Kemet, Afrocentricity and Knowledge.* Trenton, N.J.: Africa World Press, 1990.

Attali, Jacques. *Noise: The Political Economy of Music.* Trans. Brian Massumi. Minneapolis: University of Minnesota Press, 1985. Originally published in 1977.

"Attorney to Seek Bail in Cult Case as Hearing Looms." *The New York Amsterdam News*, 8 June 1932, 1.

"Bail Doubled as Cult Head Flashes Roll." *The New York Amsterdam News,* 9 March 1935, 1.

Baker, Houston A., Jr. *Blues, Ideology, and Afro-American Literature: A Vernacular Theory.* Chicago: University of Chicago Press, 1984.

_____.*Modernism and the Harlem Renaissance.* Chicago: University of Chicago Press, 1987.

Barrett, Leonard E. *Soul-Force: African Heritage in Afro-American Religion.* Garden City, N.Y.: Anchor/Doubleday, 1974.

Bell, Derrick. *Faces at the Bottom of the Well: The Permanence of Racism.* New York: Basic Books, 1992.

"Cabin and Cloister." *The Christian Science Monthly,* 10 May 1930.

Carter, Stephen L. *Reflections of an Affirmative Action Baby.* New York: Basic Books, 1991.

"Centralized Movement to Aid Jobless Gains Impetus and Support in Harlem." *The New York Amsterdam News,* 12 Nov. 1930, 2.

"Challenge for Divine." *The New York Amsterdam News,* 17 Nov. 1934, 8.

Changes in the Church." *The New York Amsterdam News,* 30 May 1923, 12.

"The Church Today." *The New York Amsterdam News,* 22 Sept.1926, 20.

"Churches and Civic Bodies Continue Relief for Harlem Poor and Jobless." *The New York Amsterdam News,* 17 Dec. 1930, 2.

"Collapsible Color Line." *The Boston Globe,* 11 March 1929.

Cone, James H. *Black Theology and Black Power.* San Francisco: Harper Collins, 1989. Originally published in 1969.

_____. *The Spirituals and the Blues.* New York: Seabury Press, 1972. Reprinted by Orbis Press.

Cosentino, Donald J. "Interview with Robert Farris Thompson." *African Arts 25,* No. 4 (Oct. 1992): 52-63.

Crenshaw, Lewis D. To President of Hampton Normal and Agricultural Institute, 15 May 1930. European Tour Papers, Hampton University Archives, Hampton, Virginia.

Crouch, Stanley. *Notes of a Hanging Judge: Essays and Reviews, 1979-1989.* New York: Oxford University Press, 1990.

"Cult Head Acclaimed by Throng." *The New York Amsterdam News,* 29 June 1932, 1.

Cushing, Edward. "Music of the Day." *The Brooklyn Eagle,* 17 April 1928.

"Descendants of Slaves Honored Africa's Friend." *The Colonist,* 14 June 1930.

"Deserving." *Musical Courier,* 24 May 1930.

Dett, R. Nathaniel. "The Authenticity of the Spiritual." In *The Dett Collection of Negro Spirituals,* 4th Group. Minneapolis: Hall and McCreary, 1936.

_____ "The Development of Negro Religious Music." *In Negro Music* (Bowdoin Literary Prize Thesis, Harvard University, 1920).

_____. "The Emancipation of Negro Music." In *Negro Music* (Bowdoin Literary Prize Thesis, Harvard University, 1920).

_____. "Negro Music." In *The International Cyclopedia of Music and Musicians.* Ed. Oscar Thompson. New York: Dodd, Mead, 1938, 1243-46.

_____, ed. *Religious Folk-Songs of the Negro: As Sung at Hampton Institute.* Hampton, Va.: Hampton Institute Press, 1927.

_____. "Understanding the Negro Spiritual." In *The Dett Collection of Negro Spirituals,* 3rd Group. Minneapolis: Hall and McCreary, 1936.

"Divine Feeds 600." *The New York Amsterdam News,* 30 March 1932, 11.

"Divine Takes Vote Battle into Court." *The New York Amsterdam News,* 6 July 1935, 1.

Doggett, Allen B., Jr. "Artistic Achievement." *Christian Advocate,* 20 Jan. 1927.

Downes, Olin. "Hampton Institute Choir." *The New York Times,* 18 April 1928.

Du Bois, W. E. B. *Darkwater: Voices from Within the Veil.* New York: Schocken, 1969. Originally published in 1920.

_____. *Dusk of Dawn: An Essay Toward an Autobiography of a Race Concept.* New York: Harcourt, Brace, 1940.

Early, Gerald, ed. *Lure and Loathing: Essays on Race, Identity, and the Ambivalence of Assimilation.* New York: Penguin, 1993.

Ellison, Ralph. *Invisible Man.* New York: Vintage, 1972.

_____. "What America Would Be Like Without Blacks." *Time,* 6 April 1970, 54-55.

Fanon, Frantz. *Black Skin, White Masks.* Trans. Charles Lam Markmann. New York: Grove, 1967. Originally published in 1952.

_____. *Studies in a Dying Colonialism.* Trans. Haakon Chevalier. London: Earthscan, 1989. Originally published in 1959.

_____. *The Wretched of the Earth.* Trans. Constance Farrington. New York: Grove Weidenfeld, 1963. Originally published in 1961.

Ferguson, Leland. *Uncommon Ground: Archaeology and Early African America, 1650-1800.* Washington: Smithsonian Institution Press, 1992.

Foucault, Michel. *The History of Sexuality,* Vol. 1. Trans. Robert Hurley. New York: Vintage, 1989.

Franklin, John Hope. *The Color Line: Legacy for the Twenty-First Century.* Columbia: University of Missouri Press, 1993.

Gates, Henry Louis, Jr., ed. *"Race," Writing, and Difference.* Chicago: University of Chicago Press, 1986.

_____. *The Signifying Monkey: A Theory of Afro-American Literary Criticism.* New York: Oxford University Press, 1988.

George, Nelson. *Buppies, B-Boys, Baps and Bohos: Notes on Post-Soul Black Culture.* New York: Harper Collins, 1992.

_____. *The Death of Rhythm and Blues.* New York: Pantheon, 1988.

Hacker, Andrew. *Two Nations: Black and White, Separate, Hostile, Unequal.* New York: Scribner's Sons, 1992.

Harper, Lucius C. "We Prefer the 'Blues' to Our Essential Causes." *The Chicago Defender,* 1 Oct. 1938, 16.

Harris, Eddy L. *Native Stranger: A Black American's Journey into the Heart of Africa.* New York: Vintage, 1992.

Harrison, Barbara Grizzuti. "Spike Lee Hates Your Cracker Ass." *Esquire,* Oct. 1992, 132-40.

Hazzard-Gordon, Katrina. *Jookin': The Rise of Social Dance Formations in African-American Culture.* Philadelphia: Temple University Press, 1990.

Higgins, Kathleen Marie. *The Music of Our Lives.* Philadelphia: Temple University Press, 1991.

Holloway, Joseph E., ed. *Africanisms in American Culture.* Bloomington: Indiana University Press, 1990.

Hooks, Bell. *Yearning: Race, Gender, and Cultural Politics.* Boston: South End, 1990.

Hughes, Langston. *The Big Sea: An Autobiography.* New York: Hill and Wang, 1963. Originally published in 1940.

"'I Taught Father Divine' Says St. Bishop The Vine." *The New York Amsterdam News,* 23 Nov. 1932, 1.

Imes, William Lloyd. "Pays Tribute to Dr. Bishop." *The New York Amsterdam News,* 6 Jan. 1926, 16.

Jones, William R. *Is God a White Racist?: A Preamble to Black Theology.* Garden City, N.Y.: Anchor/Doubleday, 1973.

Jung, Carl G. "Your Negroid and Indian Behavior." *The Forum,* April 1930, 193-99.

King, Martin Luther, Jr. *Why We Can't Wait*. New York: Mentor, 1964.

"Ku Klux Klan Robes Free." *The New York Amsterdam News*, 23 Oct. 1929, 20.

Loubser, J. A. *The Apartheid Bible: A Critical Review of Racial Theology in South Africa*. Cape Town, South Africa: Maskew Miller Longman, 1987.

Lusk, Eric. "Gardner Blasts BCC Plans." *The Daily Tarheel*, 27 Oct. 1992, 1.

Marable, Manning. *The Crisis of Color and Democracy: Essays on Race, Class and Power*. Monroe, Maine: Common Courage Press, 1992.

Miller, Kelly. "After Marcus Garvey—What." *The New York Amsterdam News*, 27 April 1927, 16.

_____. "After Marcus Garvey—What." *The New York Amsterdam News*, 4 May 1927, 16.

_____. "Preachers in Politics." *The New York Amsterdam News*, 11 May 1927, 16.

Mok, Michael. "The World Must Hear Her." *The New York Post*, 22 Nov. 1939.

Morini, Albert. To Arthur Howe [President of Hampton Institute], 5 and 6 Sept. 1935. European Tour Papers, Hampton University Archives, Hampton, Virginia.

Morrison, Toni. *Playing in the Dark: Whiteness and the Literary Imagination*. Cambridge: Harvard University Press, 1992.

Moses, Wilson Jeremiah. *The Wings of Ethiopia: Studies in African-American Life and Letters*. Ames: Iowa State University Press, 1990.

Mudimbe, V. Y. *The Invention of Africa: Gnosis, Philosophy, and the Order of Knowledge*. Bloomington: Indiana University Press, 1988.

_____, ed. *The Surreptitious Speech: Presence Africaine and the Politics of Otherness 1847-1987*. Chicago: University of Chicago Press, 1992.

Ngũgĩ wa Thiong'o. *Barrel of a Pen: Resistance to Repression in Neo-Colonial Kenya*. Trenton, New Jersey: Africa World Press, 1983.

_____. *Decolonising the Mind: The Politics of Language in African Literature.* Nairobi: Heinemann Kenya, 1986.

_____. *Detained: A Writer's Prison Diary.* Nairobi: Heinemann Kenya, 1981.

Phenix, George P. To R. Nathaniel Dett, 21 April 1930. R. Nathaniel Dett Papers, Hampton University Archives, Hampton Virginia.

Price, Al. "At Home in Africa." *Emerge,* April 1993, 58-59.

Ransom, Reverdy C. *The Pilgrimage of Harriet Ransom's Son* (Nashville: AMEC Sunday School Union, n.d.).

"Rector Hides Behind 'Smoke Screen' in Raising 'Jim Crow'." *The New York Amsterdam News,* 18 Sept. 1929, 1.

Reed, Adolph, Jr. "Steele Trap" (Rev. of Shelby Steele's *The Content of Our Character*). *The Nation,* 4 March 1991, 274-80.

"Rev. McGuire, Prelate, Dies." *The New York Amsterdam News,* 17 Nov. 1934, 1.

Roberts, E. Elliott. "Hats Off to Rev. Powell." *The New York Amsterdam News,* 9 June 1934, 8.

Rouzeau, Edgar T. "Black Israel." *The New York Amsterdam News,* 8 Sept. 1934, 9.

Saadawi, Nawal El. *The Hidden Face of Eve: Women in the Arab World.* London: Zed Books, 1980.

"Salvation Army Station Feeding 250 as Civil Groups Plan to Fight Want." *The New York Amsterdam News,* 29 Oct. 1930, 3.

Sandburg, Carl. Quoted in the Chicago *News,* 29 Sept. 1926. Quote cited in Martin Bauml Duberman, *Paul Robeson* (New York: Knopf, 1988).

Sartre, Jean-Paul. *Being and Nothingness.* Trans. Hazel E. Barnes. New York: Washington Square, 1956. Originally published in 1943.

Schultz, Mark. "Professor Explodes Myths about Slavery." *The Herald Sun* (Durham, North Carolina), 14 Sept. 1992.

Seashore, Carl E. *Psychology of Music.* New York: McGraw-Hill, 1938.

Spencer, Jon Michael. *Blues and Evil.* Knoxville: University of Tennessee Press, 1993.

_____. *Sacred Symphony: The Chanted Sermon of the Black Preacher.* Westport, Conn.: Greenwood, 1987.

_____. *Sing a New Song: Liberating Black Hymnody.* Minneapolis: Fortress, 1995.

Steele, Shelby. *The Content of Our Character: A New Vision of Race.* New York: Harper Collins, 1990.

"Supreme Court Justice Smith Succumbs after Followers of Cult Predict End." *The New York Amsterdam News,* 9 June 1932, 1.

Tait, George E. "The Church Duty." *The New York Amsterdam News,* 3 Nov. 1934, 8.

Thompson, Robert Farris. *African Art in Motion: Icon and Act.* Berkeley: University of California Press, 1974.

_____. *Flash of the Spirit: African and Afro-American Art and Philosophy.* New York: Vintage, 1983.

Thorpe, Earl E. *The Old South: A Psychohistory.* Durham, N.C.: Seeman Printery, 1972. Reprinted by Greenwood Press.

West, Cornel. *Race Matters.* Boston: Beacon, 1993.

"Young People's Fellowship of St. Philip's in Three-Day Session." *The New York Amsterdam News,* 2 May 1928, 3.

INDEX